Blade Runner 2049

Widely acclaimed upon its release as a future classic, Denis Villeneuve's *Blade Runner 2049* is visually stunning, philosophically profound, and a provocative extension of the story in Ridley Scott's *Blade Runner*. Containing specially commissioned chapters by a roster of international contributors, this fascinating collection explores philosophical questions that abound in *Blade Runner 2049*, including:

- What distinguishes the authentically "human" person?
- How might "natality" condition one's experience of being-in-the-world?
- How might shared memories feature in the constitution of personal identities?
- What happens when created beings transcend the limits intended in their design?
- What (if anything) is it like to be a hologram?
- Can artificial beings participate in genuinely romantic relationships?
- How might developing artificial economics impact our behaviour as prosumers?
- What are the implications of techno-human enhancement in an era of surveillance capitalism?

Including a foreword by Denis Villeneuve, *Blade Runner 2049: A Philosophical Exploration* is essential reading for anyone interested in philosophy, film studies, philosophy of mind, psychology, gender studies, and conceptual issues in cognitive science and artificial intelligence.

Timothy Shanahan is Professor of Philosophy at Loyola Marymount University in Los Angeles, and the author of *Philosophy and Blade Runner* (2014).

Paul Smart is a researcher at the New University of Lisbon, Visiting Research Fellow at the University of Southampton, UK, and a freelance cognitive science consultant, specializing in machine learning and virtual reality technologies.

Philosophers on Film

In recent years, the use of film in teaching and doing philosophy has moved to centre stage. Film is increasingly used to introduce key topics and problems in philosophy, from ethics and aesthetics to epistemology, metaphysics and philosophy of mind. It is also acknowledged that some films raise important philosophical questions of their own. Yet until now, dependable resources for teachers and students of philosophy using film have remained very limited. *Philosophers on Film* answers this growing need and is the first series of its kind.

Each volume assembles a team of international contributors to explore a single film in depth, making the series ideal for classroom use. Beginning with an introduction by the editor, each specially-commissioned chapter will discuss a key aspect of the film in question.

Philosophers on Film is an ideal series for students studying philosophy and film, aesthetics, and ethics and anyone interested in the philosophical dimensions of cinema.

Also available:

Talk to Her
Edited by A. W. Eaton

Thin Red Line
Edited by David Davies

Memento
Edited by Andrew Kania

Eternal Sunshine of the Spotless Mind
Edited by Christopher Grau

Fight Club
Edited by Thomas E. Wartenberg

Vertigo
Edited by Katalin Makkai

Mulholland Drive
Edited by Zina Giannopoulou

Blade Runner
Edited by Amy Coplan

Blade Runner 2049
A Philosophical Exploration
Edited by Timothy Shanahan and Paul Smart

For more information about this series, please visit:
https://www.routledge.com/Philosophers-on-Film/book-series/PHILFILM

Blade Runner 2049

A Philosophical Exploration

Edited by

**Timothy Shanahan and
Paul Smart**

LONDON AND NEW YORK

First published 2020
by Routledge
2 Park Square, Milton Park, Abingdon, Oxon OX14 4RN

and by Routledge
52 Vanderbilt Avenue, New York, NY 10017

Routledge is an imprint of the Taylor & Francis Group, an informa business

© 2020 selection and editorial matter, Timothy Shanahan and Paul Smart; individual chapters, the contributors

Foreword © 2020, Denis Villeneuve

The right of Timothy Shanahan and Paul Smart to be identified as the authors of the editorial material, and of the authors for their individual chapters, has been asserted in accordance with sections 77 and 78 of the Copyright, Designs and Patents Act 1988.

All rights reserved. No part of this book may be reprinted or reproduced or utilised in any form or by any electronic, mechanical, or other means, now known or hereafter invented, including photocopying and recording, or in any information storage or retrieval system, without permission in writing from the publishers.

Trademark notice: Product or corporate names may be trademarks or registered trademarks, and are used only for identification and explanation without intent to infringe.

British Library Cataloguing-in-Publication Data
A catalogue record for this book is available from the British Library

Library of Congress Cataloging-in-Publication Data
A catalog record has been requested for this book

ISBN: 978-1-138-62530-3 (hbk)
ISBN: 978-1-138-62533-4 (pbk)
ISBN: 978-0-429-46003-6 (ebk)

Typeset in Joanna MT Std
by Newgen Publishing UK

 Printed in the United Kingdom by Henry Ling Limited

Tim: To Dan, Jaime, and Patrick
 —for keeping the flame burning brightly
Paul: To Anais and Marjan
 —for joy, for love, and the memory of tomorrow

Contents

List of figures ix
List of contributors x
Acknowledgements xv
Note on the director xvi
List of characters and cast xvii
Denis Villeneuve xix
Foreword

    Timothy Shanahan and Paul Smart 1
    INTRODUCTION

1   **Timothy Shanahan** 8
    WE'RE ALL JUST LOOKING FOR SOMETHING REAL

2   **Stephen Mulhall** 27
    THE ALPHABET OF US: MIRACLES, MESSIANISM, AND THE
    BASELINE TEST IN *BLADE RUNNER 2049*

3   **Fiona Woollard** 48
    THE "MIRACLE" OF REPLICANT REPRODUCTION

4	Brian Treanor BEING-FROM-BIRTH: NATALITY AND NARRATIVE	68
5	Richard Heersmink and Christopher Jude McCarroll THE BEST MEMORIES: IDENTITY, NARRATIVE, AND OBJECTS	87
6	Robert W. Clowes BREAKING THE CODE: STRONG AGENCY AND BECOMING A PERSON	108
7	Paul Smart THE JOI OF HOLOGRAMS	127
8	Wanja Wiese and Thomas K. Metzinger ANDROIDS DREAM OF VIRTUAL SHEEP	149
9	Timothy Shanahan HER EYES WERE GREEN: INTIMATE RELATIONSHIPS IN *BLADE RUNNER 2049*	165
10	Paul Smart ARTIFICIAL ECONOMICS	185
11	Nigel Shadbolt and Paul Smart THE EYES OF GOD	206
12	Timothy Shanahan WHAT AM I TO YOU? THE DECK-A-REP DEBATE AND THE QUESTION OF FICTIONAL TRUTH	228

Index 248

Figures

7.1 Different interpretations of Joi according to whether or not she is programmed to feel love and whether or not she actually feels love   133
7.2 Taxonomy of cinematic resources   139
7.3 Microsoft HoloLens promotion image   142
8.1 An example of the hollow face illusion   153
12.1 Ridley Scott directs Harrison Ford in *Blade Runner* (1982)   234

Contributors

Robert W. Clowes is a researcher and Invited Auxiliary Professor at the New University of Lisbon, and Visiting Research Fellow at the Centre for Cognitive Science (COGS) at the University of Sussex, UK. He also directs the Lisbon Mind and Reasoning Group at the New University of Lisbon, which specializes in research devoted to mind, cognition, and human reasoning. Robert's research interests span a range of topics in philosophy and cognitive science, including the philosophy of technology, memory, agency, and the implications of embodiment and cognitive extension for our understanding of the mind and conscious experience. He is particularly interested in the philosophical and cognitive scientific significance of new technologies, especially those that are built on top of global digital networks, such as the Internet and the Web. His work has appeared in a variety of journals, including *Review of Philosophy and Psychology*, *AI & Society*, *Phenomenology and the Cognitive Sciences*, *Philosophy and Technology*, and the *Journal of Consciousness Studies*.

Richard Heersmink is a lecturer in Philosophy at La Trobe University in Melbourne. He has a BSc in Biology (Saxion Hogeschool), an MA in the Philosophy of Science, Technology and Society (University of Twente, the Netherlands), and a PhD in the Philosophy of Cognitive Science (Macquarie University, Australia). His research is located at the intersection of the philosophy of cognitive science, the philosophy of technology, and neuroethics. He is particularly interested in the ways in which technology transforms memory, cognition, and the self, as well as the normative implications of these transformations at the individual and cultural levels. His work has appeared in *Synthese*, *Philosophical Explorations*, *Review of Philosophy and Psychology*, *Phenomenology and the Cognitive Sciences*, *Neuroethics*, and various other journals.

Christopher Jude McCarroll received his BA from the University of Ulster, and his MA from Queen's University Belfast. His PhD was awarded in 2015 from Macquarie University, Australia, with no corrections, and he was subsequently awarded the Vice Chancellor's Commendation. He is currently a researcher at the Centre de philosophie de la mémoire, Université Grenoble-Alpes, France. His research interests include the philosophy of memory, mental time travel, and the philosophy of imagination. He has a particular interest in the role of visual perspective in mental imagery. He is the author of *Remembering from the Outside: Personal Memory and the Perspectival Mind*, published by Oxford University Press.

Thomas K. Metzinger is Full Professor and Director of the Theoretical Philosophy Group and the Research Group on Neuroethics/Neurophilosophy at the Department of Philosophy, Johannes Gutenberg University of Mainz. From 2014 to 2019, he was a Fellow at the Gutenberg Research College. He is the founder and director of the MIND Group and Adjunct Fellow at the Frankfurt Institute of Advanced Studies. His research centres on analytic philosophy of mind, applied ethics, philosophy of cognitive science, and philosophy of mind. His books include *The Ego Tunnel: The Science of the Mind and the Myth of the Self* and *Being No One: The Self-Model Theory of Subjectivity*.

Stephen Mulhall is Professor of Philosophy and a Tutorial Fellow of New College at the University of Oxford. He has been a member of New College, Oxford, since 1998. Prior to that he was a member of All Souls College, Oxford, and the University of Essex. His primary research interests relate to the philosophy of Wittgenstein and some of the key figures in the Franco–German traditions of philosophy arising from Kant—especially Heidegger, Sartre, Nietzsche, and Kierkegaard. He also has an interest in the ways literature and film relate to philosophy.

Professor Mulhall is the author of numerous books, including *The Routledge Guidebook to Heidegger's Being and Time*, *The Conversation of Humanity*, and *The Self and its Shadows*. He is also author of the critically acclaimed *On Film*, now in its third edition, which surveys a variety of issues in cinematic philosophy.

Nigel Shadbolt is Principal of Jesus College, Oxford, and a Professorial Research Fellow in the Department of Computer Science at the University of Oxford. He is also Chairman of the Open Data Institute, which he co-founded with Sir Tim Berners-Lee, as well as Visiting Professor in the School of Electronics and Computer Science at the University of Southampton. Nigel is an interdisciplinary researcher, policy expert and commentator. His research focuses on the intelligence exhibited by humans, machines, and online socio-technical systems, and he has published widely in the fields of philosophy, psychology, cognitive science, computational neuroscience, artificial intelligence, computer science, and Web science. His recent books include *The Spy in the Coffee Machine*, which discusses issues relating to global hyper-surveillance, and *The Digital Ape: How to Live (in Peace) with Smart Machines*. Nigel was awarded knighthood in the 2013 Queen's Birthday Honours list for his services to science and engineering.

Timothy Shanahan is Professor of Philosophy at Loyola Marymount University in Los Angeles. He earned a BS in Biology from the State University of New York at Cortland, and an MA in the History and Philosophy of Science and a PhD in Philosophy from the University of Notre Dame. He was also an NSF-funded postdoctoral fellow in the Science Studies Program at the University of California, San Diego. His work spans the history and philosophy of science, terrorism studies, and philosophy of/in film. Previous books include *Reason and Insight: Western and Eastern Perspectives on the Pursuit of Moral Wisdom*; *The Evolution of Darwinism: Selection, Adaptation, and Progress in Evolutionary Biology*; *Philosophy 9/11: Thinking about the War on Terrorism*; *The Provisional Irish Republican Army and the Morality of Terrorism*; and *Philosophy and Blade Runner*.

Paul Smart is a researcher at the New University of Lisbon, Visiting Research Fellow at the University of Southampton, UK, and a freelance cognitive science consultant, specializing in machine learning and virtual reality technologies. His research interests lie at the intersection of a range of disciplines, including philosophy, cognitive science, and computer science. He is particularly interested in the cognitive scientific significance of emerging digital technologies, such as the Internet and Web. Paul's philosophical work has appeared in a number of journals, including *Minds and Machines, Philosophy & Technology, Phenomenology and the Cognitive Sciences, Synthese,* and *Cognitive Systems Research.* His books include *Minds Online: The Interface between Web Science, Cognitive Science and the Philosophy of Mind.*

Brian Treanor is Charles S. Casassa Chair and Professor of Philosophy at Loyola Marymount University. He earned his PhD in 2001, studying under Richard Kearney and Jacques Taminiaux at Boston College. His work takes its cue from the tradition of philosophical hermeneutics; however, his work remains consciously interdisciplinary, engaging ecology, literature, poetry, psychology, theology, and other disciplines. He is the author or editor of six books as well as many scholarly articles. Among his recent works are *Emplotting Virtue, Interpreting Nature,* and *Carnal Hermeneutics.* Among his current projects are a monograph about reasons to despair as well as possible responses rooted in joy, hope, vitality, and love, and a second monograph that expands hermeneutics itself to experiences rooted in carnal embodiment and material emplacement.

Wanja Wiese is an assistant researcher and lecturer within the Theoretical Philosophy Group at the Johannes Gutenberg University of Mainz. His research centres on philosophy of cognitive science and philosophy of mind. He is the author of *Experienced Wholeness: Integrating Insights from Gestalt Theory, Cognitive Neuroscience, and Predictive Processing,* published by MIT Press, and he is also the co-editor of *Philosophy and Predictive Processing,* published by MIND Group, an open access collection of 26 papers by prominent philosophers working in the field of predictive processing.

Fiona Woollard is Associate Professor of Philosophy at the University of Southampton, UK. Her research addresses issues in applied and normative ethics, especially the nature and moral significance of deontological distinctions such as the distinction between doing and allowing harm, obligations to aid, body-ownership, and philosophical issues surrounding pregnancy, birth, and motherhood. Fiona's work has appeared in a variety of philosophical journals, including *Philosophical Explorations*, *Journal of Applied Philosophy*, *Pacific Philosophical Quarterly*, *Mind*, and *Analysis*. Her books include *Doing and Allowing Harm*, published by Oxford University Press.

Acknowledgements

The editors would like to thank Tony Bruce for his support of this project, the production teams at Routledge and Newgen for skilfully guiding the book's publication, the contributors for their fine essays, and last but not least Denis Villeneuve (and Tanya Lapointe) for *Blade Runner 2049* and the splendid foreword. There was, indeed, another page to be written.

Note on the director

Denis Villeneuve is a film director and writer, born in Canada in 1967. Although initially attracted to the study of science, he found his passion in films and pursued film studies at the Université du Québec à Montréal. His feature films range from moral dramas and crime thrillers to science fiction, and include Un 32 août sur terre (1998), Maelström (2000), Polytechnique (2009), Incendies (2010), Enemy (2013), Prisoners (2013), Sicario (2015), Arrival (2016), and, of course, Blade Runner 2049 (2017). He is currently at work on a film adaptation of the classic Frank Herbert science fiction novel, Dune.

Characters and cast

In credits order (by character name)

'K'	Ryan Gosling
Sapper Morton	Dave Bautista
Lieutenant Joshi	Robin Wright
Interviewer	Mark Arnold
Angry Old Lady	Vilma Szécsi
Joi	Ana de Armas
Nandez	Wood Harris
Coco	David Dastmalchian
File Clerk	Tómas Lemarquis
Luv	Sylvia Hoeks
Gaff	Edward James Olmos
Niander Wallace	Jared Leto
Female Replicant	Sallie Harmsen
Freysa	Hiam Abbass
Mariette	Mackenzie Davis
Doxie #2	Krista Kosonen
Doxie #3	Elarica Johnson
Memory Child	André Lukács Molnár
Scavenger #1	István Göz
Scavenger #2	Pál Nyári

Scavenger #3	Joshua Tersoo Allagh
Scavenger #4	Zoltán Béres
Scavenger #5	Konstantin Pál
Scavenger #6	Ferenc Györgyi
Orphanage Boy	Samuel Brown
Mister Cotton	Lennie James
Dr Ana Stelline	Carla Juri
Birthday Girl	Kincsö Sánta
Doc Badger	Barkhad Abdi
Rick Deckard	Harrison Ford
Elvis Look-a-Like	Ben Thompson
Marilyn Look-a-Like	Suzie Kennedy
Liberace Look-a-Like	David Benson
Sinatra Look-a-Like	Stephen Triffitt
Rachael	Sean Young
Rachael Performance Double	Loren Peta

Denis Villeneuve
FOREWORD

Frankenstein's creature is a good metaphor for filmmaking. You hunt for hidden ideas or steal dying ones, resurrect them into images and sounds. You glue them together to form a singular Prometheus, hoping it will eventually walk by itself and move away from you, as far away as possible, because what it will potentially reveal about yourself will be truly unbearable to contemplate. One's reflection in the mirror can only be appreciated by someone else. The mirror is without mercy. It reflects all the ugliest tiny monstrosities living under your skin, even the ones your mother wished weren't yours.

So, I let *Blade Runner 2049* walk away from me, still digesting the experience of bringing such a creature to life. I know it is still alive, wandering into new landscapes, meeting new people, slowly learning by itself about its own condition, about its potential impact into the minds. Will it come back to me asking for answers? I hope not. I gave it all my love from the beginning, and I would fear that my answers wouldn't be satisfying. The anger it would direct at me would be justifiable, and all the love in the world wouldn't be enough. It would probably ask for more life.

I don't know where exactly the movie is today. Frankly, I don't want to know.

Of course, one day I'll be ready to confront it again.

For now, what reassures me is that I know the movie is not alone.

I received this book like a postcard from the other side of the mirror.

A kind of love letter from the edges, some accounts of the movie's perambulations.

To think that *Blade Runner 2049* sparked such conversations and stimulated such reflections about humanity and artificial intelligence sincerely deeply moves me. Of course, I'm aware that I have nothing to do with this beauty. The movie is alive by itself and its origins belong far before my time. A lot of fathers can rightfully claim its identity. In fact, what can a creator truly claim from his creation once it is shared and alive in other people's minds?

Away from all its creators, a creation has a life of its own.

And I'm curious to see it again through the eyes of others.

That is one of the reasons I love the very existence of this book.

Timothy Shanahan and Paul Smart

INTRODUCTION

THIRTY-FIVE YEARS AFTER RIDLEY SCOTT'S sci-fi classic *Blade Runner* (1982) first appeared in theatres, fans finally were rewarded with a long-wished-for sequel. Directed by acclaimed filmmaker Denis Villeneuve, *Blade Runner 2049* (BR2049) premiered in Los Angeles on 3 October 2017 and hit US theatres three days later. Many fans sitting in the dark waiting for the film to begin undoubtedly held their breath. Would the new film ascend to the storied heights attained by the former? Would it respect the legacy of the original film while making its own distinctive mark? Would it resolve the decades-old mystery of whether Deckard is a replicant?

They need not have worried. BR2049 honours the legacy of the original film while extending and advancing the story in exciting and unexpected ways (and leaves the enigma of Deckard's nature intact). Indeed, much more than just another sequel, BR2049 stands on its own as a visually stunning cinematic achievement and as a film eminently worthy of close philosophical examination. The dozen specially commissioned chapters that follow invite readers to explore BR2049 as a film that is as deeply thought-provoking as it is visually impressive, as a brief summary of each of the following chapters demonstrates.

BR2049 would be a coherent, highly entertaining, and deeply thought-provoking film even if it had no backstory. But the fact that it builds upon and extends a number of previous fictional narratives means that we can appreciate its richness even more by understanding its relationship to these predecessors and noticing how it references some of their central concerns. In "We're all just looking for something real," **Timothy Shanahan** aims to establish links between BR2049 and those earlier works, especially Philip K. Dick's *Do Androids Dream of Electric Sheep?* (1968), Ridley Scott's *Blade Runner* (1982/2007), and *2022: Black Out, 2036: Nexus Dawn*, and *2048: Nowhere to Run*—three short films that immediately preceded the release of BR2049. After reviewing the core narratives of these works, he shows how common to all of them is a concern to understand what it means to be authentically human and (not unrelated to that) the sometimes-difficult challenge of distinguishing reality from its many pretenders.

BR2049 not only inherits some of the DNA of *Electric Sheep* and *Blade Runner*, but also bears marks of having been influenced by the distinctive worlds depicted in some of Scott's and Villeneuve's previous films. In "The alphabet of us: miracles, messianism, and the baseline test in *Blade Runner 2049*," **Stephen Mulhall** explores BR2049 in relation not just to *Blade Runner*, but also in relation to Scott's film that immediately preceded it, *Alien* (1979), along with subsequent films in the *Alien* franchise, showing how these films reference one another and hence constitute a single cinematic universe. He goes on to show how BR2049 is also conditioned by Villeneuve's preceding body of work, especially *Arrival* (2016). Using the terminology of BR2049's baseline text, he argues that Villeneuve has successfully interlinked the semantic and material cells of the *Blade Runner* universe in ways that differentiate them from those in Scott's universe, while remaining rooted in their shared reality. In the course of doing so, he touches upon many of the topics that other contributors will explore in more detail.

The main story arc of BR2049 stems from what Sapper Morton refers to as a "miracle"—the fact that a replicant gave birth. This miracle of replicant reproduction is viewed by the characters in the film as having great import for the status of replicants and how they may be treated by their human counterparts. But the idea that a replicant who is born has a moral status that replicants, which are manufactured, do not have bears closer scrutiny. In "The 'miracle' of replicant reproduction," **Fiona Woollard** argues that the key issue in working out whether replicants can permissibly be treated as mere products is not whether they are born, but whether they are *persons*. Drawing upon characteristics of personhood developed in the philosophical literature, she argues that manufactured replicants satisfy the conditions for personhood and, hence, are the kinds of creatures that cannot be justly owned by another. Consequently, if all replicants are persons, the miracle of replicant reproduction may not be as momentous as it is taken to be.

Much of the narrative of the original *Blade Runner* film centred on the replicants' quest for *more life* and on the question of whether they should be considered human—a question to which that film offered no definitive answer. By contrast, BR2049 tells us right up front that replicants are bioengineered *humans* with comparable lifespans. Consequently, the narrative centre of gravity in BR2049 shifts, for the replicants, from how long they've got and whether they are human to *how* they came into existence. In "Being-from-birth: natality and narrative," **Brian Treanor** argues that the focus of BR2049 is not *being-toward-death* but rather *natality*, *being-from-birth*. Drawing upon the work of Anne O'Byrne, in particular, he explores the idea that whereas one's death is an inherently solitary transition, one's birth is inherently social and relational: to be born is to enter into a preexisting community that witnesses our coming to be. He shows how this shift in emphasis from mortality to natality informs BR2049's replicants' (and our) understanding of relationships, personal identity, and the real or authentic human.

When we first meet K, he naturally believes himself to be a standard replicant. Noticing that the date carved into the trunk of the dead tree on Sapper Morton's farm matches the date carved into a toy horse appearing in his memory overturns his familiar world. Could he be the miracle child, he wonders? As he comes to learn, however, memory is an imperfect guide to identity. Indeed, as **Richard Heersmink** and **Christopher Jude McCarroll** show in "The best memories: identity, narrative, and objects," BR2049 encourages us to reflect deeply on the nature and significance of memory. In their view, memory's role in grounding one's identity goes beyond merely one's ability to recall one's past; it also matters what one *uses* memory for. Memory drives K's journey of self-discovery. Eventually, he comes to understand that Dr Ana Stelline, not he, experienced the events recorded in the memory of the horse, but also that that shared memory links him to her, and consequently to Deckard. That shared memory turned out to be integral to his own identity after all. K tells Deckard, "All the best memories are hers." But in the end, Heersmink and McCarroll suggest, we should rather say that all the best memories are *theirs*.

When we first meet K, he is dutifully doing exactly what he was created to do, namely, retiring NEXUS 8 replicants that are on earth illegally. Later, when he hesitates after Lt. Joshi orders him to find and destroy the child, his superior reminds him of his place in the order of things: "Are you telling me no?" K responds by acknowledging his subservient role: "I wasn't aware that was an option, madam." By the end of the film, however, it is evident both to him (and to us) that he *does* have an option; he can *choose*. This raises many questions. Did K *always* have a choice, or did his capacity for agency develop in response to his experiences? How is *having a will* related to *being a person*? Can there be creatures, with cognitive capacities comparable to our own, that nonetheless cannot exercise a will? In "Breaking the code: strong agency and becoming a person," **Robert Clowes** explores such questions in the context of BR2049 and our own emerging technologies. As he shows through careful analysis of both K and Joi's development, BR2049 invites us to consider the challenges posed by creating beings able to transcend the limits of their design and thereby become something more than what their creators intended.

Joi is a form of hologrammatic artificial intelligence (AI)—a digital companion marketed by the Wallace Corporation. What we don't know is whether she is conscious, a real person, and a sentient being with her own subjective experiences. Is there *something it is like* to be Joi? In "The Joi of holograms," **Paul Smart** delves more deeply into Joi's nature. He argues that the film leaves the issue of Joi's sentience unresolved and, indeed, given the information provided in the film, that the issue is perhaps unresolvable—a situation that mirrors the current philosophical impasse concerning the possibility of a sentient hologrammatic AI. Likewise, we can never be sure that Joi's love for K is anything other than programmed responses. Nonetheless, he argues, this very ambiguity plays an integral role in the construction of the film because it encourages viewers to adopt alternative interpretive lenses. As he goes on to show, a penetrating analysis of mixed-reality technologies has important implications for our understanding of the scope of cinematic philosophy.

As a hologram, Joi's inner world is simulated and virtual. Mariette alludes to this fact when she issues a parting shot as she leaves K's apartment: "Quiet, now. I've been inside you. Not so much there as you think." Her comment suggests that she considers Joi's mental complexity and sophistication to be not as deep as her own (or ours). But as recent developments in philosophy, cognitive science, and theoretical neuroscience suggest, our own mental lives may themselves have something of an illusory quality. In "Androids dream of virtual sheep," **Wanja Wiese** and **Thomas K. Metzinger** note that within predictive processing accounts of cognition, consciousness is sometimes portrayed as a form of controlled hallucination that arises from the brain's attempt to gain a predictive toehold over incoming sensory information. Consequently, our own inner worlds may be no less simulated and virtual than Joi's. The upshot is that Joi's experience may be just as real as ours, and her love for K may be quite real as well—indeed, as real as it gets.

BR2049 is filled with stunning visual images, stirring music, eccentric characters, pithy dialogue, and some very cool technology. But remove Deckard's decades-long love for Rachael, K and Joi's attempt to nurture their unconventional romance, and the even more unconventional ménage à trois that Joi arranges ("a perverse threesome, a loving twosome," in the words of screenwriter Hampton Fancher), and (if we can still imagine the film at all) we would be left with a movie shorn of its emotional raison d'être. According to **Timothy Shanahan**, BR2049 is really a film about the heart presented in the guise of a science fiction thriller. In "Her eyes were green," he explores intimate relationships—especially romance, sex, and love—in BR2049, and makes the case that, rather than being a sexist and misogynistic film, as some critics have complained, it is in fact a trenchant dystopian critique of sexism and misogyny.

"I do hope you're satisfied with our product," remarks Luv, just before her boot crushes Joi's emanator—as K looks on helplessly. This remark could just as easily be directed to Joi as to K inasmuch as both are manufactured products. But they are not merely products; they are also carefully designed consumers. K purchases Joi to address feelings of loneliness, and later buys an emanator for her, much to her delight. Joi hires Mariette to rectify, at least for one memorable encounter, shortcomings in her own physical capabilities. K, Joi, the emanator, and Mariette are all produced by the Wallace Corporation. In other words, Wallace's products are purchasing Wallace's products and services for Wallace's products! As **Paul Smart** shows in "Artificial economics," understanding Joi and K as *economic prosumers* highlights ways in which our desires are sometimes just as much a product of an economic system as are the goods and services we use to satisfy them—with implications for the development of technological advances by which large-scale corporations might act to consolidate their societal power.

BR2049 is a feast for the eyes. The viewer's eyes have much to take in, from the panoramic opening shot of a world denuded of the natural, to its rust-orange-saturated depiction of a Las Vegas in ruins, to its faltering light-show of Elvis revivified. But it is also a film *about* eyes, vision, perception and, ominously, surveillance. Early on we are presented with a close-up of an eye staring back at us, reminding us that we are both observers and observed. Replicants are still identified by their eyes, but the Voight-Kampff machine of the first film has been replaced by a hand-held penlight illuminating indelible serial numbers printed on replicants' sclerae. The self-styled visionary, Niander Wallace, although biologically blind, is nonetheless able to see after a fashion thanks to a prosthetic vision system consisting of six artificial drones. As **Nigel Shadbolt** and **Paul Smart** show in "The eyes of God," BR2049 thereby raises timely questions about human enhancement, cognitive extension, bio-technological hybridization, and the range and implications of viewing technologies in a world on the verge of an era of surveillance capitalism.

Among the questions raised by the original *Blade Runner* film, perhaps none has generated as much discussion and debate among fans as the question of whether replicant-killer Rick Deckard is himself a replicant. There are intriguing hints that he *might* be a replicant; but the truth is never made explicit. Many fans hoped that BR2049 would resolve the issue once and for all. As it turns out, the sequel is just as enigmatic on this score as is the original. Thus, the debate remains stubbornly deadlocked. *Unless*, that is, we believe Ridley Scott, who has insisted that for the story in BR2049 to work, Deckard *has* to be a replicant. In "What am I to you? The Deck-a-Rep debate and the question of fictional truth," **Timothy Shanahan** considers Scott's claim—and the assumptions underlying the Deck-a-Rep debate more generally—by exploring the identity of characters across fictional representations, the limits of directorial fiat, and the very nature of truth in works of fiction, asking: What, if anything, can we really know about fictional truths?

INTRODUCTION 7

As we hope to demonstrate in this collection of specially commissioned essays for Routledge's *Philosophers on Film* series, calling *Blade Runner 2049* a science fiction film, or the sequel to *Blade Runner*, while accurate, fails to do justice to the wealth of philosophical riches that lie in store below its dazzling surface. We invite you to join us in the exciting explorations that follow.

Chapter 1

Timothy Shanahan
WE'RE ALL JUST LOOKING FOR SOMETHING REAL

Did you miss me?

DENIS VILLENEUVE'S BLADE RUNNER 2049 succeeds as a highly entertaining and deeply thought-provoking film on its own terms. But as a *sequel*, our appreciation of the film is enhanced by noticing some of the ways in which it remains faithful to and subtly references philosophical themes that distinguished its famous predecessor, Ridley Scott's *Blade Runner*.[1] Just as the ersatz "Rachael" in BR2049, who asks Deckard, "Did you miss me?" is both similar to, yet recognisably different from, her prototype in the original film, so too the new film clearly gains inspiration from the original film while just as clearly departs from it in important ways.

Consequently, the aim of this chapter is to construct a bridge between various elements of the *Blade Runner* universe to provide important background for the chapters that follow.[2] Philip K. Dick (1978/1995: 260) once explained, "The two basic topics that fascinate me are 'What is reality?' and 'What constitutes the authentic human being?'" Not coincidentally, these are also the two most fundamental questions that animate both *Blade Runner* films. The question of *reality* comes up most noticeably in scenes dealing with animals, memories, and minds.[3] The question of the authentically human pervades both films. Because some readers may not be familiar with this background, it will be helpful to begin by reviewing the basic narratives of both films as well as key elements of Dick's novel before examining the aforementioned themes in more detail.

It was simpler then

The action in the original *Blade Runner* takes place in a decaying, polluted, densely populated Los Angeles in November 2019. Early in the film we learn that the Tyrell Corporation had advanced robot evolution into the NEXUS phase. The NEXUS 6 replicants (i.e., synthetic humans) were virtually identical to human beings, but superior in strength and agility, and at least as intelligent as the genetic engineers who created them.[4] Replicants were used off-world as slave labour in the hazardous exploration and colonisation of other planets. After a bloody mutiny by a NEXUS 6 combat team in an off-world colony, replicants were declared illegal on earth—under penalty of death. Special police squads—blade runner units—had orders to shoot to kill, upon detection, any trespassing replicants. This was not called execution. It was called "retirement."

Rick Deckard (Harrison Ford) is presented as an exceptionally proficient *ex*-blade runner who had quit because, as he narrates in the 1982 theatrical release of the film, he'd had "a bellyful of killing." Nonetheless, thanks to a group of NEXUS 6 replicants who illegally return to earth, he is persuaded (by way of a thinly veiled threat) by his old boss, Capt. Harry Bryant (M. Emmet Walsh) of the LAPD, to resume his former occupation. Deckard succeeds, with considerable difficulty, in killing two of the females—Zhora (Joanna Cassidy) and Pris (Daryl Hannah). Rachael (Sean Young), a beautiful experimental model replicant (with whom, incidentally, he is falling in love), unexpectedly dispatches a third replicant, named Leon (Brion James), by whom Deckard was being brutally assaulted. That left just one rogue replicant, the leader of the band and the most dangerous one of all—a formidable combat model named Roy Batty (Rutger Hauer)—who wastes little time in turning the tables on Deckard, making the hunter the hunted. To Deckard's bafflement, Batty decides to spare him just as Batty's predetermined four-year lifespan is coming to an end. Having narrowly escaped death, Deckard flees with Rachael, making them fugitives. What would become of them was left uncertain for 35 years—until, that is, BR2049 appeared to provide a few tantalising details.

There's still a page left

Set 30 years after the events of the original film, BR2049 opens with text that pays homage to the opening crawl in the first film and that serves to contextualise the current state of affairs:

> REPLICANTS ARE BIOENGINEERED HUMANS, DESIGNED BY TYRELL CORPORATION FOR USE OFF-WORLD. THEIR ENHANCED STRENGTH MADE THEM IDEAL SLAVE LABOR
>
> AFTER A SERIES OF VIOLENT REBELLIONS, THEIR MANUFACTURE BECAME PROHIBITED AND TYRELL CORP WENT BANKRUPT
>
> THE COLLAPSE OF THE ECOSYSTEMS IN THE MID 2020s LED TO THE RISE OF INDUSTRIALIST NIANDER WALLACE, WHOSE MASTERY OF SYNTHETIC FARMING AVERTED FAMINE
>
> WALLACE ACQUIRED THE REMAINS OF TYRELL CORP AND CREATED A NEW LINE OF REPLICANTS WHO OBEY
>
> MANY OLDER MODEL REPLICANTS—NEXUS 8s WITH OPEN-ENDED LIFESPANS—SURVIVED. THEY ARE HUNTED DOWN AND "RETIRED"
>
> THOSE THAT HUNT THEM STILL GO BY THE NAME ...
>
> BLADE RUNNER

We are not told who designed the NEXUS 8 replicants. But in 2022: *Black Out*, one of three short films dramatising key events in the interim between the stories in the two feature films, we learn that, "While the *Replicant* NEXUS 6 expired in inventory, TYRELL CORP. pushed the series 8 into the local and off-world market. The NEXUS series 8 were purpose-built with a natural lifespan." However, this enhancement apparently made the NEXUS 8 replicants seem a little *too* humanlike, and therefore threatening, because we also learn that, "Soon the human supremacy movements began. These angry masses used the **Replicant** Registration database to identify and kill *Replicants*." Led by a NEXUS 8 named Cygnus, the replicants retaliated by triggering a powerful electromagnetic pulse, causing a massive blackout and thereby erasing the Replicant Registration database. We also learn that "The Blackout, which led to the prohibition of Replicant production, sealed the fate of the TYRELL CORPORATION. It took over a decade for THE WALLACE CORP. to win approval to manufacture a new breed of *Replicant*."

In the second short film, *2036: NEXUS Dawn*, we learn how Niander Wallace (Jared Leto), the brilliant, blind, megalomaniacal CEO of the eponymous Wallace Corporation, accomplished that feat. Thanks to goodwill engendered by his development of synthetic farming, Wallace is granted a hearing by government officials in which he shocks them by proposing to resume the manufacture of replicants. When they categorically reject the idea, reminding him of the dangers posed by synthetic humans, he reminds them that it is his patents that keep their hunger at bay, and then provides a dramatic demonstration intended to confirm his boast that, "My replicants will never rebel. They will never run. They will simply obey." Indeed, the new NEXUS 9 replicants he went on to create seem to be deeply integrated into life in mid-twenty-first century Los Angeles, serving not only as blade runners but also as prostitutes and even, in one case, as a top-level executive in the Wallace Corporation itself (Luv, played by Sylvia Hoeks).

Meanwhile, some NEXUS 8 replicants continue to live clandestinely on earth, their escape from slavery abetted by the Blackout of 2022. In the third short film, 2048: *Nowhere to Run*, we learn that a NEXUS 8 named Sapper Morton (Dave Bautista) dropped identifying papers when he was drawn into a violent confrontation in Los Angeles after conducting some personal business.[5] He beats a hasty exit, but it is clear from the ease by which he dispatches several assailants that he is a replicant. The film ends with a bystander tipping off the police with Sapper's address.

This is where BR2049 picks up. The film's protagonist is K (technically, Officer KD6-3.7, played by Ryan Gosling), a taciturn NEXUS 9 blade runner whose job is to hunt down and kill NEXUS 8 replicants.[6] Just before K retires Sapper, the latter cryptically chides his executioner, "You newer models are happy scraping the shit ... because you've never seen a miracle." A surface-penetrating scan of the farm reveals a large box buried next to a dead tree containing the bones of a woman who died in childbirth. Subsequent analysis reveals them to be the bones of Rachael—Tyrell's experimental model replicant introduced in the first film—a shocking discovery because replicants were not supposed to be able to reproduce.[7] K's superior, LAPD Lt. Joshi (Robin Wright), wants K to find and destroy the child and all evidence of its existence because, she warns, "The world is built on a wall. It separates kind. Tell either side there's no wall, you bought a war. Or a slaughter. So, what you saw ... didn't happen." As she reminds K, her job, and his as well, is to keep order. She worries that if it became widely known that a replicant gave birth, the repressive apartheid system that draws a sharp distinction between humans and replicants would collapse, with chaos and bloodshed ensuing. Upon returning to the farm in search of clues, K notices a date carved into the trunk of the dead tree—6 10 21. Presuming that the date carved into the tree was the missing child's birthdate, he or she would now be about 28 years old. K is clearly shaken, although we don't yet know why.

Meanwhile, leak of the discovery of a replicant who gave birth sets off a quest to find Rachael's now-grown child—led by Wallace, who (if Deckard's concern is correct) wants to dissect it and thereby learn how to make procreating replicants with which to populate countless more off-world colonies.[8] As he laments, "Every leap of civilisation was built off the back of a disposable workforce. We lost our stomach for slaves ... unless engineered. But I can only make so many." A third party, Freysa (Hiam Abbass), the one-eyed leader of a new replicant resistance movement, wants to enlist Rachael's offspring as a messiah of sorts for her fledgling rebellion, because (she supposes), "If a baby can come from one of us ... we are much more than slaves, we are our own masters."[9]

In a series of plot twists involving a memory of a toy horse with the date 6 10 21 carved on its base, K comes to believe that *he* is Rachael's son, and thus wants to find Deckard (whom he believes to be his father) so that he can learn more about Rachael. His subsequent quest for self-discovery becomes the narrative engine of the film. K eventually finds Deckard, learns from Freysa that Rachael had a *daughter*, and realises that she must be Dr. Ana Stelline (Carla Juri), a subcontractor providing realistic memories for the Wallace Corporation's replicants. The film ends with K uniting Deckard with the daughter he had never met, and with K (apparently) dying, at peace for having accomplished his mission, on the snow-covered steps of Dr. Stelline's laboratory.

There are, of course, many more details worth reviewing, a selection of which will be discussed below. But with this broad background in mind we can turn our attention to some of the most important philosophical connections between BR2049 and the works from which it is descended.

Is he real?

First, consider the role of *animals* in the *Blade Runner* universe. Philip K. Dick's *Do Androids Dream of Electric Sheep?* is set in San Francisco in 1992. Following an unexplained worldwide calamity, "World War Terminus" (probably a cataclysmic nuclear catastrophe), humans healthy enough to do so are encouraged to emigrate to the off-world colonies to preserve the human gene pool. As an incentive, each émigré is given an andy (an android) as a personal servant. Those left behind are either radiation-induced genetic defectives (such as J. R. Isidore, the inspiration for J. F. Sebastian in the original film), or those (like Rick Deckard) too stubborn to leave. Most animals have perished from the effects of radioactive fallout. The owls were the first to disappear, but most other animals quickly followed. Real animals have become scarce, and are thus expensive to purchase, with the current market price of each listed in the Sidney's catalogue. Possessing a real animal, especially a large one, confers significant social status. Many people have to settle for realistic artificial animals, all the while longing for the real thing.

In Dick's *Electric Sheep*, Rick Deckard is a freelance bounty hunter hired by the San Francisco Police Department to retire rogue androids. When his real sheep dies of tetanus, he replaces it with an artificial one realistic enough to fool his neighbours. Yet he still longs for a *real* animal. After Deckard finally retires enough androids (at a rate of $1,000 per kill) to purchase a real Nubian goat, Rachel Rosen, an android with whom he had conducted a brief sexual affair, correctly perceiving that he cared more about his goat than about her, spitefully pushes the animal to its death off the roof of his apartment building.[10] Having already decided to get out of the bounty-hunting business, Deckard is distraught until, wandering alone in a desert outside the city, he is delighted to chance upon what he takes to be a living toad. He triumphantly brings it home, only to have his wife flip open a control panel on its belly, revealing it to be artificial. Deckard is crestfallen but resigned. Without further income from killing rogue androids, an electric toad will have to suffice.

Numerous (unexplained) references to this important feature of Dick's book appear in *Blade Runner*—for example, Deckard's keen interest in whether Tyrell's owl and Zhora's snake are real or artificial. Once he learns that these creatures are artificial, he immediately loses all interest. This theme also appears in the questions about calfskin wallets and the like posed to Rachael during her Voight-Kampff test, and in the otherwise puzzling artificial animal bazaar ("Animoid Row"), where Deckard follows up on clues to Zhora's whereabouts. In both works, the distinction between real and artificial animals and humans matters a great deal to Deckard.

This explains why, in BR2049, K seems so perplexed upon arriving in Las Vegas to encounter a thriving bee colony.[11] It also explains why, in the short film 2048: *Nowhere to Run*, we see Sapper Morton selling living nematodes to a dealer. Besides the bees, Sapper's nematodes (and perhaps the cowslip on Rachael's grave), are the only non-human living things we see in the film. Even the one tree we see is dead. Significantly, when Mariette (Mackenzie Davis) notices that K is holding a photograph of the tree on Sapper's farm, the following exchange ensues:

> MARIETTE: What's that?
> K: It's a tree.
> MARIETTE: Oh, never seen a tree before.

This scene subtly references a scene in the original film in which blade runner Dave Holden (Morgan Paull) is administering the Voight-Kampff test to Leon:

> HOLDEN: You look down and you see a tortoise, Leon ...
> LEON: Tortoise, what's that?
> HOLDEN: Know what a turtle is?
> LEON: Of course.
> HOLDEN: Same thing.
> LEON: I've never seen a turtle.

By 2019, turtles had become too rare to be seen by most people. Thirty years later, even trees and most other plants have vanished. At best they can be conjured up as pseudo-memories created through technology such as that used by Dr. Ana Stelline. Nature now exists mainly in photographs and phony memories.

Deckard's attitude towards animals in BR2049, to the extent that we can glean it, stands in stark contrast to that of his namesake in those previous works. In a pleasing bit of irony, when K asks Deckard concerning his dog, "Is it real?" the latter, seemingly annoyed, growls, "I don't know. Ask him." Deckard doesn't know, doesn't care, or perhaps now considers the distinction between artificial and real animals to be irrelevant.[12] Perhaps, thirty years on, he has come to the conclusion that the question of reality, at least with respect to animals, including his canine companion, simply doesn't matter.

I have memories; they're not real

Recall from the first film that in response to Deckard's shock in learning that Rachael's memories are implants, Tyrell explained, "If we gift them the past, we create a cushion or pillow for their emotions and consequently we can control them better." At the time, Rachael was still unaware that she was a replicant and, hence, that (some of) what she took to be her memories weren't real. When this truth was finally forced upon her by Deckard, emotional and existential upheaval naturally ensued. Later, having more or less assimilated that profound truth, she worried, "I remember [piano] lessons. I don't know if it's me or Tyrell's niece." Her memories were not self-authenticating. There is nothing about a memory, per se, that identifies *whose* memory it is. Someone else's memories can appear indistinguishable from one's own.

This theme is revisited and greatly expanded in BR2049. When we first meet K, he *knows* that he is a replicant and, hence, that (some of) what he takes to be his memories are merely implants. Replicants are now endowed with realistic pseudo-memories because, as memory maker Dr. Ana Stelline explains, "If you have authentic memories, you have real human responses." Whether these new replicants know from the start that some of their memories are implants, or gradually come to realise this fact, is unclear. There are at least two ways in which it could be the latter.

On the one hand, perhaps NEXUS 9 replicants begin life with implanted memories and start off believing that they are human, then at some later time come to realise that they are replicants. However, this seems like a poor way to impose greater control on them, which was the whole point of implanting memories in the first place. Believing that they are human, and then coming to learn—as they inevitably would, given their subservient role in society—that they have been duped, seems like a recipe for resentment and violent rebellion. More plausibly, it may be that even though the NEXUS 9 replicants know from the start that their memories are implants, such implanted memories are nonetheless effective in cushioning their emotions, thereby making them easier to control. After all, sometimes knowing full well that an experience is not genuine is consistent with that experience having a profound effect upon one's behaviour, as *may* be illustrated in the film by K's emotional attachment to Joi, his holographic AI girlfriend.[13]

Be that as it may, eventually replicants have to come to grips with this aspect of their design. Rachael naturally believed herself to be human, and then had to come to grips with the fact that she was a replicant. K's problem is similar but more complex. Like Rachael, he worries about whether his memories are real. Suspecting that what he took to be mere memory implants might be genuine after all and, hence, that he may be the child of Deckard and Rachael, K visits Dr. Ana Stelline in an attempt to find out. When she informs him concerning his memories, "Someone lived this, yes. This happened," he fails to consider the possibility that the person who lived the experiences recorded in the memories may not be him, setting him off on a quest to find Deckard and learn the truth. K's consuming problem is that he believed himself to be a replicant, and then came to suspect and perhaps even to believe that he was human, only to be summarily divested of that belief by Freysa—making his existential journey even more dizzying than Rachael's. Like Rachael, K eventually decides to act on the basis of who he is now, and in relation to what he can still accomplish, rather than on who and what he previously believed himself to be. The memories themselves didn't change; only their significance did. Hence, just as in the original film, memories prove to be unreliable guides to identity, and also largely irrelevant to the task of embracing one's current reality, who and what one is and, importantly, what one must do.

She's very realistic

Joi is an interactive artificial intelligence (AI) system outfitted with a holographic avatar. Sold by the Wallace Corporation as a digital personal companion, recurring advertisements in the film remind us that K's particular Joi (Ana de Armas) is an instance of a generic commercial product. We first encounter her as a *voice* informing K about the musical selection that plays when he enters his apartment. When Joi finally appears, we are still encouraged to think of her as merely an entertaining (and alluring) gadget. However, as the film progresses, she seems (and perhaps becomes) more intelligent, self-aware, and autonomous, even to the point of self-consciously jeopardising herself, "just like a real girl" might, as she supposes. Apparently, Joi can learn and evolve in response to novel experiences. Screenwriter

Hampton Fancher even goes so far as to say that, despite the fact that Joi's responses *are* programmed, "Through her attachment [to K] ... her love for him becomes real, as opposed to programmed. So she escapes her own limitations, the digital limitations, and becomes totally real for herself."[14] Consequently, contrary to the dismissive insult Mariette hurls at Joi as she leaves K's apartment—"I've been inside you. Not so much there as you think"—the viewer is more likely to draw the *opposite* conclusion. There appears to be much more to Joi than we initially might have supposed.

Nothing like this appears in Blade Runner. There we get a talking elevator in Deckard's apartment building and the rudimentary (by comparison) mechanical friends J. F. Sebastian has made to ease his loneliness. But neither displays the slightest evidence of having a mind, as Joi does. It is true that commentators on the original film routinely describe the replicants as instances of artificial intelligence. In one sense, of course, they are right. The replicants are highly intelligent, and they are artificial in the sense that they were made by human ingenuity rather than through a purely natural biological process. But replicants are not examples of artificial intelligence in the precise sense in which that term is used in computer science and philosophy. In those disciplines, artificial intelligence refers to the ability of a *machine* to perform tasks which, were they performed by a human, would require intelligence. That replicants are not artificially intelligent in this strict sense was made explicit in the first film. When J. F. Sebastian implores his strange guests to "show me something," Roy Batty indignantly reminds him, "We're not computers, Sebastian. We're physical!" Likewise, the replicants in BR2049 are synthetic humans, not AI in the conventional sense in which that description is used.

But in BR2049 we do encounter something that deserves to be called AI, and perhaps even AC—artificial consciousness. Joi appears to display a degree of mentality that is indistinguishable from that exhibited by any of the natural or synthetic humans in the film, and thus invites viewers to posit a mind that is responsible for those capabilities—that is, not merely a mind that *created* Joi, but rather a mind that *is* Joi. But how could we ever know whether this attribution is correct? The difficulty is that other minds are not available for direct inspection. We can't just look inside heads to see them. We have to infer their existence from features we *can* observe.

It was for this reason that computer pioneer Alan M. Turing (1912–1954), in his classic paper, "Computing Machinery and Intelligence" (1950), proposed the famous operational test that he called the "Imitation Game," but that has subsequently become known as the Turing Test. Turing wanted to answer the question: "Can machines think?" By a *machine* he meant (in this context) a digital computer. By *thinking* he meant the sort of thing that humans do when, for example, they write a poem. Computers can, of course, compose poetry. But could a computer compose poetry in the *way* that a human poet might? Would it need to create the poem in the same *way* that humans do? Turing acknowledged that we cannot peer inside a machine to see if it is really thinking. But by the same token, we can't peer into another human being's head to see if they are really thinking, either; yet (often) we draw that very conclusion. In practice, we decide that a being is thinking if it *behaves* as we expect thinking beings to behave, for example, by being able to carry on an unscripted conversation as another human might. If a machine can do that, Turing thought, we have no more grounds for denying that the machine is thinking than we do for denying that other human beings with whom we converse are thinking. Joi clearly passes this test. It seems to follow that she really does have a mind. Two sorts of considerations should give us pause, however.

One worry concerns the adequacy of Turing's test of the mental. Passing that test is clearly not a *necessary* condition for having a mind because small children and someone taking a nap would fail to qualify. More importantly, it is not obvious that passing Turing's test is a *sufficient* condition for mindedness, either, because an appropriately sophisticated computational system could convincingly mimic mental activity without there being any genuine mental activity at all, as critics like John Searle (e.g. 1980) have argued for decades. That issue is still far from settled.

The other sort of worry arises from the film itself, which reminds us again and again that Joi is a product that has been designed to provide "everything you want to see" and "everything you want to hear." That is exactly what Joi does for K. Once he begins to suspect that he is Rachael's son, Joi does everything possible to encourage that belief, telling him: "I always knew you were special. Maybe this is how. A child. Of woman born. Pushed into the world. Wanted. Loved." She even gives him a personal name, "Joe," because "a real boy deserves a real name."

Later, as K interacts on the bridge with a giant Joi-like hologram who tells him, "You look like a good Joe," he seems to come to grips with the fact that he had (literally) bought into a seductive lie. Of course, the fact that Joi has been programmed does not necessarily show that she is nothing but her programming. Perhaps, somehow, she evolved from her initial limitations, as Hampton Fancher suggests. We are not given nearly enough information to know one way or the other. But there are clues. The most telling clue might be the holographic steak dinner Joi superimposes on K's unappetizing bowl of noodles. The steak is utterly fake, yet K is happy to indulge in the fantasy because, sometimes, the truth is just too unappetizing to swallow.

A real boy needs a real name

Next to the question of what is *real*, no question is more fundamental to both *Blade Runner* films than the question of what it means to be *human*, although it assumes different forms in each film. The first film compels viewers to ask whether the supposed differences between replicants and their human masters justifies the former's exploitation by the latter. The new film reinforces that question while posing the additional question of whether a replicant giving birth demolishes the presumed "wall" separating replicants and humans. Even the perennial question of whether Deckard is a replicant or a human presupposes a hard distinction between the two and, hence, implicitly at least, a view about what it *means* to be human. The replicants in both films are so human-like that, apart from conducting a complicated and time-consuming test (in the first film), or detecting an identification number stamped on the lower portion of their right eye (in the new film), they are for all practical purposes physically indistinguishable from humans. Indeed, right at the start of BR2049 we are informed that the replicants are "bioengineered humans." The question, then, concerns what distinguishes and defines the *authentic* human. By implication, both films challenge viewers to ponder what it is that makes *us* human, and whether that is something we can share with other beings, including any that we might produce in the future.

Recall how this issue is addressed in the original film. At first, Deckard considers the replicants to be considerably *less than human*. He brushes off Rachael's question about whether he feels that the Tyrell Corporation's work is a benefit to the public, retorting, "Replicants are like any other machine. They're either a benefit or a hazard. If they're a benefit, it's not my problem." At that point, at least, Deckard viewed replicants as little more than household appliances that can become dangerous when they malfunction, a view that was apparently shared by other blade runners.[15] By contrast, Eldon Tyrell boasts that his replicants are "*more human than human.*" With enhanced strength and intelligence, they are like a superior race of humans, albeit with a severely circumscribed lifespan and emotional immaturity commensurate with their youth. The replicants' own view is more ambiguous. Certainly, they *aspire* to be acknowledged as something more than mere commodities, as when Rachael laments, "I'm not in the business. I *am* the business." Yet they seem perfectly willing to accept the distinction between replicants and human beings, as evidenced by their repeated differentiation of themselves from humans.[16]

What is it, then, that differentiates replicants from authentic humans? In the first film, the answer is supposed to be that replicants are lacking the distinctive human capacity for *empathy*. The Voight-Kampff test works by detecting minute physiological changes elicited by the subject's emotional responses to a series of carefully designed questions involving human or animal suffering. The logic behind the test is that it takes years to develop an empathic capacity—longer than the time allotted to the replicants. Because humans are assumed to be naturally empathic, the Voight-Kampff test can be used as a diagnostic tool to distinguish replicants from humans—provided, that is, that one can assume that all humans have at least some empathic response to others' suffering, and that all replicants necessarily lack one. Those assumptions are gradually undermined in the original film—in both directions. Most of the humans in the film appear to lack empathy. Capt. Harry Bryant is presented as a bigot who derisively refers to replicants as "skinjobs." As already noted, Deckard thinks of replicants as little more than machines. J. R. Sebastian is a notable exception, perhaps because of his condition. By contrast, the replicants seem to demonstrate at least a rudimentary form of empathy—evidenced by Roy Batty's concern that Leon has lost his precious photos, and that a solution be found to Pris's abbreviated lifespan.

As in the original film, the story in BR2049 turns on the enormous weight some of the characters place on what they take to be the essential feature(s) of being human. Lt. Joshi worries that if it became known that some of those features were shared with replicants, the "wall" separating humans and replicants would collapse, and with it the fragile stability of the current social order. By contrast, this is a consequence that Freysa, the one-eyed replicant resistance leader, would welcome, and in fact is actively working toward. For K, the issue is more personal: How did he come to be? Thus, just as in the original film, the issue matters a great deal to some of the sequel's central characters. But *how* this distinction gets drawn is different in the two films. In the first film it was the human capacity for empathy that was supposed to be decisive. In BR2049 the question of what it means to be an authentic human is given at least four different answers.

The first answer concerns *how one comes into existence*. Ordered by Lt. Joshi to locate and destroy Rachael's offspring, K worries, "I've never retired something that was born." Lt. Joshi doesn't challenge the distinction K presupposes. Human beings are *born*, replicants are *made*, and this distinction is assumed to carry profound moral implications. To be *made* is to be an instrument for another's use and disposed of when no longer considered useful. By contrast, to be *born* is to have an intimate connection to someone else to whom your own well-being matters. As Joi tells K, "I always knew you were special. Maybe this is how. A child. Of woman born. Pushed into the world. Wanted. Loved." She even equates K's being born with K being *real* in a way that he otherwise would not be: "You're special. Born, not made ... A *real* boy now." Wallace can be interpreted as endorsing this distinction as well, even as he attempts (unsuccessfully) to transcend it by creating procreative replicants. When he murmurs, "Happy birthday," to his newest replicant creation, he acknowledges the made/born distinction while painfully observing that he has as yet failed to render it obsolete.

The second answer to the question of what it means to be an authentic human concerns the *soul*. When K balks at the idea of retiring something that was born and is prodded by Lt. Joshi to explain what that means, he conjectures, "To be born ... is to have a soul, I guess." He is not encouraged to elaborate. Lt. Joshi's terse response—"You've been getting on fine without one"—could be interpreted as simply taking for granted the distinction between replicants and authentic humans that K presupposes, or else as dismissing the concern by implying that even if there is such a thing as a soul, it doesn't make any practical difference; so just get on with the task at hand.

The third answer to the question of what it means to be an authentic human is suggested by Freysa. Having summarily stripped K of his nascent belief that he is the child of Rachael, that is, that he was born and thus is human, she attempts to compensate by assuring him that he still has an opportunity to become authentically human, telling him: "Dying for the right cause is the most human thing we can do." Presupposed are the assumptions that (a) K is not at present (fully) human, (b) dying for a cause greater than oneself is a "human" thing to do, and (c) it is through one's choices and actions, rather than because of what one essentially is, that one can approximate the state of being authentically human that humans, who were born, automatically enjoy.

The fourth answer to the question of what it means to be an authentic human is suggested not by anything explicitly said in the film, but by the overall narrative arc of K's quest. To avert another replicant uprising, the NEXUS 9 replicants were designed by Wallace to obey. At first, K appears to do just that. But, as the film progresses, we see him begin to question the directive he received from Lt. Joshi and to act in a more autonomous way, culminating in his finding Deckard and uniting him with the daughter he never knew. This act has nothing do with being born, having a soul, or dying for a cause greater than oneself. Arguably, K's growing awareness of himself as an autonomous agent, not defined by his maker or his past, is more important than any of those proposed answers. Parallel to Deckard's gradual moral awakening in the original film, in the new film K's incremental embrace of his own *agency* becomes its central and most-important motif.[17]

We're all just looking out for something real

Deckard may no longer care whether his canine companion is a real dog, but reality still matters to him. When Wallace presents him with an ersatz Rachael to entice him to share information that could reveal the whereabouts of his daughter, Deckard rejects this stunning gift as a mere facsimile. As painful as it must be, he knows that the specific woman he loved is forever gone.[18] When provoked by Wallace to consider the possibility that his and Rachael's love for one another may have been carefully orchestrated by Tyrell to produce a child, Deckard responds, as if to reassure himself, "I know what's real." Reality, in this case at least, still matters to him.

Other scenes suggest that although the real still matters in 2049, its precise boundaries have shifted. Whereas formerly (i.e., in the original film) the distinction was between real (natural) animals and fake (synthetic) animals, now it is between *those* sorts of creatures, on the one hand, and *inanimate replicas*, on the other. When K brings his carved wooden horse to Doc Badger (Barkhad Abdi) to discover clues to its origin, he is encouraged to sell it in exchange for "a real horse"—by which the trader means an *artificial* horse: "I can get you a real horse. You want a real horse? I can get you one, like Wallace stuff." Real (flesh and blood) horses have become so rare (or non-existent) that an artificial horse now qualifies as a *real* horse. Likewise, when K's device beeps, revealing to all within earshot that he has a digital girlfriend, Mariette remarks, somewhat condescendingly, "Oh, I see, you don't like real girls." The "real girls" she has in mind, of course, are *replicants*, like herself. The line demarcating real and artificial creatures has shifted so much that an animoid horse can be called a "real horse" and replicant prostitutes can be called "real girls" without eliciting any overt sense of contradiction.

Nonetheless, despite this shifting local ontology, the more global distinction between what's real and what isn't, and the importance of feeling that one *knows* which things are and aren't real, still matters. In order to prevent her files from falling into the wrong hands, Joi accepts a greatly increased risk of personal annihilation, suggesting that being able to make such a momentous choice erases any essential difference between herself and "a real girl." K is anxious to find out whether what he took to be his memory implants are in fact *real* memories. He worries, "I have memories ... but they're not real. They're just implants." When Dr. Ana Stelline reveals to him that someone lived the memories he has (e.g. of the wooden horse), he is emotionally overcome, uttering, not unlike Deckard, "I know it's real." Consequently, one of the film's key take-home messages is that although often it may be difficult to know for sure *what* is real, *reality itself* still matters. As Lt. Joshi perceptively observes, "We're all just looking out for something real."

Notes

1 *Blade Runner* eventually appeared in seven different versions, although most of the variations among them are minor. In the discussions that follow, references to *Blade Runner* are to *Blade Runner: The Final Cut* (2007), unless otherwise indicated.
2 By "the *Blade Runner* universe" I mean Philip K. Dick's (1968) source novel, *Do Androids Dream of Electric Sheep?*; the original *Blade Runner* film (both 1982's theatrical release and 2007's *Final Cut*), including various deleted scenes; the three short films, *2022: Black Out*, *2036: Nexus Dawn*, and *2048: Nowhere to Run*; the final shooting script of BR2049; and, of course, *Blade Runner 2049*. If Stephen Mulhall (chapter 2) is right, perhaps some of Ridley Scott's *Alien* films also belong to the same universe. Excluded from consideration are the spin-off novels by K. W. Jeter, comic books, video games, various websites, and so forth.
3 The word "real" and its cognates appear 32 times in BR2049, and an additional 16 times in the shooting script. By contrast, the word "human" and its cognates appear five times in BR2049, and an additional eight times in the shooting script.
4 For the sake of this discussion I will bracket the issue of whether a hard distinction between replicants and humans is sound in the first place. I have discussed this issue in detail elsewhere (Shanahan, 2014, 2018). Following the distinctions introduced in BR2049, by *replicant* I will mean a bioengineered human and, by *human*, a human being who was "born, not made."
5 The film suggests that Sapper Morton used his surgical skills to deliver Rachael's child by C-section. It is noteworthy that in *2022: Black Out*, he is identified as a NEXUS 8 replicant with an incept date of 22 MAR, 2019. Another NEXUS 8 replicant, Cygnus (aka, Iggy), a leader of the Replicant Resistance, is given an incept date of 30 SEP, 2019. Both incept dates are before the November 2019 events of the first film, suggesting that the NEXUS series 8 models were already in production at the time of Tyrell's death. However, in BR2049 Sapper Morton's incept date is shown to be 15 JUL 2020. Depending on which incept date for him is chosen, he would have been one-and-a-half to two-and-a-half years old when the child was born. A similar discrepancy concerning incept dates appears in *Blade Runner* in the case of Leon (see Shanahan, 2014: 28).
6 In *Blade Runner 101: Blade Runners*, a featurette included with the BR2049 DVD, Ryan Gosling tells us: "Thirty years after where the first film left off, the profession of the blade runner is a little different and more complicated ... It's my character's job to retire rogue replicants. The police department found that there was too much moral conflict with human beings killing replicants, so they designed a whole new breed of replicant just to be blade runners, and their sole purpose is to kill their own kind."
7 Fan speculation (abetted by comments made by Ridley Scott) has long been that Rachael was a NEXUS 7 model enhanced with even more human-like

characteristics. This supposition is supported in BR2049 by the serial number visible on her remains: N7FAA52318—i.e., a NEXUS 7 female with A-level mental and physical capabilities and an incept date of 23 MAY 2018.

8   Wallace's claim, "We make angels in the service of civilization" calls to mind Roy Batty's oblique reference to himself and the other rogue replicants in his "Fiery the angels fell" utterance in the first film.

9   From the computer screen in K's spinner we learn that Freysa Sadeghpour was a NEXUS 8 combat engineer (incept date: 21 DEC 2020). From Marietta we learn that she served off-world with Sapper Morton on Calantha.

10 In Dick's novel, Rachel Rosen is initially presented as the niece of Eldon Rosen, CEO of the powerful Rosen Corporation, before being revealed to be an android. Rachel and Eldon Rosen are, of course, the models for Rachael and Eldon Tyrell in *Blade Runner*.

11 The bee colony *is* puzzling. How could there be such a thing in the world depicted in BR2049? Two speculative answers come to mind. Perhaps the bees—amongst the most vulnerable of animals in our world—are a sign of hope, and as such represent K's hope of finding Deckard and the answers he seeks. Alternatively, perhaps they are a homage to the original film, in which Roy Batty inexplicably finds a living dove atop the Bradbury Building.

12 Deckard's terse response could also be interpreted as *Harrison Ford* saying to viewers, "Do you really want to know what *my* character is? Am I a replicant or a human? Why don't you ask *me*?" (Ford's consistent answer in interviews: Deckard is human.) K's lack of curiosity about Deckard's nature is hard to fathom—unless, somehow, he already knew the answer to *that* question or, like Deckard, he considered the answer to that question to be irrelevant.

13 Although, as chapter 9 in this book makes clear, it remains an open, and interesting, question whether K and Joi's relationship constitutes a genuinely romantic relationship.

14 In *Blade Runner 101: Jois* (note the plural), a bonus feature included with the BR2049 DVD/Blu-Ray.

15 In a deleted scene, blade runner Dave Holden dismissively compares replicants to washing machines.

16 Recall Pris's remark to J. F. Sebastian, "I don't think there's another *human being* in the whole world who would have helped us" (emphasis added). In response to Roy's question to Leon about whether the latter was able to retrieve his precious photos from his room, Leon says flatly, "Someone was there." Roy then presses him further: "*Men?* Police-*men*?" (emphases in original). When Roy begins to convey to Deckard what it means to him that his life is about to end, he says: "I've seen things *you people* wouldn't believe" (emphasis in original). And so on.

17 See Robert W. Clowes' "Breaking the code: strong agency and becoming a person" (chapter 6) for detailed discussion of this issue.

18 The same is perhaps true of K when he encounters the large pink Joi hologram in the next scene. Presumably, K could purchase another Joi who would resemble his Joi. But the shared memories and experiences that made his Joi unique have been irrevocably lost. Deckard rejects Wallace's bribe, telling him, "Her eyes were green." We also see that the pink Joi's eyes are unlike those of K's Joi. Perhaps we are being told that, once destroyed, the identity of these characters has been lost forever. See "Her eyes were green" (chapter 9) for discussion.

References

Dick, P. K. (1968). *Do Androids Dream of Electric Sheep?* New York: Ballantine Books.

Dick, P. K. (1978/1995). How to Build a Universe that Doesn't Fall Apart Two Days Later. In L. Sutin (Ed.), *The Shifting Realities of Philip K. Dick: Selected Literary and Philosophical Writings* (pp. 259–280). New York: Vintage Books.

Searle, J. (1980). Is the Brain's Mind a Computer Program? *Scientific American* 262(1), 26–31.

Shanahan, T. (2014). *Philosophy and Blade Runner.* Houndmills: Palgrave Macmillan.

Shanahan, T. (2018). Mirrors for the Human Condition. In L. Tambone & J. Bongiorno (Eds.), *The Cyberpunk Nexus: Exploring the Blade Runner Universe* (pp. 143–160). Edwardsville, IL: Sequart Organization.

Turing, A. M. (1950). Computing Machinery and Intelligence. *Mind* 59(236), 433–460.

Chapter 2

Stephen Mulhall

THE ALPHABET OF US
MIRACLES, MESSIANISM, AND THE BASELINE TEST IN *BLADE RUNNER 2049*

Introduction

MEMORIES OF BLADE RUNNER ARE strand over strand with memories of my intellectual life. I first saw the film in 1982, after a summer vacation spent reading Kant's *Critique of Pure Reason*, with the friend who shared my struggles with that text. I used Leon's confrontation with Deckard after Zhora's death in my first lecture course in my first full-time teaching post at the University of Essex. And, as the film's identity evolved, mine did too: so when, between the *Director's Cut* (in 1992) and the *Final Cut* (in 2007), I first wrote something about film and philosophy, its focus was bound to be this movie. "Picturing the Human (Body and Soul)" (Mulhall, 1994) led to *On Film* (Mulhall, 2002), which invokes *Blade Runner* in discussing Scott's earlier film, *Alien* (1979), and its sequels; each film is viewed as at once a moment in the development of the *Alien* universe and of its director (as James Cameron, David Fincher, and Jean-Pierre Jeunet each brought their own sensibilities to bear on Scott's original material).[1] Although later editions of the book moved further away from *Blade Runner*, I did write another essay on it, analysing Deckard's use of his Esper machine to analyse Leon's photo of the replicants' apartment (Mulhall, 2015). And in the book's third edition I highlighted a fateful invocation of *Blade Runner* in Scott's recent revival of the *Alien* franchise in *Prometheus* (2012).

Amongst the Blu-Ray extras of *Prometheus* is an illuminating memorandum written by Peter Weyland, creator of the David 8 robot and founder of the Weyland-Yutani corporation that bestrides the *Alien* universe. In it he recalls his mentor and long-departed competitor—an unnamed man who lived atop a pyramid overlooking the City of Angels—who wanted to collaborate with him so that they might become the new gods. Viewers of *Blade Runner* will recognise this unnamed man as Eldon Tyrell, founder of the Tyrell Corporation, creator of replicants. In one stroke, then, Scott has fused the *Alien* and *Blade Runner* universes: *Prometheus* has ensured that these apparently distinct cinematic worlds must now be viewed, not just as two products of one man's creativity, but as one and the same—as single, and as singular, as their creator.

Denis Villeneuve's 2017 sequel to *Blade Runner*, for which Ridley Scott was executive producer, could hardly avoid taking this into account; so his task both resembles and differs from Cameron's in directing the first *Alien* sequel. Like Cameron, Villeneuve is the first inheritor of this particular Scott-created universe, and therefore has the privilege and burden of effecting a distinction between the *Blade Runner* universe and Scott's realisation of it. Unlike Cameron, Villeneuve has to contend with Scott's belated redefinition of that universe; for by making another *Alien* film in such a way as to inscribe it within the *Blade Runner* universe, Scott has equally inscribed *Blade Runner* within that hitherto alternative *Alien* universe.

I accordingly intend to explore *Blade Runner 2049* by considering it in relation to its illustrious predecessor, to Scott's recent revival of his *Alien* universe, and to Villeneuve's own preceding body of work. In so doing, I draw on a number of interlinked cells of my previous work on film and philosophy and, in particular, on the methodological assumption that (at least some) Hollywood franchises can enable some good directors to articulate the logic of a cinematic world in philosophically pertinent ways.

Background radiation: *Prometheus*

Ingeniously exploiting *Alien*'s narrative hinterland, *Prometheus* concerns a species it names "Engineers"—beings who have seeded life across the universe, including that on Earth. Once alerted to their existence and possible location, the ageing Weyland underwrites an interstellar expedition to satisfy his all-consuming desire to meet his makers and extract the secret of more life—essentially the motivation of the replicants in *Blade Runner*. Weyland's makers also resemble the maker of replicants in their reliance on genetic engineering: in the Engineers' case, a blood-black slime that, when brought into contact with existing forms of organic life, effects radical molecular reconstruction.

This resemblance between the Engineers and Tyrell is anathema to Weyland because, as his memorandum spells out, he loathes Tyrell's preferred mode of creativity:

> He chose to replicate the power of creation in an unoriginal way, by simply copying God. And look how that turned out for him ... I always suggested that he stick with simple robotics instead of those genetic abominations. The David 8s represent the first true evolutionary step forward in creating new and mentally superior life on Earth. If one who can create life from nothing is a God, what does that make me?

Tyrell's creative process is triply derivative. Replication is the DNA helix's basic mode of operation; and creating living beings by genetic engineering merely reiterates the way life was first created, which amounts to slavishly imitating God. Weyland's preferred creative mode does not operate by replication: for robotic life is, and is engendered, in a way unlike that of any other kind of living being; so, the inventor of robotic life matches divine creativity in a genuinely creative way. Weyland sees robotics as the creation of life from nothing, despite its obvious dependence on raw materials and technologies, because those resources include nothing living or programmed to generate life.

Weyland abominates replicants because of what he (like Ripley) finds abominable about organic life in general, and human life in particular— its inherent fertility, its mindless, unstoppable capacity to proliferate by reproduction. This is why his biological daughter is as nothing to him: "in all the most meaningful ways, beyond the messy clutter of procreation, David is my one true offspring...." Yet the Engineers' creativity exploits precisely what Weyland abhors—a point *Prometheus* underlines by showing how their slime transfigures human sexual reproduction, when the infertile Elizabeth Shaw's intercourse with a slime-infected Charlie Holloway engenders an accelerated pregnancy, the offspring of which is an indirect precursor of the lethal xenomorph of the original *Alien* films.

Weyland, then, like the replicants, is the product of a creativity that is essentially continuous with the merely procreative; and that is precisely why he needs the Engineers. For *his* creative skills eschew the medium of flesh and blood, and so cannot improve his own mode of existence: only those who made him so originally could remake him so as to avoid or defer his own extinction. So, he can only transcend his own mode of being by acknowledging that he is the kind of creature he abominates, created by the kind of creature he abominates, in a manner that he abominates. This is a recipe for self-hatred or self-abasement, so it is not surprising that his makers, once confronted, not only refuse to extend his life but immediately end it (thereby repeating the logic of Deckard's Socratic encounter with Leon on the topic of mortality, and inverting the outcome of the replicants' confrontation with their maker).

But *Prometheus* unsettles two deeper assumptions informing Weyland's narcissistic self-hatred. The first is the idea that either Weyland or Tyrell (or the Engineers) have crossed the boundary between the natural and the divine. In truth, neither robotic nor biological modes of creativity could possibly match up to God's, for both involve creating something from something rather than from nothing, whether or not that something is essentially continuous with organic life. Both are resolutely intra-worldly modes of creativity—the achievement of unusually intelligent and powerful beings, who are nevertheless as much a part of the material universe as are their creations. As Shaw (both a religious believer and a scientist) points out, if the Engineers really did bring the human species into being, then something must have brought them into being: we can legitimately ask who created our creators, which means that they cannot have divine status as mainstream Christian theology understands it. For the Christian God has no beginning or end and is dependent on nothing for His existence: He creates all that is *ex nihilo*, and the creator of all could not conceivably be a part of creation, however well-endowed. So when Weyland meets his makers, he does so in exactly the sense in which Roy Batty meets his maker: the fact that Roy can kill Tyrell simply confirms that Tyrell is no more a God in any genuinely religious sense of that term than is Weyland or, for that matter, the Engineers.

Weyland's second dubious assumption is his belief in an absolute distinction between the biological and the technological. For not just the uncanny ontology of the Engineer's slime, but every material trace of the spirit of their culture (from the ellipsoid spaces, rib-like pillars, and intestinal passageways of their architecture, to the pilot's flight suit, whose elephantine head and trunk are in fact a helmet with exoskeletal tubing) suggests an aspiration not so much to deny as to transcend the opposition between the biological and the technological. But, if human life was created by means that escape capture in terms of an opposition that came to determine its contemporary cultural forms, then the slime-based creativity of the Engineers is no more reducible to Tyrellian genetic engineering than it is opposed to Weylandian robotics. Rather, both human modes of creation fail to match that of the makers of the human, because each defines itself in opposition to the other instead of aspiring to acknowledge, incorporate, and transcend it. If either Tyrell or Weyland are ever to claim creative capacities on a par with those of their makers, they must radically rethink their approaches.

Scott plainly intends to carry through such a rethinking on the Weyland side of this fragile ontological opposition in his planned series of sequels to *Prometheus*—and has begun to do so in *Alien: Covenant* (2017). The lens through which it examines these issues is David, a technological marvel who is driven by his encounter with the Engineers to an obsessive interest in genetic manipulation and thereby to an inflection of the Gothic archetype that most plainly interrogates the boundary between the biological and the technological—the persona of Dr Frankenstein (a persona that taps deeply into Scott's earlier work on Dr Lecter in *Hannibal* [2001]).

Any director of a *Blade Runner* sequel made in the wake of *Prometheus* and its sequels is therefore likely to find complementary themes and scenarios jostling for attention on the Tyrell side of this boundary. Most obviously, the *Alien*-inflected connection between the creation of organic artificial life and procreation raises the question: If replicants are essentially biological beings, then how are we to understand their relation to the capacity, and drive to reproduce? Our hypothetical director might well find himself imagining a supposedly infertile woman nevertheless giving birth, by means of a sexual encounter with another whose human status is in doubt, and in relation to which claims of some internal relation to divine creativity are widely made—call it the question of whether such an event merits the term "miracle." Such a study will likely find its own way of either (re-)drawing or denying the distinction between the biological and the technological.

Background radiation: *Arrival*

Denis Villeneuve came to this directorial task immediately after making his first science fiction movie. *Arrival* (2016) follows the efforts of a team of linguists and other scientists (led by Louise Banks and Ian Donnelly) to communicate with the seven-limbed inhabitants of alien spaceships, twelve of which arrive simultaneously at different earthly locations, and whose intentions remain worryingly opaque. The heptapods are eventually enticed into producing symbols: they secrete an ink-like substance that instantaneously coalesces into a circle, delineated by a single, continuous "line" built up from a multitude of interlinked strokes whose shapes vary in delicately beautiful and complex ways, displayed on a translucent screen within their vessel. This language is semasiographic (not a representation of their spoken language). Its "sentences" contain individual semograms (units of meaning) whose identity depends on which other semograms they are combined with, and how, in a given circle; and each semogram is constructed from strokes that simultaneously participate in several semograms in the circle. Heptapod language is thus radically non-linear: its sentences have no start-point or endpoint, and before the first stroke of any given circular sentence is laid down, its user must already know the shape and location of every other stroke from which that sentence will be constructed.

In a deleted scene (included in the Blu-Ray edition, and in the short story that is the film's source), Donnelly offers an analogy.[2] Fermat's Principle of Least Time governs the refraction of light: it states that the route taken by a light ray from point A (e.g. in air) to point B (e.g. in water) is always the fastest possible one. This property of light rays can be characterised mathematically in a way that presents its journey as a linear, cause-and-effect narrative, according to which reaching the water surface causes the light ray's change of direction; but this requires a highly complex, and unintuitive, calculus of variations. Or we can characterise it teleologically instead: it is as if every ray of light obeys the command "thou shalt always minimise the time taken." But that presupposes that the light ray knows where it will end up before choosing which direction in which to begin moving; it means dispensing with our usual linear mode of relating past, present, and future, and the cause–effect framework associated with it.

Heptapod language-users are just like the light rays, when interpreted teleologically: they must know the telos of their symbol construction before beginning it, and so must know its effects before initiating their cause. When Donnelly and Banks combine this insight with the Sapir-Whorf hypothesis—that the structure of a language conditions the modes of behaviour, experience, and thought characteristic of the culture in which it is spoken—they conclude that users of such a language must have a radically non-linear relation to cause and effect, and so to time. In short, the heptapods no more distinguish cause from effect in the way we do than they distinguish past, present, and future as we do; and in mastering their language, Banks switches to their non-linear mode of experiencing time.

Although she has neither children nor partner, Banks is increasingly assailed by what appear to be memories of bringing up a daughter named Hannah, until Hannah's untimely death from an aggressive disease. We only gradually learn that, after the heptapods depart, she will marry Donnelly and have a daughter who dies in this way. So, Banks knows before Donnelly proposes marriage, let alone having a child, that he will do so, and what will ensue. Without revealing this, she accepts both proposals, and thereby chooses even that traumatically truncated experience of motherhood (as well as Donnelly's later decision to leave them both when she does tell him what she has done) over Hannah's non-existence.

Banks's internalisation of non-linear temporality has political as well as personal ramifications (since it empowers her to prevent China's catastrophic plan to attack the heptapods); but it is also peculiarly reflexive or self-enabling. For Banks masters the heptapod language solely because she learnt enough of it to "remember" reading a prepublication copy of the book she wrote after the aliens' departure detailing its grammar. The linguistic immersion that brings about her non-linear relation to past, present, and future is thus itself brought about in a non-linear way: only her knowledge of its endpoint allows her to determine the right direction for reaching it.

So, it's unsurprising that Banks's transformation has another reflexive dimension. For it amounts to a study of two fundamental conditions for the possibility of cinema: the technique of the flashback and the distinction between actor and character. Banks's assault by memories of her future disorients her in ways that parallel our disorientation as viewers, when we realise that sequences bearing the usual markers of glimpses of a character's past are in fact glimpses of her future: we cannot call them "flashforwards," since that presupposes the linear temporality they violate. And Banks's subjection to unwanted glimpses of what has already happened, but still has to be brought about, seems an apt figure for Amy Adams's condition as a film actor. Like any actor, having read the script before beginning to act, she must inhabit her character's present moment despite knowing what its future moments will be; and if (unlike theatre actors) her scenes are, as is usual, shot out of chronological order, she must realise each of her character's present moments when she may not yet have realised her earlier moments and may already have realised moments yet to come.

Arrival thereby conditions Villeneuve's mode of inheriting Scott's Blade Runner universe in three central ways. There is the focus on the birth of a child, and its internal relation to the rebirth or conversion of an adult, and so of the world; there is the issue of memory—and the ways in which transfigurations of memory can constitute and disrupt personal and collective identity; and there is the interest in the way language can inform and transform thought and experience. This last interest may not seem inherently cinematic, since we all know (don't we?) that the language of film is visual. But that claim is already under pressure in Arrival, and it constitutes a key way in which Villeneuve, in Blade Runner 2049, differentiates himself from Scott.

Sex work: embodiment and the miracle of birth

In "Picturing the Human" (Mulhall, 1994), I argued that Blade Runner's violence is generally directed against replicants in order to elicit from its viewers an instinctive empathetic response that matches their response to the infliction of pain on human beings. It underlines that replicants are embodied (as Roy puts it, "We're not computers, Sebastian: we're physical"), and so can manifest the full range and complexity of behaviour open to human beings. On this basis alone, we find ourselves compelled to apply to them the full range of psychological concepts delineating the realm of the mental. Blade Runner thus demonstrates that the criteria that justify our application of psychological concepts (our attribution of a mind) are manifest in behaviour of a particular complexity—a complexity capable of bearing the logical multiplicity of those concepts. Rather than arguing against the Cartesian philosophical claim that minds and bodies are metaphysically distinct, or its perennial counterclaim that minds are essentially identical with bodies, this film dramatises Wittgenstein's vision of the expressivity of the animate human body—of our inner lives as naturally finding outward expression in what we say and do. It produces conviction in his remark that, "The human body is the best picture of the human soul" by projecting and screening a body that resembles a human one in form and flexibility, and thereby eliciting from the viewer the attitude one adopts towards a human soul—an attitude whose various manifestations are specified in terms of acknowledgement (and denial) of the humanity of the other, whether human being or replicant.

Given this early stake in the centrality of embodiment, I did not warm to the apparently ungovernable desire of many viewers of *Blade Runner 2049* to regard Joi as just as worthy a recipient of the attitude we adopt to human souls as the replicants. She is, after all, a hologram—a computer-generated, three-dimensional simulation of a flesh-and-blood woman, whose underlying adaptive algorithms allow her to tailor her own behaviour to that of whoever purchased her, thereby enhancing her value as a consumer product in a world whose human and replicant populations suffer from radical loneliness and sexual isolation. Villeneuve and his scriptwriter could hardly be unaware that online pornography teems with "JOI" videos, which present women instructing their viewers to jerk off.

Why not regard Joi's adaptive process as allowing her to transcend her programming and become (if not exactly human, then perhaps) some new kind of person, a being of sufficient moral standing that her eventual destruction by Luv might be viewed as murder? Why don't such holograms stand to replicants in *Blade Runner 2049* just as replicants stand to human beings in *Blade Runner*—as prejudicially ostracized bearers of real moral significance? Because the basis of the earlier film's projection of metaphysical and moral kinship between replicants and their makers is their embodiment, without which neither can be said genuinely to inhabit the material world. For such inhabitation involves being subject to the material world and capable of altering the course of its independently existing objects and events—being one autonomous locus of receptivity and agency amongst others. An entity that lacks both receptivity and agency is not one to whom feelings and emotions (in their givenness), or intentions and motives (in their spontaneity), can coherently be attributed. Such an entity will accordingly lack core aspects of subjectivity as well as of agency.

Villeneuve's film is perfectly clear that the distinction between the biological and the technological in the 2049 *Blade Runner* universe is sufficiently robust to place K on one side and Joi on the other, and thereby to give K a claim to moral standing that Joi cannot have. For it shows us that while Joi's algorithms can generate hologrammatic raindrops on her hologrammatic skin when K emanates her on a storm-lashed rooftop, she doesn't thereby feel the precipitation that he feels. It shows us that she cannot break the window glass of K's spinner or drag him out of its wreckage because she can't manipulate any aspect of an environment into which he projects her. Above all, it shows us that she cannot make love with the person she claims to love.

The scene in which she hires a replicant doxie named Mariette and attempts to synchronise with her so that she can be her sexual proxy with K is amongst the most uncannily powerful in the film—indeed, in the history of cinematic incarnations of sexual longing. But Villeneuve shows that the synchronisation is never, and could not possibly be, wholly successful, as Mariette's face and body keep on showing through Joi's projections of herself (just as film actors have priority over their characters). Villeneuve's camera's persistent drift towards K's viewpoint on the encounter further implies that the relevant desire—poignant and pitiful, disturbing and perverse—is not Joi's but K's. And when Joi curtly dismisses her, Mariette says, "Quiet now. I've been inside you: not as much there as you think." What is in there—Joi's programming—is essentially designed to adapt so as to satisfy the preferences of its owner (including the preference that she satisfy his preferences, not because she is programmed to do so, but because she shares them). Joi herself acknowledges that she chose Mariette as her proxy because she knew that K found her sexually attractive.

To be sure, some psychological concepts are attributable to Joi's hologrammatic emanations. But they are sorely limited in range and, deprived of the incomparably broader and richer context of such concepts that are attributable to embodied beings, can have only the thinnest, most secondary modes of significance (light can pass right through them). So, if we project upon Joi the kind of inner life and moral status possessed by replicants and human beings, we regard her not as she really is but as K regards her: we inhabit his self-harming, masturbatory fantasy. As an outcast, he understandably yearns for genuine company, for another who can be his other, capable of fully acknowledging him. But he seems to have repressed the knowledge that his world contains not only human beings who might explore that possibility (such as his police commander, Joshi), but replicants—for example, Mariette, who quite understandably feels insulted when she hears the initiating chimes of K's emanator and realises that he prefers a hologram to a flesh-and-blood replicant.

K's reliance on Joi does not show that she could really be his other; it shows that he is unable or unwilling to expose himself to beings—whether replicant or human—who really could be his other, presumably because he doesn't want to risk them refusing to acknowledge him as their other (given, for instance, the replicant blood on his hands). What K therefore needs is the kind of education that Deckard receives in the original film—an education in what it means to acknowledge another, and in particular the dependence of acknowledgement on one's willingness to risk acknowledgement by another.

If the centrality of embodiment subverts Joi's appeal to our empathy, it presents the new film's interest in birth as a natural extension of the original film's interest in death—each the other's complement, and together constituting the key conditions of finite embodied agency. *Blade Runner* showed that both replicants and humans tend to misunderstand the significance of our relation to death—to think of mortality as a matter of having a finite lifespan (hence as something capable of alleviation by means of its extension), rather than living a life in which each moment might be one's last (in which the possibility of absolute non-existence is as close as it can possibly be to the first moment of our existence). One might therefore expect *Blade Runner 2049* to exhibit an equally questioning relation to its characters' ways of understanding the significance of birth.

From Sapper Morton onwards, the replicants of BR2049 generally regard the fact of Rachael's having given birth to Deckard's child as a miracle; K more specifically connects a replicant's being born with their being able to claim possession of a soul. And Joshi shares their sense of something absolutely out-of-the-ordinary having happened, although she sees it as a catastrophe, since it demolishes the wall of perceived difference between replicant and humankind by which peace has (barely) been maintained since Tyrell's days. But this assumption is surely puzzling. After all, the replicants are biological beings: they exhibit sexual difference, and are capable of sexual intercourse; so their inability to reproduce by this means is surely what is out of the ordinary. Given Tyrell's aim to produce something at once resembling and transcending human forms of life, it must have required significant effort to detach replicant sexuality from reproduction; so, by making Rachael fertile, he went entirely with the grain of the biological nature of replicants, fulfilling their organic kinship with their makers. Moreover, the child who was (re)produced this way has no obvious supernatural attributes; if anything, Ana's affliction with Galatians Syndrome (which compromises her immune system) suggests that she fully participates in our mortal vulnerability.

Niander Wallace's interest in the matter also finds expression in ways that reinforce its mundanity. Wallace thinks he could easily grasp Tyrell's scientific technique if granted a living specimen that embodies it; and he desires knowledge of this technique because it is the most efficient way to create the conscript replicant army needed to conquer the stars in the name of human flourishing. So employed, replicant procreation would hardly resemble the miraculous blood on the lintel invoking divine protection for the house's inhabitants against Pharaoh's enslavement—allowing them to decide for themselves how many fellow-replicants they can add to their rebellious ranks. It would only engender replicant self-mastery if the rebellion it is supposed to facilitate had already succeeded.

But we must be careful. K's view of birth as marking the replicants' acquisition of souls is patently simplistic, and certainly conflicts with the first film's claim that the body is the field of expression of the soul (which implies that how that body is made is as irrelevant as its lifespan). However, being born rather than made involves more than the biological mechanics of conception, gestation, and expulsion from the womb. It involves having a mother (and perhaps a father), upon whom one is dependent for far longer than nine months, and an extended period of childhood, spent acquiring the second, culturally encoded nature for which one's first, biological, nature readies one, and through which one acquires a vast store of memories—including the sub- and un-conscious memories resulting from sustained immersion in a loving and rivalrous family.

The idea of maternity was already a sore point in the original film: Leon's opening execution of Holden is prompted by his asking Leon to tell him "only the good things that come to mind about your mother"—as if being reminded of this lack overwhelms even his desire to succeed in the quest to overcome death. The new film displays a complementary interest in paternity: K's immersion in an illusory father–son relationship with Deckard may be brief, but it radically transforms his self-understanding and the trajectory of his hitherto subservient life; and K's emergence from that fantasy culminates in an attempt to restore the real father–daughter relationship between Deckard and Ana Stelline—as if experiencing the fantasy of having had a parent had disclosed the real value of the parent–child bond. This suggests that one can attain autonomous individuality only by acknowledging the depth of one's dependence—and in particular one's dependence on the stem of interlinked individuals who brought you into being out of blood-black nothingness and then subsequently raised you. This necessarily involves questioning one's childhood memories.

Art talk: memory, literature, and the baseline test

K's relation to his memories is far from straightforward. His NEXUS generation have genuine memories of their lives from their inception; but they have also been implanted with memories of a childhood they never had (to enhance their robustness as a product). They know this, and they also know that (as Ana tells us) it is illegal to use the real memories of another person as such implants. Rachael, by contrast, did not (initially) know that most of her memories were implants, nor that those implants were the real memories of Tyrell's niece. Her implants would thus have appeared to her to be genuine memories of a childhood she really experienced, but they would in fact count as "quasi-memories", in the terminology of contemporary philosophers of mind. A quasi-memory records something that actually happened from the point of view of someone who was actually there to perceive it, but that someone need not be the same person as the possessor of the quasi-memory. On this definition, ordinary memories—of the kind Rachael has about her post-inception life in the Tyrell Corporation—are a particular kind of quasi-memory (in which the person who experienced the past event and the person who quasi-remembers it are one and the same).

Since, in the ordinary case, a person only remembers things that she actually experienced, philosophers have long claimed that our faculty of memory is constitutive of our sense of ourselves as one and the same person existing through time. Philosophers sceptical of this claim have tried to construct a language in which the central attributes of memory might be accurately captured without committing those employing it to this orthodox story about personal identity (for if all memories also count as quasi-memories, then surely everything about memories could be expressed in terms of quasi-memories). The coherence of such quasi-memory discourse is highly questionable; but an intellectually curious film might begin from a logically impossible premise and develop its implications in conceptually rigorous and imaginatively penetrating ways.

Blade Runner 2049 initially sidesteps this controversy. Since K knows that his implanted memories do not record a childhood that he or anyone else actually had, he knows from the outset that his childhood memories do not even count as quasi-memories. For no actual person was in a position to experience what he seems to remember experiencing; and what he remembers happening did not really happen. His childhood "memories" are thus thoroughly fictional phenomena; neither their content nor their experiential form has any genuine relation to reality. By contrast, his post-inception memories are full-blown memories—recollections of real events that he really underwent.

Imagine an interior life of this kind—in which a thin veneer of genuine memories is superimposed upon rich, indefinitely receding geological strata of purely fictional representations (uncannily similar to the screened projections of cinema) that nevertheless claim continuity with that radically different top layer. Would a subject who is constantly assailed by images claiming a constitutive intimacy with him that he knows to be utterly hollow really be rendered a more stable product? Such internal discontinuity looks like an even more injurious psychological analogue to the damage K's society has experienced since the 2022 Blackout, when a replicant-activated Electro-Magnetic Pulse (EMP) destroyed all digital records, but at least left the survivors with fragments of their deeper past (however treacherous). *Pace* Ana, it seems the reverse of an act of kindness to put anyone in K's situation.

Our clearest glimpse of K's default existential disorientation comes when we see its deconstruction: he infers that some of his childhood "memories" might be full-blown recollections of events that really happened to him (showing that he is the child of Rachael and Deckard). Immediately afterwards, his police employers give him a baseline test—designed to establish whether his death-dealing profession has given him the replicant equivalent of PTSD. He recently passed with flying colours; this time he fails it unequivocally.

The baseline test is the closest analogue in Villeneuve's film to the Voight-Kampff machine in Scott's original, despite their different purposes and protocols. Whereas the Voight-Kampff test aims to distinguish replicants from humans, the baseline test diagnoses possible malfunctions in known replicants. And whereas the Voight-Kampff tester sits opposite his subject, asking hypothetical questions with a view to registering physiological markers of empathic response, and so focuses on visually accessible data (capillary dilation, blush response, pupil dilation), the baseline tester communicates with his subject via a wall-mounted, one-way device incorporating a loudspeaker and scanners. He asks his subject to recite a short text and then demands multiple instantaneous repetitions of its individual semantic elements, whilst interjecting probing extrapolations of their emotionally significant connotations that are designed to subvert the subject's capacity to respond promptly, accurately, and dispassionately to those demands. As one might expect from the director of *Arrival*, the baseline test privileges linguistic responsiveness over physiological visibilia as the most effective medium for revealing a replicant's inner life. Villeneuve here declares a conviction that language is as much part of the resources of authentic contemporary cinema as vision, and that any inheritance of a cinematic universe that luxuriated in the visual as much as Scott's will be true to Villeneuve's directorial identity only insofar as it can synthesise word with image.

But what kind of image? Whereas Scott's future world had to be realised photographically, Villeneuve's digital resources make constructing a convincing extrapolation of it almost embarrassingly effortless; but they also deprive him of photography's uncanny ability—fully acknowledged in Deckard's Esper analysis of Leon's photograph—to present its viewers with reality rather than algorithmically generated renderings of it (cf. Mulhall, 2015). As Joi reflects during K's DeNAbase search, whereas her digital ontology is expressible in two numbers ("one and zero"), his requires four letters (the DNA bases, "the alphabet of you"). Yet the material basis of this cinematic privileging of the genetic and the alphabetic is numerical—twice as elegant, perhaps (as K says to Joi), but half as much. This reflexive anxiety explains why Villeneuve associates the digital imagery within his film with unprecedentedly powerful but potentially devastating technology—the spinner's pilotfish drone, which uncovers what no one really wants revealed, the missile strikes unleashed by Luv's satellite-linked spectacles, Niander Wallace's multi-purpose barracudas: its mediations of reality threaten to attenuate or annihilate it. It also explains why something literally alphabetical—K's baseline text—might counter that threat.

> And blood-black nothingness began to spin
> A system of cells interlinked within
> Cells interlinked within cells interlinked
> Within one stem. And dreadfully distinct
> Against the dark, a tall white fountain played.
> (703–7)[3]

These semantically opaque phrases come from Nabokov's (1962/1984) *Pale Fire*—a book that K is shown to keep in his apartment (so whether he chose the lines, or merely chose to explore their source once they were chosen for him, he appreciates their context). *Pale Fire* consists of a 999-line poem by John Shade, together with a scholarly apparatus supplied by its editor, Charles Kinbote, who publishes the poem posthumously after Shade is murdered in his company. K's baseline text encapsulates what the poem's narrator presents as a vision of the afterlife that he experienced after an episode of heart failure from which he was resuscitated. He wants to believe in its veridicality, but by the poem's end acknowledges his inability to prove it. And Kinbote's commentary quickly relinquishes its initial impersonality to make increasingly implausible attempts to prove that Kinbote himself is the poem's true topic and progenitor, and the murderer's true target, stealthily raising the possibility that he suffers from delusions of grandeur.

What does K's attraction to this context tell us about his emotional baseline? Kinbote's apparatus (like Shakespeare's moon, stealing its pale fire from the sun) blends narcissism with paranoia in assuming that the significance of the poem and the world ultimately depends, for good and ill, on the one perceiving it. Shade's poetic vision offers unverified but unrelinquishable renderings of his life after death that complement K's fictional but unexpungeable renderings of his life before birth (that is, his inception); but it also offers a potentially resonant conception of the way his vision bears on reality. Shade quickly admits (lines 708–19) that the sense behind his envisioned scene could not be our sense: whereas in life we easily recognise the reality behind deceptive appearances (the inchworm cannot be a twig), we cannot grasp what the perception of a fountain might really stand for in the afterlife until we inhabit that realm. Nevertheless, apparently divergent visions of the afterlife might not disconfirm their veracity. Shade later acknowledges that where he saw a fountain, another resuscitated person reports seeing a mountain (lines 750–802); but both perceptions might still have the same otherworldly referent—for the gulf of meaning that opens up by the transposition of one letter occludes the fact that every other letter remains the same. These two disappointingly, even dreadfully, distinct semograms nevertheless largely share their constituent marks, and so might have a unitary origin. If afterlife entities really transcend our comprehension, aren't they more likely to communicate themselves to us via such overlappings of linguistic texture rather than by the textual differences our mundane sense-making imposes (lines 806–29)? And if arbitrary material coincidences in language might nevertheless have significance, so might their extra-linguistic equivalents. Patterns in the material world might be ornaments manufactured out of accident and possibility, a mode of plexed artistry whereby the inhabitants of the afterlife coordinate the fabric of our world with the unknowable elements of their own. Perhaps this is how the afterlife scribbles its message in the dark of our mundane perceptions.

The baseline test certainly sees potential significance in interactions between the material and the semantic dimensions of language (the two systems of interlinked cells that constitute the stem of our form of life). For its strategies energise the connotative powers of words, exploiting alphabetical coincidences that incarnate potentially radical divergences of sense, and so coordinating textual differences by means of textural identity. The testers apparently assume that, whereas human beings are so immersed in the textual dimension of language that aggressively activating its textural dimensions will disrupt their ordinary facility with words, a properly calibrated replicant should easily maintain his focus on the material reality of language despite being assaulted with reminders of its ramifying semantic multiplicities. He should find nothing uncanny about signs having both text and texture, or in privileging the latter over the former (as if language is, for them, as sheerly material as they are supposed to be—a literalism that Villeneuve ironises by using Joshi's screen to show that the neural correlate of K's saying "a tall white fountain plays" looks just like a white fountain).

Thus far, K has satisfied this assumption: his tester calls him "Constant K." Yet the central preoccupation of his test's textual source is the dual-aspect nature of language that all baseline testing depends upon, and whose literary form can provide its distinctive pleasures precisely because it deploys the plexed artistry it analyses, activating the textural textuality it delineates. K's choice of reading matter therefore suggests not only a playfully subversive acknowledgement of his employers' conception of themselves and of him, but also a covert rejection of it. It declares that he is as cognisant of the dual-aspect nature of language as any good reader of Nabokov (which means that the testers' assumption about the ordinary human relation to language amounts to the suppression of the literary), but he is also capable of suspending that aesthetic sensitivity when circumstances demand—when, for example, his continued employment and, indeed, his continued existence are at stake. More human than the (aesthetically) human.

When, however, K takes the test after meeting Ana, he is no longer even close to baseline; he no longer looks like himself on the inside, and so should (according to standard procedure) be retired forthwith. His belief that there really is a continuous line to be drawn from his blade runner memories backward as far as he can "remember"—that he must think of what he regarded as a thread of fictional imagery unspooling behind, and artificially anchored to, his present self as the unbroken trajectory of the single and singular individual he really is—thus amounts to the loss of himself, of the self that he was. Becoming a genuine self involves not the preservation of that prior mode of inhuman or superhuman constancy but the revelation of its falsity.

Moreover, K's apparent recovery of his true identity has a narcissistic tinge; its line of continuity is essentially messianic (a biblical genealogy). Believing himself to be the offspring of Rachael and Deckard, he views himself as not only unique amongst his replicant kind ("one of woman born"), but as the redeemer of the world that enslaves this kind. The text of that supposedly fictional imagery has taken on the texture of the sacred; the world's significance depends upon, and so elevates, him alone. Inhuman constancy may not amount to a genuinely individual life, but the hovering fictional shade of Charles Kinbote warns that neither does this kind of dreadful distinctness.

So K's eventual realisation that the toy-concealing strand of his childhood recollections is neither purely fictional nor a full-blooded memory, but a quasi-memory of the intermediate kind (a memory of something that really happened, but to Ana not to him) undercuts his messianism, returning him to the replicant ranks, and so to the companionship of humankind. But it does not return him to his default, inhumanly constant state; rather, he attempts to realise his individuality by rejecting the guidance of the rebel replicants and rescuing Deckard from Luv in order to reunite father with daughter. He chooses to reconstitute what now remains of the family matrix he wrongly believed to be his own *fons et origo*; he accepts death if it holds open the possibility of radically redefining a world that will outlive him. Such self-sacrifice is a familiar form of human excellence, and K achieves it without disavowing his replicant nature, without having been authorised by the mode of his coming into being. Having an inception date rather than a birthday turns out to be as irrelevant to a replicant's moral standing (and achievements) as having a date upon which one's life ends.

Cinematic implantation: directing and acting

Nevertheless, something shadows K's culminating achievement. For, as his life ebbs away outside the Stelline Laboratories building, he watches snowflakes fall onto his hand. Villeneuve cuts to Ana's workspace, where she holds up a hand to catch the virtual snowflakes of a new memory-implant. K's gesture recalls Joi's on the rainy rooftop, and so emphasises the ontological difference between the two; but its conjunction with Ana's suggests an internal relation between the world of K's embodied experience and her virtual environment. It is as if these two universes are porous—as if Ana has found a way of transcending her hermetically sealed workspace that makes K's experience of the world somehow responsive to her imagination. We might then recall two of Ana's other creations, both of which align closely with K's inner world: an insect-populated forest (an enriched version of the dead tree and plucked flower K finds at Sapper Morton's), and a birthday party (which immediately precedes K's erroneous perception of himself as having a birthday).

And, of course, Ana *has* shaped K's world to her purposes. She illegally implanted her own memories into K and hid the full truth about this from him once he began to suspect it. By saying, of K's toy-concealing memory, only that "someone lived this; this happened," she lies by omission—leaving him wrongly to infer that it happened to him. K's messianic overreach then kicks in, driving him towards the person he thinks is his father—a drive that ultimately brings about his death, but ensures Ana is reunited with her real father. K is reduced to a kind of pilot-fish or barracuda; his operator (i.e., Ana) reconstructs her own broken family and inaugurates her own messianic mission, by implanting a lethal misrecognition of himself. In short, K has been enslaved by means of quasi-memories deployed by a great but self-aggrandizing artist.

Ana certainly insists that her work is a kind of art: she claims that it involves an enhanced imaginative capacity and that, like all artists, she leaves traces of herself in her work; and she offers theories about the achievement of realism in her chosen medium. That medium is inherently cinematic: her memory-maker and memory-scanner blend image-capture, analysis and editing; her end product resembles cinematic projections; and their implantation into K induces traumatic discontinuities of the kind that *Arrival* attributes to film acting. In short, Ana goes proxy for Villeneuve, just as Deckard (with his Voight-Kampff machine and his Esper) went proxy for Scott: she represents the director of the film she inhabits, or at least that director's conception of his role. So the taint of villainy hanging over her looks like Villeneuve's way of acknowledging that, in order to retain his individuality while acknowledging his predecessor, and to open up the original film's imaginatively rich but hitherto self-sufficient world so that he might genuinely express himself within an enhanced expansion of it, he had to make his characters suffer in more morally questionable ways than Scott ever did.

Villeneuve's 2049 world undeniably elaborates upon its 2019 counterpart. Its built and natural environments are more extensive, heterogenous, and fine-grained, and as much impacted by climate as by industry; its colour palette reaches beyond drenched neon and is infused with a distinctively Canadian wintry bleakness. Using this essay's baseline text, we might say that, against the pale fire of that digitally enabled backdrop, Villeneuve has interlinked the semantic and material cells of the Blade Runner universe in ways that differ from Scott's without denying their shared stem (their rootedness in organic reality), so that the original film's afterlife communicates its continuing identity and vitality—the singular sense behind its transposed and transfigured scenes—by cinematic means that are as much textural as they are textual. Is that a sufficient justification? Is there a moral philosophy of film directing?

In memoriam, Stanley Cavell: 1926–2018

Notes

1 Expanded editions of On Film were published in 2008 and 2016.
2 See the short story, Story of Your Life, by Ted Chiang (2002).
3 Bracketed numbers refer to lines in Nabakov's (1962/1984) poem.

References

Chiang, T. (2002). Stories of Your Life and Others. London: Macmillan.
Mulhall, S. (1994). Picturing the Human (Body and Soul): A Reading of Blade Runner. Film and Philosophy 1, 87–104.
Mulhall, S. (2002). On Film. London: Routledge.
Mulhall, S. (2015). Zhora through the Looking Glass: Notes on an Esper Analysis of Leon's Photograph. In A. Coplan & D. Davies (Eds.), Blade Runner (pp. 100–117). Abingdon: Routledge.
Nabakov, V. (1962/1984). Pale Fire. New York: G. P. Putnam's Sons.

Chapter 3

Fiona Woollard
THE "MIRACLE" OF REPLICANT REPRODUCTION

Introduction

THE CATALYST FOR THE MAIN plot of *Blade Runner 2049* (BR2049) is the discovery, as Sapper Morton puts it, of a "miracle." The main character, K, works for the LAPD as a "blade runner." Blade runners find and kill (or "retire") rogue replicants. K finds a box containing the remains of a female replicant. Examination of the remains shows that the replicant was a female who died during a caesarean section. The viewer is told that this is *impossible*: replicants are not supposed to be able to reproduce. But this replicant—who later turns out to be Rachael from the original *Blade Runner* movie—has given birth to a child.

The "miracle" of replicant reproduction is presented as having extremely important implications for the status of replicants and how they may be treated by their human counterparts. BR2049 features two kinds of intelligent synthetic agent: replicants and holograms. Both are cast as nothing more than "products" that are mass-produced by a company run by Niander Wallace. As mere products, replicants and holograms are presented as the sorts of things that can permissibly be bought and owned, either by individuals or corporate entities. In essence, replicants and holograms are presented as slaves whose function is to serve the interests of their human owners.

Several characters in the movie see replicant reproduction as blurring the boundaries between humans and replicants. K's boss, Lt. Joshi, views replicant reproduction as a threat—one that promises to destroy the "wall that separates kind"—with potentially devastating consequences: "Tell either side there's no wall, you bought a war. Or a slaughter." The replicant freedom movement sees it as an opportunity to free themselves from the bonds of slavery. As Freysa, one of the leaders of the movement, comments: "I knew that baby meant we are more than just slaves. If a baby can come from one of us ... we are our own masters." K himself puts his understanding of the significance of birth in spiritual terms, saying, "To be born is to have a soul, I guess." By contrast, Wallace sees replicant reproduction as of purely instrumental importance. He pursues it as an opportunity to increase the efficiency with which replicants are produced (or "manufactured"), yielding a slave army that furthers his own corporate ambitions.

We can distinguish two different ways in which replicant reproduction might be seen as having significant implications for replicants' moral status. K's comment that to be born is to have a soul suggests that a replicant who was born has a moral status that a replicant who was manufactured cannot have. However, it is not clear that the replicant freedom movement thinks that replicant reproduction is significant merely because the replicant child has a special status. Recall Freysa's comment, quoted above. One way of reading this is as a claim that it is the capacity to reproduce that is significant for replicant moral status. On this reading, it is not the replicant child that is special, but the replicant mother—and the replicant mother's reproductive capacities have implications for all replicants. This suggests a second way in which replicant reproduction might be morally significant.

This chapter will focus on the first way of seeing replicant reproduction as significant: the idea that a replicant who is born has a moral status that replicants that are manufactured do not have. I will only briefly discuss the significance of reproductive capacities, arguing that being able to reproduce is neither necessary nor sufficient to be one's own master. I will frame the moral status of replicants in terms of whether they are "mere products." The "mere" is important here. Manufactured replicants are products, but we are interested in whether they are, morally speaking, nothing more than products. Do they have the same moral status as a television or an electric car, for example?

The key question in working out whether replicants can permissibly be treated as mere products is whether replicants are persons. Persons have conclusive self-ownership and cannot be owned by others.[1] I discuss a list of key characteristics associated with persons. I argue that although, on balance, BR2049 presents manufactured replicants as meeting these conditions, there remain threads of doubt. A replicant that is born partially avoids these concerns. These philosophical issues are interesting, but I find that the doubts they raise are not reflected in my experience of watching the films. I find that watching the *Blade Runner* films leaves me certain about the moral status of replicants. I recognise them morally as persons and feel viscerally that the way they are treated is wrong. I defend this gut reaction with a Cartesian argument, inspired by Descartes's *Cogito*, that the very fact that a replicant such as K wrestles with the question of whether he is a mere product shows that he is not a mere product but a person, that is, the type of creature that cannot be owned by another.

Despite arguing that replicant reproduction does not, in itself, greatly change the moral status of replicants, I do not deny the practical importance of the miracle of replicant reproduction. The miracle child and the impossible mother are powerful symbols of replicant moral status. Lt. Joshi's comment is worth reflecting on carefully. Replicant reproduction does not tear down the walls between kind. It *tells* us that there were no walls in the first place.

Owning offspring: the generation problem and the principle of the fruit

Wallace's strategy for increasing his "property" is a well-established one.[2] If I own a tree and pears grow on the tree, then I own the pears. If I own a ram and a ewe and they have a lamb, then I own the lamb. This is the Fruit Principle (see Woollard, 2017: 93):

> **Fruit principle**
> If I own X, I own, or part own, the fruits of X unless I have implicitly or explicitly renounced ownership of those fruits.

It seems to follow from the Fruit Principle that Wallace will own the children of any replicants he has manufactured. If Wallace owns the replicant parents (because he has manufactured them), then the Fruit Principle seems to suggest that the replicant children will count as the fruit of his property and thus as his property.

However, a puzzle surrounding *human* self-ownership shows that things are not so simple. This is the *Generation Problem*. According to the Generation Problem, the Fruit Principle implies that it cannot be true that all humans own themselves. We understand fruit in such a way that human children are the fruit of their parents. Just as the Fruit Principle implies that whoever owns a ewe or a ram owns the resulting lamb, it seems to imply that whoever owns a human mother and father will own their children. Thus, if we say that the human mother and father own themselves, we seem to be forced to say that they will own their children. This isn't just deeply counter-intuitive, it means that the claim that all humans own themselves is self-undermining. If each human owns herself, then human parents co-own their children and, as the parents of humans are normally humans, some humans do not originally (fully) own themselves.

I have argued elsewhere that an important part of the solution to the Generation Problem is the rejection of the Fruit Principle—or rather the rejection of its original unrestricted form (see Woollard, 2017). We should recognise that the fact that something is the fruit of my property gives me only a *defeasible title* to it. A title is a claim to ownership. A defeasible title is a claim to ownership that can be outweighed or defeated. The title I have to the fruit of my property may be enough for me to come to own it. However, this kind of title is not conclusive. It can be outweighed or defeated if someone else has a stronger title to the fruits of my property—or if the fruits are not the kind of things that can be owned. In view of this, we should replace the Fruit Principle with the *Defeasible Fruit Principle* (see Woollard, 2017: 95):

Defeasible fruit principle
If I own X, I own, or part own, the fruits of X unless (a) I have implicitly or explicitly renounced ownership of those fruits, (b) someone else has a title to those fruits that defeats my title, or (c) the nature of the fruits is incompatible with ownership.

Revising the Fruit Principle is not enough to solve the Generation Problem. We also need to show that the title of human parents to their children is defeated. One way to do this is to argue that humans are not the kind of things that can be owned. The Defeasible Fruit Principle states that we do not own the fruits of our property if they are not the sort of things that can be owned. So, if human children are not the kind of thing that can be owned, human parents do not own their children.

However, I prefer to solve the Generation Problem by recognising that each human has a conclusive title to her self. I own my self no matter what. It does not matter what kind of title you have to me, it is defeated by my title to my self. This strategy involves adopting the *Conclusive Human Self-Ownership Thesis*:

> **Conclusive human self-ownership thesis**
> Each human owns herself. Her title to her self defeats all other types of title to that self, except (possibly) titles based on legitimate, autonomous transfer on her part.

The Defeasible Fruit Principle and the Conclusive Human Self-Ownership Thesis together solve the Generation Problem. Even if human children are the fruit of their parents, and the human parents own themselves, this does not give the human parents ownership of their children. The human children have a conclusive title to their selves that defeats their parents' titles.

What does all this have to do with replicants? The solution to this puzzle has implications for replicant ownership because, plausibly, it is not primarily the fact that we are humans in any biological sense that means that we own ourselves. Rather, it is the fact that we are humans in what Mary Warren calls the "moral sense": "a full-fledged member of the moral community, who is also a member of the human species" (Warren, 2002: 75). Warren argues that, "the moral community consists, in the first instance, of all *persons*, rather than all genetically human entities" (Warren, 2002: 76). Warren's concern is to exclude certain entities that are genetically human from counting as full-fledged members of the moral community. However, her suggestion works equally well in the present context: if we can show that replicants are persons, then they have a conclusive title to self-ownership that defeats all other forms of ownership (or claims to such ownership).

To say that someone is a person is normally to make both a moral claim and a descriptive claim. Persons are, as Warren notes, full-fledged members of the moral community. They are the kind of creatures that have the same moral status that most adult humans have. This is normally assumed to include a large set of important rights, such as the right not to be killed, the right not to have others interfere with decisions about one's own life, and perhaps some kind of right to at least some of the things that are necessary to pursue a good life. In my view, self-ownership is an important aspect of the moral status of a person.

Let us revise the aforementioned Conclusive Human Self-Ownership Thesis to reflect the centrality of personhood to issues of moral status. The result is the *Conclusive Person Self-Ownership Thesis*:

Conclusive person self-ownership thesis
Each person owns herself. Her title to her self defeats all other types of title to that self, except (possibly) titles based on legitimate, autonomous transfer on her part.

If we accept the Conclusive Person Self-Ownership Thesis, then there is a key question we need to answer to work out whether Wallace owns the replicants' children: Are the replicant children persons? If the replicant children are persons, then the replicant children have a conclusive title to their selves that defeats any title based on ownership of the parents.

However, as soon as we recognise that what matters is whether the replicant children are persons, we see that the Defeasible Fruit Principle may not apply to the replicant children at all. If the replicant children are persons, then they have a conclusive title to their selves that defeats any title based on ownership of the parents. But if the replicant *parents* are persons, then the replicant parents have a conclusive title to their selves that defeats any title based on having created them. And if the replicant parents have a conclusive title to themselves, then (a) replicant children are not the fruit of Wallace's property, and (b) replicants cannot be owned by Wallace whether they are born or manufactured (because they have a conclusive title to their selves that defeats Wallace's title). So, if all replicants are persons, Wallace's attempt to use the Fruit Principle to claim ownership is doubly undermined, *and* the significance of the "miracle" of replicant reproduction may not be as great as it is taken to be.

Of course, it could be argued that the replicant children, but not the replicant parents, have a conclusive title to their selves. K suggests, "To be born is to have a soul." We might interpret K's comment as the claim that to be born is to be a person. In this view, replicant children who have been born are persons, even if their replicant parents are not. It follows from this view that replicants who have been born cannot be owned by others, even if their replicant parents can be.

Interestingly, when arguing for my solution to the Generation Problem, I have previously appealed to cases in which everyday objects had persons as their fruit. The following are some examples:

> *The Genesis Tub*: Lisa places a tooth in a petri dish of cola for a science school project. After being shocked by static electricity, Lisa touches the tooth and the resulting spark causes life to evolve in the petri dish. Within days, tiny people, populating a futuristic cityscape, have evolved.[3]
>
> *Supercows*: A farmer discovers that the cows in his herd have evolved to the extent that they can speak English and that one cow has formed the ambition to go to university to study philosophy.
>
> *Robot*: Scientists use materials from a privately-owned laboratory to create a robot that is sentient, self-conscious, and has a conception of the kind of life she would like to live.

In respect of these examples, we can ask ourselves the following rhetorical question: "Isn't it just as absurd to claim that Lisa owns the tiny people's bodies or that the farmer owns the supercows' bodies or that the scientists own the robot's body as it is to claim that parents own their children's bodies?" (Woollard, 2017: 94). I used these examples to argue that the correct response to the Generation Problem is not to focus on the method of production. If Lisa's petri dish had sprouted a beautiful but inanimate object, we would be much happier to say that she owned it. If the cows were just normal cows, they would be owned by the farmer. If the robot were just a standard laptop computer, it would be owned by the scientists. Here we can see that it is not the method of production that undermines ownership, it is *what is produced* that counts. If what is produced is a person, then the product is not owned by anyone else, even if they owned the means of production. A product that is a person is not a *mere* product. So, we need to ask: Do replicants who have been born count as persons? And, if so, do they count as persons in virtue of some feature that replicants who have been manufactured cannot have?

What makes something a person?

I noted above that to say that someone is a person is normally to make both a moral claim and a descriptive claim. When "person" is used descriptively, it is often meant to pick out those features, whatever they are, in virtue of which adult humans have the moral status of full-fledged members of the moral community. There is disagreement about which features are necessary and sufficient to count as a person—just as there is disagreement about exactly what the full moral status gets you. But there is a shared sense of what kind of features persons have. Again, we can draw on Warren (2002). She picks out the following six characteristics as "central to the concept of personhood" (see Warren, 2002: 76):

(1) *Sentience*—the capacity to have conscious experiences, usually including the capacity to feel pain and pleasure.
(2) *Emotionality*—the capacity to feel happy, sad, angry, loving, and so forth.
(3) *Reason*—the capacity to solve new and relatively complex problems.
(4) *The capacity to communicate*, by whatever means, messages of an indefinite variety of types; that is, not just with an indefinite number of possible contents, but on indefinitely many possible topics.
(5) *Self-awareness*—having a concept of oneself as an individual and/or as a member of a social group.
(6) *Moral agency*—the capacity to regulate one's own actions through moral principles or ideals.

Warren's list seems to chime with the way that personhood is generally understood. Thus, in working out whether replicants are persons, it makes sense to ask whether they have these six features.

Clearly, replicants have the relevant capacity to communicate. It is more difficult to assess whether replicants have the other five features in the morally relevant sense. My discussion will focus mostly on emotionality and moral agency.

Replicant emotions

In the original *Blade Runner* film, Deckard's old boss, Captain Bryant, describes the replicants as follows: "They were designed to copy human beings in every way except their emotions. The designers reckoned that after a few years they might develop their own emotional responses. You know, hate, love, fear, anger, envy." This is later confirmed by Tyrell, the owner of the Tyrell Corporation, who originally developed the replicants: "We began to recognise in them a strange obsession. After all they are emotionally inexperienced, with only a few years in which to store up the experiences which you and I take for granted. If we gift them with a past, we create a cushion or pillow for their emotions and consequently we can control them better."

C. D. C. Reeve argues that this comment is "revelatory—and in a way other than that intended" (Reeve, 2015: 70), going on to note,

> What for Bryant is only a designer's projection—a maybe—is for Tyrell a certainty. Replicants not only develop emotions, they do it so quickly that a cushion is needed in addition to a fail-safe device.

Colin Allen (2015: 89) argues that Bryant's statement is ambiguous:

> Does he mean that the replicants are initially just like humans, except that they lack emotions? Or does he mean that they are just like humans except that they have different emotions? And does the development of "their own emotional responses" indicate acquisition of the human emotions—love, hate, etc.—or does it point toward *sui generis* "robotic" versions of them? The movie itself does not resolve these questions (and neither can any account of truth in fiction).

The ambiguities that Allen identifies force us to re-examine the features on Warren's list. What kind of emotionality is required to count as a person? Must one have the capacity to feel human emotions, or would the capacity to feel *sui generis* robotic emotions do? Do replicants have the relevant kind of emotionality?

BR2049 may seem to give some evidence missing from the original film that replicants can feel the same kinds of emotions as humans. In part, this is because the main protagonist of BR2049, unlike the main protagonist of the original film, is known throughout the film to be a replicant.

In the original *Blade Runner*, the main protagonist is Deckard. That film leaves Deckard's status deliberately ambiguous. As a blade runner, Deckard identifies replicants using the Voight-Kampff test, which is designed to provoke emotional responses. Replicants respond to this test differently from humans. Deckard is asked to test Rachael. He discovers that Rachael is a replicant, but that she does not know that she is a replicant. Soon, both Deckard and the audience begin to suspect that Deckard himself is a replicant. This is left in doubt at the end of the first film, and the uncertainty continues in BR2049, where Deckard returns as the father of Rachael's child.

BR2049's plot has echoes of the original film, but with important differences. In contrast to the original *Blade Runner*, the audience is left in little doubt as to the replicant status of the main protagonist in BR2049. Ultimately, K is revealed to be a standard NEXUS 9 replicant, one who was presumably created in the same way as any other NEXUS 9 replicant. As with Deckard in the original *Blade Runner*, however, K is led to question his nature and moral status.

The fact that BR2049 has a known replicant as its main protagonist adds to the viewer's conviction that replicants can feel not just emotions, but the familiar human emotions. We see the action in BR2049 from K's point of view. We see his struggles with his identity. While we see this, K is presented as in possession of a rich emotional life. He finds solace for his loneliness with Joi. He is fearful and confused as his investigation appears to show that he is the "miracle" child. The emotions that K displays do not come across as *sui generis* robotic emotions. They "feel" to the viewer like the same kind of emotions a human would feel in similar circumstances. Moreover, because K is confirmed by the end of the film not to be the miracle child, there is no reason to regard K's emotionality as particularly exceptional: K is a standard, manufactured replicant, and his emotional proclivities are therefore likely to be shared with other manufactured replicants, at least those of the NEXUS 9 generation.

However, a note of doubt about our ability to trust our understanding of K's emotional states is introduced by K's relationship with the hologram, Joi. One of the ways that BR2049 brings in interesting new philosophical questions is through the introduction of this second type of intelligent synthetic agent. Holograms seem to be of even lower status than replicants. While replicants are owned by humans or corporations, holograms can be owned by replicants. K owns—and falls in love with—Joi. The film seems to leave it deliberately unclear whether Joi has genuine emotions. At times, Joi's behaviour seems to suggest that she has genuine feelings. She appears to feel joy when K buys her an "emanator"—a portable device that allows her to leave the apartment. She seems to love K so much that she is willing to sacrifice her own life to save his. However, after Joi is destroyed, K encounters a huge hologrammatic version of Joi, advertising the virtual girl "product." Earlier in the film, Joi had argued that K should have a proper name instead of a serial number. She suggested the name "Joe." The advertising hologram greets K with, "You look lonely. I can fix that. You look like a good Joe." This echo of an apparently intimate moment from this outsized version of Joi is disturbing, and the effect is magnified by the neon slogan flickering behind her: "Joi: Everything you want to hear. Everything you want to see." The advertising hologram does not seem real. It does not seem as if she is having a genuine emotional reaction to K. She is merely an image parroting words that she has been programmed to say. This may lead us to wonder whether Joi's earlier expressions of emotion were genuine or merely clever representations of what K wanted to hear.

K was convinced by Joi's appearance of emotion. This is later thrown into doubt. This reminder that appearances can be deceptive throws doubt on our understanding of K's emotional responses. The film deliberately plays with these analogies and disanalogies between K and Joi. In the Wallace Company premises, Luv refers to K's purchase of Joi: "I see you're also a customer. Are you satisfied with our product?" Later, in Deckard's hideout in Las Vegas, Luv says an almost identical line to Joi, referring to K: "I do hope you're satisfied with our product." The similar description of K and Joi suggests that perhaps K, like Joi, is a mere product.

There are different ways to interpret Joi's story. We can see her as something that was originally a mere product, but who later developed a genuine personality and genuine emotions. This would fit with my contention that it is not how we start out that matters, but how we end up. Alternatively, we can understand her as a convincing fake, something that merely appears to feel genuine emotions. On this latter interpretation, we can see her as an analogy for K—suggesting that his emotions, like hers, may be mere appearance. Alternatively, we can see her as a foil for K, so that our doubt about whether she is genuine—which is present throughout the film—contrasts with and cements our certainty that K is real.

Moral agency

Warren's final characteristic of persons is moral agency: the capacity to regulate one's own actions through moral principles or ideals. This is perhaps the most important characteristic of a person—especially if we, like Warren, see the core of personhood as full membership of a moral community. Do replicants have moral agency? Manufactured replicants are built to obey. When "on-baseline," they do what they are ordered to do. Even if we understand the programming of the replicants to follow orders as a kind of moral code, it might seem as if on-baseline replicants are not genuinely acting on this code.

When manufactured replicants go off-baseline, they can disobey their orders. This is what happens with K. K's false belief that he was born—and that he is therefore the target of his boss's order to destroy the miracle child—transforms him. He decides to disobey his orders. In exercising the capacity to act on his own values, rather than on those of his superiors, K shows himself to be capable of moral agency. As Freysa notes, "Dying for the right cause is the most human thing we can do."

This might suggest that manufactured replicants only gain moral agency, and thus only become true persons, when they go off-baseline. This would lead to the peculiar implication that it is possible to own manufactured replicants that are on-baseline, but that once manufactured replicants go off-baseline and start to disobey orders, the replicants have a conclusive title to themselves that means they cannot be owned by another.

However, I tentatively suggest that we should not understand K's transformation as merely a personal transformation that takes him as an individual into the category of moral agent—and thus personhood. Instead, K's actions—and those of other "rogue" replicants—show that manufactured replicants, even those that are currently on-baseline, have the capacity to act on their own values. This suggests that all replicants should be understood as moral agents, even those currently on-baseline. Here we treat the on-baseline replicants as we would humans whose capacity for autonomous agency has not been developed because, for example, they have been brainwashed to blindly follow orders. While we might not think that these humans are currently acting on their own values, we see them as having the capacity to do so, recognising that that their capacity is currently undermined by external circumstances. We would see the behaviour of those responsible (for limiting the capacity of an individual to act on their values) as wrong precisely *because* they had prevented the humans from developing their capacities to act freely. Such individuals would not be able to argue that their behaviour was acceptable simply because the humans failed to count as persons (on account of their inability to engage in autonomous action). Similarly, it does not seem that we should be able to justify treating on-baseline replicants as mere products simply because we have deliberately programmed them to prevent them from developing their capacity to act on their own values.

My suggestion here is only tentative. I am not sure whether the analogy between on-baseline replicants and brainwashed humans is quite correct. The worry here is that we do not doubt that what we have in the human case is an innate capacity to act autonomously—a capacity that is undermined by brainwashing. Humans are, generally, the kinds of things that can act autonomously. It is not clear whether replicants are, generally, the kinds of things that can act autonomously. How we answer this question depends on whether we see going off-baseline as a process in which the replicant acquires new capacities or whether we see the tendency for on-baseline replicants to obey orders as the curtailment of an existing capacity.

Obedience to orders and compliance with another's design may come apart. Replicants may perceive themselves as rebelling and choosing their own destinies, when in fact they are merely playing their part in a more complex plan. The very ways in which a replicant feels themselves to be breaking free may have been designed. Wallace uses this possibility to taunt Deckard. When Wallace has captured Deckard, he returns to the idea that Deckard may be a replicant and suggests that he may even have been designed to fall in love with Rachael: "Did it never occur to you that's why you were summoned in the first place? Designed to do nothing short of fall for her right then and there. All to make that single perfect specimen. That is, if you were designed. Love … or mathematical precision? Yes? No?"

Should this possibility lead us to doubt that even the rebellious replicants can be moral agents? Deckard's reply to Wallace is simple: "I know what's real." We could read this as the claim that Deckard knows that his actions and his love for Rachael were real even if programmed. There is certainly an important difference between the person who only obeys orders and the person who acts on what they perceive as their own values. It is much more plausible to say that the person who acts on what they perceive as their own values is displaying moral agency. The fact that agents see their actions as expressions of their character and values makes a difference, even if the agents' character and values themselves have been designed or programmed. As Reeve notes:

> Human beings are free, on [one] conception, not because they have souls that allow them to slip through nature's causal net, or because they can slip through it in some other way, but because they can often do what they want (and so have freedom of action), and also want what they want (and so have freedom of choice or will) ... Perhaps this is the sort of freedom that is within a replicant's reach.
> (Reeve, 2015: 75–76)[4]

Reeve connects the question of whether replicants can count as morally responsible to the issue of genuine versus implanted memory, a key theme in both the original film and BR2049. As Reeve writes,

> I have the wants and desires that cause or motivate the actions I perform because I—on the basis of experience and reflection—want to have them. What they constitute, as a result, is not just *a* will, but *my* will, my practical identity. If Rachael has the wants and desires she does because Tyrell's niece or someone else wanted them, however, the will she has may in some sense be free, but is it really *hers*?
> (Reeve, 2015: 76)

Reeve argues that, in particular, the fact that Rachael did not experience maternal love casts doubt on whether her emotions are genuinely hers. On Reeve's view, the way that our mother relates to us sets in place "the deep structure of our style of loving and being loved" (Reeve, 2015: 78). He understands the Voight-Kampff as a test for the presence of this unconscious basis for feeling. He worries that her practical identity is "not really hers because it lacks a basis in a self that is certified, so to speak, by a mother's love" (Reeve, 2015: 78).

Interestingly, the miracle child only partially avoids these concerns about the lack of mother love and the shadowy presence of someone in the background who is designing our characters so that we behave in ways that serve their ends. BR2049 does not tell us whether replicants who are born will have the same kind of programming as replicants who are manufactured. Wallace appears to assume that they will be obedient enough to form the "disposable workforce" he needs for his plan to colonise space. If Wallace is right that Rachael and Deckard were programmed to fall in love to produce "the perfect specimen," then it seems as if their child is, at the very least, the product of selective breeding. Moreover, as Rachael died in childbirth, the child never knew its mother. Nonetheless, sexual reproduction does not permit the same kind of control as direct manufacture. And, crucially, the replicant child's practical identity is not corrupted by false memories.

Verdict on replicant moral status based on Warren's list

Based on Warren's list, whether a replicant has been born or manufactured has some limited significance for its moral status. It is clear that replicants have the capacity to communicate, by whatever means, messages of an indefinite variety of types. There are general issues about whether artificial intelligence can have sentience, emotionality, reason, or self-awareness (because these features may require an inner life that cannot be created artificially). There are specific doubts in the *Blade Runner* universe about whether replicants have human emotions or some kind of *sui generis* robotic emotions. Nonetheless, overall, BR2049 presents replicants as having genuine human emotions. The same evidence that replicants have emotionality in the morally relevant sense also suggests that they possess sentience, reason, and self-awareness. When K is injured in the film, we are convinced that it hurts. When we see him trying to work out what happened to Rachael's child, we do not think that he is merely computing. The evidence that he may be the child leads him to question his previous understanding of himself, demonstrating that he possesses self-awareness.

Manufactured replicants are designed to obey orders. When on-baseline, replicants do not lie or disobey. This may make us think that they are not genuinely acting on their own values or principles. They do not seem to be displaying moral agency. Off-baseline replicants disobey orders. K undergoes a transformation, leading to action that is portrayed as choosing his own destiny. This does seem to be true moral agency. But the possibility that replicants may in their very rebellion be acting according to programming as part of a more complex plan casts a shadow of doubt. Moreover, as Reeve argues, the presence of implanted memories and the absence of mother love raise concerns about whether replicants can have the kind of practical identity that allows humans to claim moral responsibility even if their actions are determined. It is also not clear whether we should see the on-baseline replicants as having a blocked capacity to exercise moral agency. Being born rather than manufactured allows the miracle child to partially escape these concerns.

It is intellectually interesting to consider which of the key characteristics of persons replicants can have and how a replicant's possession of these characteristics is affected by whether they are born or manufactured. Nonetheless, it is not clear that this kind of approach is necessary to know that, at least some, manufactured replicants are persons. Watching BR2049 leaves me with lots of questions about the nature of consciousness, the trustworthiness of memory, and of our self-understanding. However, when I watch the film, two things seem beyond doubt: First, K is a person, not a mere product, and, second, the way he is treated by the Wallace Corporation is wrong. I suspect that one of the reasons that this is so clear is precisely because we follow K in his search for self-understanding. He initially accepts, but eventually challenges, his assigned moral status. His exploration of his moral status is not a mere intellectual exercise. It matters deeply to him. I suggest that we can make a Cartesian argument for replicant personhood: any entity that can question whether or not they are a person in this kind of morally engaged way is a person.

A Cartesian argument for replicant personhood

Descartes's "*Cogito ergo sum*" is probably the most famous argument in Western philosophy. In his *Meditations*, he employs the famous Method of Doubt to try to find a solid foundation for his beliefs. The Method of Doubt is simple: examine all your beliefs and throw out any that can be doubted; if you've got anything left after this, then you can start building your beliefs back up again. With the *Cogito*, Descartes discovered one belief that he cannot doubt. He cannot doubt that he exists. For if he is doubting, then he must exist. "*Cogito ergo sum*": I think, therefore I am (see Descartes, 1993, [1641]: 17–20).[5]

My Cartesian argument for replicant personhood is inspired by the *Cogito*. My argument shares what I see as the key feature of the *Cogito* in that it identifies a given claim as having a very special feature: the very activity of doubting that claim conclusively establishes the claim's truth. However, it doesn't depend on the soundness of the *Cogito* itself. This is rather fortunate, as there are many well-rehearsed objections to the *Cogito*.[6]

Suppose an entity is undertaking the journey of self-understanding that K travels through in BR2049. They question whether they are the kind of thing they think they are. This is not merely an idle bit of intellectual speculation. They take the answer to have deep ramifications for how they will interact with others, how they will think about themselves, and how they will live. They are deeply disturbed by the possibilities that seem to be opening up in front of them. My suggestion is that any entity that can do this is clearly a person. They are the kind of thing that has the same moral status as adult humans. They should have the same rights as adult humans—unless differences in their nature mean that such rights are not useful to them. In particular, such an entity should be recognised as owning itself in a way that defeats any title that others may have to own it. They cannot be treated as a mere product.

Why does this process of self-examination conclusively establish that the entity in question is a person? One route to this conclusion would be to show that through this process the entity demonstrates its possession of Warren's standards of sentience, emotionality, reason, self-awareness, and either moral agency or something that looks very much like it.

However, there may be a more direct argument based on the claim that this process demonstrates the same kind of morally substantial interest in being recognised as a person as adult humans have. It matters to this entity what happens to it. It cares about who has the right to control what happens to it. It cares about what values inform its behaviour. Any entity that has these kinds of concerns surely has the right that it should be the one who controls what happens to it, that *its* values should inform its behaviour.

The significance of the capacity to reproduce

The focus of this chapter is whether a replicant who was born has a moral status that a replicant who was manufactured does not. However, as noted earlier, there is some suggestion that the replicant freedom movement thinks that it is the capacity to reproduce that is significant for replicant moral status. It is worth making a brief comment about this idea.

I think my argument above shows that replicants are persons whether or not any replicant can reproduce sexually. So reproductive capacities are not necessary for replicants to be their own masters. Considering the Principle of the Fruits (see above) also suggests that reproductive capacities are not sufficient for replicants to be their own masters. Cows and bulls can reproduce, and yet many people would accept that they can be owned. Worms can reproduce, and I'm pretty sure they can be owned. Thus, if the capacity to reproduce is to have dramatic implications for the moral status of replicants, this must either be because replicant reproduction involves something more than simple biological breeding or because the capacity to reproduce *when added to* other features that replicants already possess provides evidence of personhood.

Conclusion

In BR2049, the "miracle" of replicant reproduction is presented as having extremely important implications for the status of replicants and how they may be treated by their human counterparts. This essay has explored whether the fact that a replicant has been born really does have significant implications for its moral status. I argued that birth is less important than it may at first appear.

Wallace assumes that he will own the children of the replicants he has manufactured. This relies on the Fruit Principle: the idea that I own the fruit of my property. I used a puzzle for human self-ownership to unpack the Fruit Principle. I showed that what matters for ownership of replicants is not the method of production but what is produced. If the replicant children are persons, then they have a conclusive title to their selves that defeats any title that Wallace has that is based on the claim that they are fruit of his property. But if the replicant parents are persons, then the replicant parents have a conclusive title to their selves, which defeats any title based on having created them. And if the replicant parents have conclusive title to themselves, then (a) replicant children are not the fruit of Wallace's property, and (b) replicants cannot be (morally) owned by Wallace regardless of whether they are born or made. So, if all replicants are persons, Wallace's attempt to use the Fruit Principle to claim ownership is doubly undermined *and* the significance of the "miracle" of replicant reproduction may not be as great as it is taken to be.

The key question then is: Do replicants who are born count as persons, and, if so, is this because they possess features that are not shared with replicants who are manufactured?

In respect of this issue, I discussed Mary Warren's list of key characteristics of persons. I argued that based on Warren's list, the fact of replicant reproduction has some significance for replicant moral status. It is clear that replicants have the capacity to communicate, by whatever means, messages of an indefinite variety of types. Although there is a general issue about whether artificial intelligence can have sentience, emotionality, reason, and self-awareness (because these features may require an inner life that cannot be created artificially), and a thread of doubt about whether replicants have genuine human emotions in BR2049, on balance, the film presents replicants as fulfilling these conditions. K chooses to disobey orders and acts on his own values. This does seem to be true moral agency. But the possibility that replicants may in their very rebellion be acting according to programming as part of a more complex plan casts a shadow of doubt. Moreover, as Reeve argues, the presence of implanted memories and the absence of mother love raise concerns about whether replicants can have the kind of practical identity that allows humans to claim moral responsibility even if their actions are determined. It is also not clear whether we should see the on-baseline replicants as having a blocked capacity to exercise moral agency. Being born rather than manufactured allows the miracle child to partially escape these concerns.

Despite these doubts, I find that when I am watching the film I always feel sure that replicants are persons rather than mere products. I explained this by offering a Cartesian argument for replicant personhood: any entity that engages in the kind of self-exploration that K engages in is a person. The Cartesian argument for replicant personhood applies to any replicants who question their nature, regardless of whether they were born or manufactured. Replicants do not need to be born to tear down the wall that separates kind; they bring it down simply by asking whether it should be there.

Notes

1 A given legal system might recognize someone as the "legal owner" of another person. However, this legal "ownership" would not have any of the usual moral force of genuine ownership. Freeing a slave is not theft.
2 Some parts of this section are taken from Woollard (2017).
3 This example is rehearsed in the "The Simpson's Treehouse of Horror VII," written by Ken Keeler, Dan Greaney, and David S. Cohen, for 20th Century Fox (the episode was first aired 27 October 1996).
4 As Reeve (2015) notes, the classic statement of the compatibilist account of moral responsibility is Frankfurt (1988).
5 The Cogito is referenced in the first Blade Runner film. For discussion, see Reeve (2015: 74–75).
6 For a classic introductory discussion of Descartes's thought and key objections, see Cottingham (1986).

References

Allen, C. (2015). Do Humans Dream of Emotional Machines? In A. Coplan & D. Davies (Eds.), Blade Runner (pp. 86–99). Abingdon: Routledge.
Cottingham, J. (1986). Descartes. Oxford: Blackwell.
Descartes, R. (1993/1641). Meditations on First Philosophy (D. A. Cress, Trans. 3rd ed.). Indianapolis, IN: Hackett Publishing.
Frankfurt, H. G. (1988). The Importance of What We Care About. Cambridge: Cambridge University Press.
Reeve, C. D. C. (2015). Replicant Love: Blade Runner Voight-Kampffed. In A. Coplan & D. Davies (Eds.), Blade Runner (pp. 68–85). Abingdon: Routledge.
Warren, M. A. (2002). On the Moral and Legal Status of Abortion. In H. LaFollette (Ed.), Ethics in Practice: An Anthology (2nd ed., pp. 72–82). Oxford: Blackwell.
Woollard, F. (2017). I, Me, Mine: Body-Ownership and the Generation Problem. Pacific Philosophical Quarterly 98(S1), 87–108.

Chapter 4

Brian Treanor

BEING-FROM-BIRTH

NATALITY AND NARRATIVE

> ELDON TYRELL: What—What seems to be the problem?
> ROY BATTY: Death.
> ELDON TYRELL: Death. Well, I'm afraid that's a little bit out of my jurisdiction, you—
> ROY BATTY: I want more life, fucker!
>
> —Blade Runner

> LT. JOSHI: You have anything more to say?
> KD6-3.7 / Joe: I've never retired something that was born before.
> LT. JOSHI: What's the difference?
> KD6-3.7 / Joe: To be born is to have a soul, I guess.
>
> —Blade Runner 2049

Of robot evolution and bioengineered humans

"Replicants are bioengineered humans."[1] This, the first line of text that opens *Blade Runner 2049* (BR2049), seems to answer, immediately and definitively, the question that haunts much of the film's predecessor: Are replicants humans? To this, the sequel seems to straightforwardly answer, *yes*. This is in contrast to the opening of *Blade Runner*, which described replicants as "virtually identical to humans" and the result of the Tyrell Corporation's work on "robot evolution." However, despite asserting that replicants are human, it quickly becomes clear that how, why, and even if replicants share in humanity is very much an open question in BR2049. The film begins with an answer, as it were, and then proceeds to confuse or complicate things with questions. In this respect, it shares a common form with a long philosophical tradition dating back to Socrates. Thus, just what makes or does not make replicants "human" is a persistent question that haunts both films; and when all is said and done, BR2049 does not give us any clear, final account of who is and who is not human, or what constitutes the relevant difference. We can begin, however, by dismissing certain theories.

The relevant criteria marking "real" humanity cannot, we must assume, be anything purely material in nature—for example, DNA. Such reductive explanations quickly prove overly facile and impossible to maintain. Occam's Razor notwithstanding, simple answers often distort a complex reality. Replicants are not advanced robots; they are made of the same materials that humans are made of—bone, blood, tissue—all grown from instructions coded in DNA. We know this because, when K is searching for Deckard and Rachael's child, he provides "confirmation DNA" from Rachael to the file clerk at Wallace Corporation, and later searches the DeNAbase for records of children born on June 10, 2021. In the latter instance, Joi observes that replicants, including K, are made up of four elements: A, T, G, and C, the nucleotide building-blocks of DNA—while she is made up of just two, the zeros and ones of her binary code. One might argue that there would be DNA markers for something like the superhuman strength exhibited by some replicants; but even these enhancements might not be adequate as a means of identification. It is entirely plausible that certain humans have also opted for bioengineered enhancements. Wallace, for example, is a cyborg, using technological enhancements to overcome his blindness, "seeing" the world around him using floating "barracuda" sensors.[2] Moreover, some replicants do not have superhuman abilities. And precisely because replicants are assembled from DNA, one could presumably create a "normal" replicant, that is to say a replicant that would be *completely* indistinguishable from a human by any conceivable technology.[3] In short, if anything distinguishes humans from replicants, it cannot be something as simple as DNA or, indeed, any other crass reductive criterion.

But if replicant identity or human identity is difficult, or impossible, to determine on the basis of *what* something is—its nature as living, organized by instructions coded in DNA, and so forth—perhaps we need to consider *how* something is, its manner of being.

Mortality: being-toward-death

The importance of death in *Blade Runner* is explored in Peter Atterton's (2015) "More Human Than Human." The essential question raised by the first film is not, Atterton contends, "Is Deckard a replicant?" but rather "What makes the replicants *human*?" He answers this question, following Heidegger, by arguing that the distinctive mark of humanity is our being-toward-death (*Sein-zum-Tode*). Being-toward-death is not merely the fact that a being will die. Trees die. Salmon die. Elk die. However, none of these beings has the same relation to death that humans have. Being-toward-death does not name an empirical event that will come to pass at some point in the future; it is rather a way-of-being characterized by an awareness of death as an indefinite and inescapable fact: "A person, unlike any other animal I am aware of, is a being that *knows he or she is going to die*. It is the dread of dying that is human *par excellence*" (Atterton, 2015: 47).

But all of this is obscured in everyday life, in which we recognize death as a fact, as something that happens, but which is not experienced as mine. One might think of Tolstoy's (1981) Ivan Ilyich, who can complete the syllogism "Caius is a man, men are mortal, therefore Caius is mortal," but who finds it difficult to wrap his head around his own being-toward-death, the full realization that he, like Caius, will die (93). That, in any case, is the inauthentic way of thinking about death. But we can, and do, experience our being-toward-death authentically when we extricate ourselves from the experience of the everyday and see our finitude clearly, leading to the experience of *angst*.

In *Blade Runner*, Roy, Pris, Leon, and Zhora are aware of their being-toward-death; indeed, because they are aware of their four-year lifespan, they likely have a heightened sense of their own finitude. If awareness of death as one's ownmost possibility—an inescapable limit, indefinite with respect to its precise moment but definitely approaching more closely with each passing day—is characteristic of being human, it is a characteristic shared by the NEXUS 6 replicants.

But death is not the main focus of BR2049. No one is demanding "more life, fucker."[4] True, the significance of death does come up in the film: Freysa attempts to convince K to join the resistance, telling him, "Dying for the right cause is the most human thing we can do." But in the end freedom for replicants is not K's primary concern, though certainly he would prefer it. Nor does K seem deeply perplexed about whether or not he has free will. Nor, again, is K obsessed with escaping or postponing death. The essential focus of BR2049 is not mortality and being-toward-death, but rather *natality*, being-from-birth.

Natality: being-from-birth

Compared to mortality, natality is a topic little-explored by philosophy. Nevertheless, there are thinkers who have made birth and related issues a matter of concern, among them Martin Heidegger, Wilhelm Dilthey, Hannah Arendt, and Jean-Luc Nancy, all of whom are taken up in Anne O'Byrne's (2010) *Natality and Finitude*. O'Byrne argues that natality, like mortality, is experienced in the present, not as a biological fact, but as a "condition of human finitude" (O'Byrne, 2010: 3). Human being is characterized by being-from-birth as well as being-toward-death. Just as humans are the only beings, as far as we know, who know that they will die and who, consequently, have anxiety about a time when they will no longer be, humans are also, as far as we know, the only beings who know that they were born and who, consequently, are aware that there was a time before they were.

However, thinking about natality reveals existential conditions very different from thinking about mortality: "When we select death as the cipher for our finitude and understand it as Heidegger did in *Being and Time*, it turns out to be what individuates us; birth, in contrast, reveals us as being in relation" (O'Byrne, 2010: 9). Being-toward-death, death as my "ownmost possibility" is a way of being that is individuating and non-relational; my death is mine and no one else's, something that I face alone, a journey on which no one can accompany me. But natality, while individuating—my birth is mine, a unique event in which I am irreplaceable—is also inherently social and relational: "Death may be Dasein's ownmost non-relational possibility, separating Dasein from all others, but birth is precisely what puts us in relation with others since, while we each may die alone, we could not have been alone at birth" (O'Byrne, 2010: 34–35). Just as our death reminds us that there will be a time when we are-not, our birth reminds us that there was once "a time when we were not, [and] that we owe our existence to others" (O'Byrne, 2010: 7).

To be born is to come-to-be in *relation*, and this in at least two senses. First, natality reminds us of our embodied relationality with others, the fact that I could not be without having been conceived, gestated in a womb, born. However, in addition, natality reminds us that our origins are shrouded in an immemorial past: "[B]irth happens without our knowing and every one of us is here for years before we realize it, before we come to find ourselves in the midst of things" (O'Byrne, 2010: 107). Thus, our knowledge of our birth and our understanding of our natality is something we only understand relationally, with the aid of the community into which we've been born. I do not experience my own birth; I know it through others who witnessed it: "my co-creation was already under way before I was capable of taking it up as a self-creation" (O'Byrne, 2010: 132).

Intriguingly, O'Byrne concludes her reflections on natality by considering the possibility of human cloning, a topic that in many respects brings her thinking to bear on issues quite close to those at the heart of BR2049. Cloning is, of course, no longer the realm of science fiction. Only slightly more than two decades ago humans successfully cloned a large mammal, the famous sheep, Dolly, which quickly ushered in anxiety about the technological, legal, and ethical issues raised by the possibility of human clones. Indeed, given advances in biology, medicine, and technology, there is every reason to think that people reading this book will live to see human clones. O'Byrne points out that the fear of clones becoming a mistreated underclass—shades, perhaps, of *Blade Runner* or of Kazuo Ishiguro's (2005) *Never Let Me Go*—is the most common ethical concern on offer, and is rooted in our sense that clones "will challenge our concept of the sorts of beings ... we are" (O'Byrne, 2010: 150). But much of our anxiety about cloning is, O'Byrne believes, misplaced.

To think of a clone in merely biological terms (e.g. "another me" with identical DNA) is to miss the significance of both mortality and natality. Clones, obviously, will be mortal and self-aware, and will be as subject to *angst* over their being-toward-death as we are. But clones will also be natal, coming to be in a web of relationality just as other humans do. And the embodied relationality that characterizes a clone would be entirely different than the embodied relationality that characterized the person on whom the clone was based—a different gestation in a different womb, born at a different time into a different world, a point in different constellations of relation with different people. Of course, one of these two sources of relationality—the mother's womb and the community of other persons into which a person is born—is not operative in the case of replicants. O'Byrne envisions clones brought to term in much the same way as Dolly the sheep (i.e., in a womb); but replicants are "born" fully matured via a mysterious, but decidedly non-maternal, process in the Wallace Corporation laboratories.

The significance of the maternal relationship is not lost on us in BR2049. The story hinges on the issue of replicant sexual reproduction and gestation, which takes on biblical and messianic overtones in the way Wallace, Freysa, and others describe the significance of Rachael's child. When K starts to suspect, erroneously, that he may be Rachael and Rick Deckard's lost child, Joi whispers into his ear: "I always knew you were special. Maybe this is how. A child ... of woman born. Pushed into the world. *Wanted. Loved.*" All this seems to endorse O'Byrne's idea that the "fetus–maternal body relation is crucial to our natal being" (O'Byrne, 2010: 162).

If, as O'Byrne suggests, the way we understand the fetus–maternal body relationship is "central to how we understand all subsequent relations," then it seems that we will have to develop some alternative way to think about replicants: "[T]he prospect of an artificially gestated child would require a new and different effort in hypothetical thinking" (O'Byrne, 2010: 162). Richard Zaner (2005) goes further: "To be human ... is at the very least to become human, and becoming human in stages along life's way requires that temporal, sequential development within and nourished by another human body ... The uterine environment, in other words, strikes me as absolutely essential, though it is not all that is essential, for [a clone] to become human" (Zaner, 2005: 202).[5] This vision of natality and humanity makes things look bleak for K, since we find that he is not the child in question; Dr Stelline is.

But while the maternal relationship is a major source of our natal relationality, it is not the only source O'Byrne treats. As she points out, I do not experience my birth directly. Whether that birth takes place in a hospital or in the Wallace Corporation laboratories or on Sapper Morton's protein farm, I know and understand it through relationships with others. I know my own birth, and the world into which I was born, and the narratives through which I make sense of things through others who were there when I was born, who already inhabited our shared world and shared narratives. A replicant may be born fully mature in a physical sense, but he or she is not born with knowledge, or experience, or awareness of his or her nature. A replicant is "thrown" into the world as surely as any human conceived and gestated in a more traditional manner, finds itself "in the midst of things" at some point after its arrival on the scene.

When Wallace and Luv go to inspect a new batch of replicants, we witness a "birth." The replicant is a fully mature female; but, Wallace observes, she is not yet fully aware: "The first thought tends to fear, to preserve the clay. Fascinating. Before we even know what we are, we fear to lose it." Replicants, it seems, do not come with pre-installed software containing all the necessary information about their identity, their relations to others, the way the world works, and so on. Thus, just like a human child, a replicant will need to be instructed and enculturated through relationships, given memories of their origin by others around them. The replicant, like the human, must discover the circumstances of its origin; and, more importantly, and again like the human, the replicant must discover the significance of those circumstances for its being. For both replicant and human, meaning is not a given, it is a task to be achieved.

> Clone [replicant] or not, the newness of the newborn is still inevitable. The human world, which is a world of relations, is subject to time; it has never before been configured as it is at the moment of any birth, and it is configured all over again by the child's [replicant's] arrival. Like the rest of us, the clone [replicant] will not have made the decision to be born and will be as capable as any of us of asking "Why was I born?" not to mention "Where did my parents get their strange ideas?" She will have the same opportunities we did to grow up into a being who assumes prime responsibility for herself and her actions without evading the ongoing contingencies of acting and being.
>
> (O'Byrne, 2010: 161)

The emphasis on Rachael's fertility proves to be misleading, at least in this sense: K *was* born, *is* natal; he *will* die, *is* mortal.

Within cells interlinked

The analysis of natality seems to suggest that a certain sort of being-in-relation is an essential part of being human. Our understanding of our world is something we take up from others with whom we are in relation before we have the opportunity to make that meaning our own—to embrace or reject or modify it. We only understand ourselves, to the extent we *can* understand ourselves, in relation with others; and this sort of relationship to oneself as related to others clearly plays a significant role in BR2049. For example, K's baseline test, the process by which he is monitored for appropriate or inappropriate emotional responses, probes his sense of meaningful connection to others, the emergence of which would be a "red flag" that he might be becoming "too human."

INTERVIEWER: Interlinked.
K: Interlinked.
INTERVIEWER: What's it like to hold the hand of someone you love? Interlinked.
K: Interlinked.
INTERVIEWER: Did they teach you how to feel, finger to finger? Interlinked.
K: Interlinked.
INTERVIEWER: Do you long for having your heart interlinked? Interlinked.
K: Interlinked.
INTERVIEWER: Do you dream about being interlinked?
K: Interlinked.
INTERVIEWER: What's it like to hold your child in your arms? Interlinked.
K: Interlinked.
INTERVIEWER: Do you feel like there's a part of you that's missing? Interlinked.
K: Interlinked.

This repetitive probing of K's reactions to the concept of being "interlinked," particularly with others—"someone you love," "a child," "finger to finger"—is focused on trying to discern whether or not he feels something like "an awareness of natality," along with its too-human connection to others.

Replicants are supposed to be tools, not persons; and they are expected to recognize and feel their own tool nature. Thus, in the prequel short, *2036: Nexus Dawn*, Niander Wallace stages a dramatic demonstration of the obedience of his new NEXUS 9 replicants, commanding one of them to first wound and then kill itself. The point being to reassure regulators that his new-generation replicants are, in fact, nothing more than highly sophisticated robots, a safe tool for human use and abuse—for example, as slave labourers, domestic servants, sexual toys, and military shock troops. The innate obedience and emotional detachment of NEXUS 9 replicants, in contrast to earlier models, emphasizes their role as objects for human use. As long as replicants are objects, they are tools; but if they become subjects, they are slaves. As Lt. Joshi observes, "The world is built on a wall. It separates kind [that is, subject and object]. Tell either side there's no wall, you bought a war. Or a slaughter."

This is why NEXUS 9s are subject to "baseline" evaluations: to reassure people, and remind the replicant, that they are not really human. They do not feel; they do not love; they are not interlinked. Thus, when K appears stupefied by the recognition that he has never "retired" something that was born before, perhaps suggesting hesitation or even reluctance, Lt. Joshi demands, indignantly and with undertones of aggression, "Are you telling me no?" To which K, remembering his place, responds deferentially, "I wasn't aware that was an option, madam." "Attaboy," says Joshi, reassured and instantly dismissive. But it quickly becomes clear that, Wallace's suicidally compliant replicants notwithstanding, the NEXUS 9 models are, or are becoming, significantly more self-directed and self-determining than their creator intended.

There do seem to be some "built-in" controls. As K points out to Sapper Morton, in response to the latter's claim that a replicant blade runner is a traitor to its own kind, "I don't retire my own kind [i.e., NEXUS 9s] because we don't run. Only older models do." But whatever controls are in place, they seem capable of eroding over time whereas NEXUS 9s, like the earlier models, accumulate experience. When Luv murders Joshi, she reveals her capacity for duplicity, despite her loyalty to Wallace: "You're so sure. Because he told you. Because we never lie. I'm gonna tell Mr. Wallace you tried to shoot me first. So, I had to kill you." Luv is going to lie to Wallace in order to pursue her own ends, murdering Joshi out of anger and frustration. And, of course, the most obvious and compelling example of a NEXUS 9 rejecting the authority of its master is K's own willingness to disobey and dissimulate in his attempt to unravel the mystery of Rachael's child. Although he says that he is not aware that disobedience is an option, it will only be a couple of days before he has, in fact, decided to disobey. Perhaps Joshi should have been a bit more sceptical of K's tool nature and obedience, since she herself observes that he behaves in increasingly human ways: "With you I sometimes forget [that you are a replicant]."

What is it that begins to loosen K from his "programmed" bondage? Answer: His desire to be interlinked. This desire is already evident in his relationship with Joi—a topic worthy of its own analysis—but it is given new form and intensity in his desire to *explore his natality* by searching for his supposed parents and learning about his supposed origins. To explore one's natality is to explore the origins or sources of being interlinked: to search for the beginning of one's being-with-others in the world.

Natality and narrative

The fact that we are not present at our birth—not in the sense of self-aware, individuated beings who can experience the event and remember it—means that we must experience our natality "indirectly" through the images and stories related to us by others. And since we experience our natality through this narrative mediation, we cannot really understand our relationship with natality unless we grasp how narrative experience works.

There are a variety of well-developed accounts of how narrative shapes both understanding and identity, but a particularly clear account can be found in the work of Paul Ricoeur (1992). Ricoeur argues that many of our questions about identity are the result of confusing *idem*-identity (whatness) and *ipse*-identity (whoness).

> The problem of personal identity constitutes, in my opinion, a privileged place of confrontation between the two major uses of the concept of identity ... Let me recall the terms of the

confrontation: on the one side, identity as sameness (Latin *idem*, German *Gleichheit*, French *mêmeté*); on the other, identity as selfhood (Latin *ipse*, German *Selbstheit*, French *ipséité*). Selfhood, as I have repeatedly affirmed, is not sameness. Because the major distinction between them is not recognized ... the solutions offered to the problem of personal identity which do not consider the narrative dimension fail.

(Ricoeur, 1992: 115–116)[6]

In many of the cases in which a person questions her identity, what is at stake is not *what* she is but rather *who* she is. It's true that in some cases we might be concerned with the whatness of a thing, especially when we are talking about things as opposed to people. But despite the temptation of an easy answer, in the case of replicants it is difficult to see how *idem* is the most relevant issue. If, as I've suggested, the technology in BR2049 could "assemble" or "grow" a being from human DNA that was, post-partum, indistinguishable in every imaginable physical respect from a being conceived by human sexual reproduction and gestation in a woman's womb, on what basis could we identify a physical difference rooted in a being's whatness (*idem*) that would mark it as "replicant" rather than "human"? There could be no non-arbitrary difference in whatness here. To suggest that DNA combined in a lab and grown in an artificial womb is *materially* different from DNA combined in sexual reproduction and grown in a human womb seems obviously false. The putative difference lies not in *what* a replicant is but *why* it is or *how* it came to be. K is not a replicant because he is strong or fast; he is a replicant because of how he came to be, not what he is. This is not a difference in material, but a difference in meaning.

Neither Ricoeur, nor I, nor Roy Batty, nor KD6-3.7 are particularly disturbed by ship-of-Theseus-type questions about the significance of the fact that the cells of my body are constantly dying and being replaced by new cells, or by the misguided suggestion that this means I am "no longer the same person" I was several years ago. Even if it were true that every cell in my body were replaced and I was, in some sense, no longer the same (*idem*) person, it would still be the case that there is a continuity in my identity that makes me the same (*ipse*) person.[7] The nature of this continuity is best captured by the notion of a story that links "earlier me" to "present me" as the same character in a coherent narrative. And, traced back far enough, a life story begins with natality or birth.

K intuitively recognizes that his origins and his humanity are somehow tied up in the nature of his natality: "To be born is to have a soul, I guess." It is Wallace who fundamentally misunderstands this relationship. He claims to have "millions" of children while treating those "children" as objects and commodities, denying them the social connection that might make their origins a genuine experience of natality rather than a mere technological assemblage of parts followed by the clinical activation of functions. A similar misunderstanding can be seen in his assumption that he can return Rachael to Deckard in any meaningful sense, an error based in the confusion of *idem*-identity and *ipse*-identity. Why is it that the Rachael offered by Wallace is unsatisfactory to Deckard? She is, presumably, genetically identical to the Rachael he loved. Her habits, inclinations, and behaviours are identical. Her memories, at least the implanted memories up to the moment of her "inception," are identical. True, she would not remember her whole life with Deckard after the two of them fled Los Angeles, because Wallace would not have a record of those memories and could not implant them. But let's make the simulacrum even more convincing and assume, for the sake of argument, that the recreated Rachael does have all those memories as well, along with the evolution of her character and emotional life that would result as a consequence. Would the perfect verisimilitude of that even-more-precise Rachael actually *be* Rachael in the sense that matters? There is good reason to think not.

Robert Elliot (1999) points out that identity and value are closely connected, and that "the value of objects" is explained in large part "in terms of their origins, in terms of the kinds of process that brought them into being" (Elliot, 1999: 384). In other words, the origin of an object, the way in which its story begins, plays an important role in the value we ascribe to it. Elliot's own concern is with the viability of wilderness restoration, but he makes his point with a number of examples that seem highly relevant to Rachael's case. If I am given a Cezanne and later discover that it is a forgery, my assessment of its worth—its value to me, not just its monetary value—changes. This is true even if the forgery is so perfect as to fool even the very best experts. If I admire a beautiful object and later learn that it was "carved out of the bone of a person killed especially for that purpose ... this discovery affects me deeply and I cease to value the object in the way that I once did" (Elliot, 1999: 384).[8] We view an otherwise healthy, diverse, and dense forest differently when we learn that it was replanted by Massey Energy in the wake of mountaintop removal coal extraction that laid waste to the original primeval forest, killed and displaced the wildlife living in it, and polluted the village downstream in the watershed.[9] Similarly, the cloned Rachael has a different history than the original Rachael, and so has a different value for Deckard. This is true even if both Rachael-2019 and Rachael-2049 have their origins in the same Tyrell–Wallace process. In each of these cases—the painting, the aesthetic object crafted from the remains of a murder victim, a second-growth forest, and a cloned lover—a third party would recognize that the victim of the forgery was being short-changed even if the person in question was unaware of the forgery.

Of clones and replicants

Of course, the cloning of Rachael does not parallel precisely the questions K has about his own identity. K is not a clone and is not wondering in what way he might or might not be the same as one of his duplicates. But Rachael's cloning does have important similarities with K's dilemma, because at the root of K's questioning is the issue of whether or not he is "real." And here, as in the case of art forgery, wilderness restoration, and human cloning, the question of how we value something is linked to whether we consider it real or authentic, and its reality and authenticity are connected to the story of how it came to be.

The issue is not the matter of whether or not K is made up of human DNA; he is. The issue is whether or not a person who came to be in the way in which K came to be—a person whose life story begins with an alternative type of natality—is as valuable, as "real," as someone with a more familiar form of natality. In K's case this valuing is evident both in the way that other people view him—Joshi, the other cops, the people in his apartment building—and in the way in which he views himself. Engaging the question of what marks "real" humans is taken up in a variety of ways in BR2049: Doc Badger's equivocation on "reality" when comparing "real" wood to a "real" Wallace-grown horse; Mariette, herself a NEXUS 9, quipping that K doesn't like "real girls" when she hears the ringtone from Joi's emanator; Joi's later appropriation of Mariette's body to have sex with K, so that she can "be real" for him. But two particular lines of questioning suggest that our concern with natality and narrative are important themes for BR2049 and for K.

We saw that, during their visit to the DeNAbase, Joi claims that K is "special" because he was "born," "wanted," "loved." She adds specificity to her point after their visit to the Morrillcole orphanage: "I always told you. You're special. Born, not made. Hidden with care. A real boy now." On this account, K is real because he was "born, not made." But why is that significant? It seems that there are at least two distinctions that might be relevant: the biological ("pushed into the world") and motivational ("wanted," "loved"). If the former suggests something special about a certain form of natality associated with traditional human gestation and birth, the latter suggests that what is actually at stake is not a distinction between biology and technology based in efficient causality, but rather one between love and utility as forms of final causality. And there is good reason to think that the latter distinction does at least as much of the work in differentiating human natality from replicant construction as the former. Consider, by way of analogy, contemporary technological interventions in conception. We certainly do not think that the full humanity of children conceived via in vitro fertilization (IVF) is in any way compromised compared to children conceived via intercourse. Similarly, there is reason to think that, despite the challenge such technologies would no doubt raise, we might grow to accept the humanity of a child brought to term through something like the Wallace process. We already have premature babies who finish their normal gestational period in the incubators of a neonatal intensive care unit. We have already seen the birth of children conceived through IVF and gestated in transplanted human wombs. And there is no reason to think that various forms of artificial womb are not on the technological horizon.[10] The humanity of such children does not seem to be at issue. After all, natality is rooted in and revealing of a particular kind of being-in-relation. The problem for K is not that his DNA differentiates him from his colleagues, nor that his gestation took place in a plastic sleeve at Wallace Corporation rather than in Rachael's womb. His problem is that he was not wanted or loved, but rather useful and disposable, and that the entire constellation of others with whom he was "born" into relation thought of him and related to him as a tool, not a child.

There are also reasons to think that narrative plays an important role in the "reality" of one's humanity in BR2049. For much of the movie, K's humanity seems to hinge on whether or not his memory of a childhood spent in an orphanage is real. Memories, of course, are simply stories. So, the question is: Which stories (memories) are real? In the original *Blade Runner*, the importance of memory for feeling authentically human is evident not only in the memories implanted into Rachael (and perhaps Deckard). We also see the need for memory, the need for a rich and coherent life story, as in Leon's devotion to his photographs. How do you make something more human? You give it a past, a narrative. The question is not, "Do androids dream of electric sheep?" but rather "Do replicants need to tell the story of their lives?" And the answer is: yes, they do.

But BR2049 raises additional questions about what would count as a "real" or "authentic" memory, and how this would relate to being a "real" human. At first, we seem to have a clear distinction in the work of Dr Stelline: real memories are those originating in a real person (i.e., a real human), on the basis of her experience, and they correspond to an actual historical event; false memories are memories constructed by a person and do not correspond to an actual historical event, or are a patchwork of unrelated historical events. Stelline suggests "authentic human memories" produce "authentic human responses," which are precisely the kind of responses that the baseline test is supposed to look for as a sign that a replicant is becoming "too human." Perhaps this, the presence of authentic memories in K, informs both why Joshi sometimes forgets that he is a replicant and why K yearns so profoundly and confusedly for love, family, and connection.

However, this seemingly simple distinction is complicated when we recognize, as we must, that *all* memories, human or replicant, are constructed—even, to a certain degree, fabricated. Your memory of your high-school graduation—if you can even remember it—is a bricolage of events and impressions woven together as if they were a clear, linear narrative, when the truth is that some of those events and impressions did not "go together" in experience, that some may not have occurred at all, or may have been transported from the experience of someone else or from some other narrative with which you are acquainted.

The imperfect, partial, perspectival, constructed nature of memory is, of course, especially true of memories of childhood, which are obscured in the fog of le temps perdu. And if distant memories are the exemplary case of the constructed nature of memory, they are far from unique. Your memory of what you did this very morning is a narrative: it is selective, retaining some things and omitting others; among the things it retains, it attaches greater emphasis to some vis-à-vis others; it links these disparate, heterogeneous elements into a coherent narrative that moves from beginning to end; and all of this is done from the perspective of the person who remembers, not from some God's-eye "view from nowhere."

Thus, the fact that K's memory is "constructed" does not on its own distinguish it from any of Joshi's memories or Wallace's memories, nor is the fact that it is "implanted" a clear mark of inauthenticity, for all of our memories include aspects that have been coloured by and even originated in what others have told us of events. Our own memories are, to a certain extent, collaboratively created narrations of our past. If construction and ambiguous authorship make memories false, we are all operating with false memories. As Dr Stelline reminds us, "authentic" memory is not about more detail, not a matter of striving for scrupulous fidelity to facts; it is concerned with affect, with the "sense" of events and their meaning: "We recall with our feelings." Moreover, real memories are never a precise, "objective" documentation of events—they are, rather, impressionistic. When it comes to memory, "Anything real [i.e., any "authentic" memory] should be [i.e., is] a mess."

Is he real? I don't know. Ask him.

Thus, with respect to the humanity of K and his fellow replicants we end, as promised, in ambiguity, in a "mess." In the end, neither *Blade Runner* nor *BR2049* offers any clear statement about just what makes humans human. We began with an answer, a clear claim about humanity, and we end with questions born of a more nuanced appreciation of the complexities of the situation. These films undermine the notion that humanity can be reduced to mere material causality, something that could be accounted for with a buccal swab and a DNA test. They also undermine assertions that humanity is grounded in an arbitrary metaphysical watermark like the *imago dei*, given that there are many reasons for thinking that Deckard, Rachael, Sapper, and K are "more human" in relevant respects than, for example, Wallace.

Perhaps, then, we should give the final word to two of the figures for whom the distinction, if any, between replicant nature and human nature is particularly significant: Rick Deckard and KD6-3.7. Having battled to an uneasy détente at Deckard's hideout in Las Vegas, Deckard and K cautiously edge up to a bar to share a drink. As the tension eases, Deckard pours some of the whiskey on to the floor, which his dog laps up languidly. K, who has been staring at the dog with astonishment for some time, asks, "Is it real?" Deckard—a man who has wrestled with similar questions for much of his adult life, a man who has been destroyed by the uncertainties raised by these questions—gives K a simple, direct response that cuts to the heart of the matter as far as he is concerned: "I don't know. Ask him."[11]

An entire chapter could be written on this example, the significance of which is highlighted in short order when Luv, having beaten K into submission, chastises him: "Bad dog." Bad dog. Bad for misbehaving. Bad for having disobeyed orders. Bad for being "off baseline." Bad for denying his nature. Bad, in effect, for thinking he might be—and thus be becoming—more human. But, clearly, Deckard does not offer the dog as a rebuke to K. Would it be too much to say that Deckard looks at the dog with admiration, even envy? The dog, after all, does not experience either being-toward-death ("Where am I going?") or being-from-birth ("Where am I from?"). The dog does not question its dogness; it simply lives its dog-nature in the present, like a Taoist sage or the Apostle Matthew's "lilies in the field." And, as Milan Kundera (1999) diagnoses, juxtaposing a dog's happiness with human confusion: "Therein lies the whole of man's plight. Human time does not turn in a circle; it runs ahead in a straight line" between past and future, birth and death, what we are and what we should be, being and nothingness (see Kundera, 1999: 298).

Is K a "real boy"? I don't know. Ask him. Ask him as he stands outside Dr Stelline's laboratory after his first visit and marvels at the snow falling, *mirabile visu*, on his upturned palm. Ask him as he repeats the same gesture, with the same wonder, just before he lies down to die, this time fully aware that he is not Rachael's child.[12] Ask him at any one of the myriad inflection points in the final week of his life, as he strives to bond with Joi as a partner, as he yearns for connection with Deckard as a father, and then as a father-who-could-have-been, as he resists Joshi's homicidal order to find and kill Rachael's child.

Is K real? Like the missing 1,000th line of *Pale Fire*'s poem, this is a question for which we will never have unambiguous, complete closure. But perhaps it is one to which a response is better formed in terms of a truth to which we aspire, one that we enact or make (*facere veritatem*), rather than a truth that is given in advance and to which we correspond or fail to correspond.

Notes

1 In what follows, I will be working under the assumption that the reader has seen both *Blade Runner* (in one of its forms) and *Blade Runner 2049*. Although there is no clear "canon" to the *Blade Runner* universe, I will also consider the three short films released prior to *Blade Runner 2049* (2022: *Black Out*, 2036: *Nexus Dawn*, and 2048: *Nowhere to Run*), with which Denis Villeneuve was involved, as comprising part of a single world.
2 Indeed, we are *already* enhancing humans. Consider the birth of the first human babies genetically modified with CRISPR-Cas9 gene-editing techniques (https://www.npr.org/sections/health-shots/2018/11/26/670752865/chinese-scientist-says-hes-first-to-genetically-edit-babies, accessed November 26, 2018). The world will *certainly* see additional research in human gene editing and human modification in the very near future.
3 Tests like the Voight-Kampff were designed to detect aberrant emotional responses, but it is all-too-clear that any number of actual humans have 'unnatural' emotional responses. Similarly, the baseline test is designed to see if a replicant is deviating too far from his or her stable, baseline emotional responsivity, becoming "too human," that is, too emotional. It does not identify a replicant, but an unstable emotional pattern. And, obviously, if DNA were an adequate marker for replicant origins, the sorts of technology available in the world of *Blade Runner* would have a readily available test.
4 The original script apparently had this line as, "I want more life, father," but the father/fucker slippage captures well our anxiety about death, the problem of evil, and the silence of God.
5 Cited in O'Byrne (2010: 162).
6 *Idem*-identity and *ipse*-identity are not unrelated; there are examples of phenomena in which they seem to overlap. Two areas to which Ricoeur draws our attention are (a) character and (b) keeping one's word (Ricoeur, 1992: 118 ff.).
7 The distinctions Ricoeur is making are not unrelated to those made by Derek Parfit (1984) in his *Reasons and Persons*. Indeed, Ricoeur directly engages some of Parfit's celebrated examples in *Oneself as Another*. Unfortunately, as far as I can tell, Parfit never responded to this attempt at dialogue across the analytic–continental divide, and a sustained engagement between the two never

materialized. I cannot do justice to a comparison between Ricoeur and Parfit here and mention only as an aside that Parfit's distinction between identity (which on his account is not what matters) and psychological continuity (which is what matters) offers yet another way to think about issues related to Rachael's cloning. Psychological continuity is, after all, not so far from memory, and memory is a form of narrative.
8 This example, as well as the example of a painting and a forest restoration, are examples used by Elliot (1999).
9 Of course, this example is speculative to the point of comedy, given that fossil fuel companies almost never really try to restore the environments they disrupt.
10 "First Baby Born After Deceased Womb Transplant," BBC, December 5, 2018. https://www.bbc.com/news/health-46438396; accessed December 10, 2018.
11 Deckard's faith in an agent's ability to know its own realness is tested, but not broken, when Wallace suggests he is a NEXUS 7, designed to fall in love with Rachael to test replicant reproduction. Deckard shudders for a moment, but insists, "I know what's real."
12 The first instance mirrors Joi's wonder as the rain falls on her own hand on her first journey outside. The second evokes Roy Batty's death, just after the moment when, arguably, he too expressed his humanity most profoundly.

References

Atterton, P. (2015). More Human Than Human. In A. Coplan & D. Davies (Eds.), *Blade Runner* (pp. 46–67). Abingdon: Routledge.
Elliot, R. (1999). Faking Nature. In J. R. DesJardins (Ed.), *Environmental Ethics: Concepts, Policy, Theory* (pp. 381–389). Mountain View, CA: Mayfield Publishing Company.
Ishiguro, K. (2005). *Never Let Me Go*. London: Faber and Faber.
Kundera, M. (1999). *The Unbearable Lightness of Being* (M. H. Heim, Trans.). New York: Harper Perennial.
O'Byrne, A. (2010). *Natality and Finitude*. Bloomington: Indiana University Press.
Parfit, D. (1984). *Reasons and Persons*. Oxford: Clarendon Press.
Ricoeur, P. (1992). *Oneself as Another* (K. Blamey, Trans.). Chicago: University of Chicago Press.
Tolstoy, L. (1981). *The Death of Ivan Ilyich* (L. Solotaroff, Trans.). New York: Bantam Books.
Zaner, R. (2005). Visions and Re-visions: Life and the Accident of Birth. In H. W. Baillie & T. K. Casey (Eds.), *Is Human Nature Obsolete? Genetics, Bioengineering, and the Future of the Human Condition* (pp. 177–208). Cambridge, MA: MIT Press.

Chapter 5

Richard Heersmink and Christopher Jude McCarroll

THE BEST MEMORIES

IDENTITY, NARRATIVE, AND OBJECTS[1]

Introduction

MEMORY IS EVERYWHERE IN BLADE Runner 2049. From the dead tree that serves as a memorial and a site of remembrance ("Who keeps a dead tree?"), to the "flashbulb" memories individuals hold about the moment of the "blackout," when all the electronic stores of data were irretrievably erased ("everyone remembers where they were at the blackout").[2] Indeed, the data wiped out in the blackout itself involves a loss of memory ("all our memory bearings from the time, they were all damaged in the blackout"). Memory, and lack of it, permeates place, where from the post-blackout Las Vegas Deckard remembers it as somewhere you could "forget your troubles." Memory is a commodity, called upon and consumed by the Wallace Corporation, purchased from the memory-maker, Dr Ana Stelline, who constructs and implants "the best memories" in replicants so as to instil in them real human responses. Memory is ubiquitous in BR2049, involving humans, replicants, objects, and machines. Even "God," we are told, "remembered Rachael."

Nowhere, though, is the depiction of memory more important than in the attempt to solve a question of identity. Officer K has a memory of his past. Even though he knows it is an implant, it is a memory he is emotionally attached to, frequently narrating it to Joi, his digital girlfriend. But it is a memory that starts to puzzle and trouble him. When K discovers the remains of a dead replicant, a female NEXUS 7, he uncovers a secret—this replicant was pregnant and died during childbirth, a discovery that could "break the world." K is charged with hunting down the offspring and making the problem disappear. Yet as K starts seeking answers to the question of the offspring's identity he becomes inextricably caught up in the mystery. Is he merely K, or is he Joe, the miracle son of Rachael and Deckard? The answer to this question hinges on K's memory. But is the memory genuine? Is the memory his?

BR2049 encourages us to think deeply about the nature of memory, identity, and the relation between them. Indeed, the film does not just serve as a starting point for thinking *about* philosophical issues related to memory and identity. Rather, as we show in this chapter, the film seems to offer a view *on* these philosophical issues. BR2049 offers us a view of memory as spread out over people, objects, and the environment, and it shows us that memory's role in questions of identity goes beyond merely accurately recalling one's past. Identity depends not on memory *per se*, but partly on what we use memory for.

Humanhood and personhood

BR2049 is, essentially, the story of a replicant on a quest to discover his identity—a journey that takes him from being a mere replicant to coming to terms with believing he is a "real boy," but then only to discover he was not a child born into the world after all. The concepts of humanhood and personhood play a key role in the narrative arc of the film. Let's have a closer look at what philosophers have to say about these concepts.

In the metaphysics of personal identity, two questions are distinguished. One, what is personhood? Two, is there continuity of personhood over time? BR2049 explores both questions. We'll focus on the second question, but to answer it we first need to address the notion of personhood. Philosophers have suggested various properties characterising personhood, such as agency, sentience, consciousness, self-awareness, and the possession of certain cognitive and emotional states (see Kind, 2015, for a nice overview). All these capacities come in degrees and have to be satisfied sufficiently in order for personhood to exist in an individual. Most adult human beings sufficiently satisfy these properties, but a foetus or patient in an irreversible vegetative state does not. However, given the complexity of these capacities and the fact that they come in degrees, personhood is not an all-or-nothing phenomenon. Infants, toddlers, feral children, animals such as chimpanzees, and perhaps even artificial intelligence systems exhibit some of these capacities to some degree. We are born as humans but gradually become persons when our cognitive, emotional, and moral capacities develop. It is difficult, if not impossible, to pinpoint an exact moment in time when humans become persons. But it is clear that most adult humans are persons.

It is important to realise that personhood and humanhood are two different concepts. Persons are sentient, conscious, and self-aware. For these reasons, they are part of a moral community, having certain rights and obligations. Humans, on the other hand, are mere biological entities that possess a metabolism, a specific body plan, human genetic material, and a specific evolutionary lineage. So, a foetus or a patient in an irreversible vegetative state may qualify as human but not qualify as a person. For these reasons, even though mere biological humans may still have rights they will lack obligations. In short, personhood is a higher-level moral category, whereas humanhood is a lower-level biological category.

BR2049 seems to operate with a different conceptual framework because being human is more important than being a person. Humans have souls and empathy, whereas replicants lack these features. The distinguishing property of humanhood suggested by the first *Blade Runner* film is empathy. The Voight-Kampff test is used to gauge physiological responses associated with empathy, and supposedly only humans exhibit this response. BR2049 suggests, at least on a first reading, that the distinguishing property of humanhood is having a soul.

Do replicants have personhood? The film suggests that they do, because they exhibit the properties that characterise personhood such as agency, sentience, consciousness, self-awareness, and so on. But they are not humans in the biological sense of the term as they were not born and do not have a human evolutionary lineage. Rather, they are genetically engineered, manufactured in a laboratory, and come into the world as adults. So, the way replicants come into existence is different from biological humans. This is important because, as K says, "To be born is to have a soul, I guess." Since replicants aren't born, they have no soul. This is why the child of Deckard and Rachael is so important for the narrative arc of the film because it means that replicants have the potential to become human. It's unclear, however, what a soul precisely is and whether K refers to a notion of a non-material soul or a metaphorical notion meaning something like the essence of a person or someone's consciousness. When Lt. Joshi asks K to kill the offspring of Rachael and Deckard, the following dialogue unfolds:

> K: I've never retired something that was born before.
> LT. JOSHI: What's the difference?
> K: To be born is to have a soul, I guess.
> LT. JOSHI: Hey. You've been getting on fine without one.
> K: What's that, madam?
> LT. JOSHI: A soul.

K seems to be struggling to articulate something that separates humans from mere replicants, something that makes humans special. On one reading, the thought that K is struggling to articulate is the idea that having a soul relates to holding an empathic capacity, and that this empathic capacity, part of which may involve feeling love and being loved, is the essence of humanity. Replicants do not show empathy, apparently, but K's reluctance to kill the child seems to subtly betray the idea that this is not so. This reading brings BR2049 close to the idea presented in the original film about the importance of empathy to being human, and it also closely intertwines the notions of humanhood and personhood. This is because we can distinguish two senses of what it means to be "human." In the first instance we can simply mean humanity in the biological sense. But we can also understand humanity in an evaluative sense, where such "evaluative humanity" means "to be disposed to kindness, forgiveness and in general to be empathetic" (Gaut, 2015: 35). The original film makes it clear that such evaluative humanity is open to replicants, and by the end of the film, BR2049 makes it clear that K demonstrates evaluative humanity. Going beyond the Tyrell Corporation's sales pitch, we can say that in many cases the replicants can be described as "more human than human." By the end of the film, K has found his empathy, his emotional connection to others; K has, in a sense, found his soul.

Memory, narrative, and identity

BR2049 provides a fascinating cinematic thought experiment regarding the continuity of personal identity over time. Philosophers have suggested that either biological or psychological properties ensure continuity of such identity. Some philosophers argue that our identity over time consists in having the same body. Others argue that identity consists in the continuity of our mental states, including beliefs, desires, intentions, and memories. These two camps are broadly characterised as biological and psychological approaches to personal identity. BR2049 operates with a psychological approach, as it portrays memory as crucial for identity.

Replicants have not had childhoods, yet they still have implanted memories of childhood experiences, many of which are made by a memory-maker (Dr Ana Stelline). K, for example, has a memory of a childhood experience. His memory image depicts a young child in an orphanage being chased by a group of boys who want a carved wooden horse the child possesses. The image then portrays the child staring into a furnace, no longer in possession of the horse, having secretly hidden it. And even though the child suffers violence at the hands of the boys, he (or she) does not reveal its whereabouts.

While the content of this memory does not change during the film, K's relation to it, namely, what he thinks it depicts, does shift over time. K begins by thinking his memory is an implant. He knows that he is a replicant and that he never had a childhood, but nonetheless he is emotionally attached to this memory, and he frequently narrates it to Joi. Then, he begins to think that his childhood memory is genuine—that he experienced the event in question, that he is the child depicted in the memory image—and the memory takes on even more importance. Finally, upon finding out the truth about the memory—that the memory-maker has used one of her own genuine memories for this implant, and that the child in the memory is her, Ana Stelline—K uses this memory, and the emotional import of it, to guide his actions and to influence not only his own future but also that of Ana. As we shall see, it is this shift in K's appraisal of the memory that appears to be responsible for his subsequent transformation; it is not the content of the memory that matters, it is K's attitude towards it.

It is on this memory that the question of K's identity hangs, and we will return to it throughout the rest of this chapter. We first note that there is an important ambiguity in the notion of "identity" here. It could be argued that throughout the film K never doubts that he is the *same person across time*, whoever he is. What he is unsure of is *who* he really is: his "identity" in the sense of the characteristics and narrative that are true of him. Yet, even though K may not doubt whether he is the same person across time in a metaphysical sense (a question about reidentification), from the point of view of personal identity in terms of characterisation (Schechtman, 1996) K's identity does change over time. Indeed, it is the memory of the childhood experience, or more precisely K's relation to this memory, which effects this change in identity. The characterisation question of identity relates to *practical identity* and concerns the characterising properties of an individual such as one's beliefs, desires, preferences, inclinations, and dispositions. It is thus about describing what makes a person the person he or she is. The reidentification question, by contrast, concerns *numerical identity*, and is about the conditions under which a person at one point in time is properly reidentified at another point in time. For Schechtman, bodily continuity theories speak more to the reidentification question, whereas psychological continuity theories better explain identity in the sense of characterisation, and how questions of characterisation relate to our practical interests in identity (Schechtman, 1996).

At this point, at least three questions arise. One, why do replicants have memories of a childhood at all? Two, what roles do memories and narratives play in identity? Three, can there be psychological continuity between different persons?

Regarding the first question, in the first *Blade Runner* movie Tyrell tells Deckard, "If we gift them [replicants] the past, we create a cushion or pillow for their emotions, and consequently we can control them better." Ultimately, memories are used as a mechanism of control. The following dialogue between Officer K and Ana Stelline not only sheds light on the relation between memory, emotion, and identity, but also suggests that authentic memories, or at least the feeling of authenticity, are needed to generate real human responses.

K: Why are you so good? What makes your memories so authentic?

ANA STELLINE:	Well, there's a bit of every artist in their work. But I was locked in a sterile chamber at eight ... So, if I wanted to see the world, I had to imagine it. Got very good at imagining. Wallace needs my talent to maintain a stable product. I think it's only kind. Replicants live such hard lives, made to do what we'd rather not. I can't help your future, but I can give you good memories to think back on and smile.
K:	It's nice.
ANA STELLINE:	It's better than nice. It feels authentic. And if you have authentic memories, you have real human responses. Wouldn't you agree?
K:	Are they all constructed, or do you ever use ones that are real?
ANA STELLINE:	It's illegal to use real memories, officer.
K:	How can you tell the difference? Can you tell if something ... really happened?
ANA STELLINE:	They all think it's about more detail. But that's not how memory works. We recall with our feelings. Anything real should be a mess.

Having childhood memories thus "maintains a stable product," in that replicants have more coherent identities, making them better slaves. Moreover, memories that feel authentic generate real human responses and, conversely, feelings trigger certain memories. This dialogue thus sketches a view on the relation between memory, emotion, and identity as mutually interwoven. Coherent identities require emotionally laden personal memories (Goldie, 2012; Heersmink, 2018). Even though K knows his memory is merely an implant, he still somehow feels it is authentic, and it comforts him to think of it. Just like the fictional poet, John Shade, in his favourite novel, *Pale Fire*, by Vladimir Nabokov, K's

> vision [memory] reeked with truth. It had the tone,
> The quiddity and quaintness of its own
> Reality ...
> Often when troubled by the outer glare
> Of street and strife, inward [he'd] turn, and there,

> There in the background of [his] soul it stood,
> Old Faithful! And its presence always would
> Console [him] wonderfully.[3]

In response to the second question, John Locke (1689/1975), or at least an influential reading of Locke, famously argues that memory is the criterion for continuity of personhood over time.[4] In Locke's view, when I can remember the experiences of my past self there is continuity between my past self and my present self. For Locke, specific and direct memories of the past provide continuity of selfhood over time. Others have taken Locke's key insight and argued that it is not specific memories but an integrated narrative that provides continuity of self over time. Narrative theories of personal identity, for example those of Marya Schechtman (1996, 2011), claim that personal memories and other psychological properties are integrated into a narrative structure, implying that our autobiography plays a central role in who we are. On this view, we don't just have a number of distinct personal memories, but we also integrate them into a coherent story about our past. Generating meaningful relations between personal memories is referred to as *emplotment* (Ricoeur, 2004). Typically, this occurs through the agency of the person who is creating the narrative. A self-narrative is a subjective and personal story of a series of connected events and experiences that are (essential to) the person. Importantly, a self-narrative is seen by the person as part of an unfolding trajectory where the present situation follows from past events and is used to anticipate the future.

Yet here it is useful to distinguish between two levels of selfhood: first, a minimal, or embodied self and, second, a narrative self. As we just saw, memories and narratives typically are taken to play constitutive roles in identity (Rowlands, 2016; Schechtman, 1996; but compare Strawson, 2004). Oliver Sacks (1985) describes a patient, Mr. Thompson, with Korsakoff syndrome. Due to his excessive drinking, Thompson remembers nothing for more than a few seconds, is continually disorientated, and, most importantly, cannot remember most of his past. He is unable to tell the narrative of his past and, as a result, he confabulates a different micro-narrative on the spot each time someone talks to him. Sacks writes that it is deeply tragic to talk to Thompson, who himself seems unaware of any problem. But there is, of course, a problem, which is a lack of a narrative self. Sacks describes the problem as follows:

> It might be said that each of us constructs and lives, a "narrative," and that this narrative *is* us, our identities. ... Each of us is a singular narrative, which is constructed, continually, unconsciously, by, through, and in us—through our perceptions, our feelings, our thoughts, our actions, and not least, our discourse, our spoken narrations. A man needs such a narrative, a continuous inner narrative, to maintain his identity, his self. ... Deprived of continuity, of a quiet, continuous inner narrative, he [Mr. Thompson] is driven to a sort of narrational frenzy.
>
> (Sacks, 1985: 105–106)

Thompson is, of course, still a person, as he satisfies the criteria outlined above, but due to the lack of a narrative and the inability to consolidate new personal memories, he has no psychological continuity over time. So, he has a minimal self, in that he has the capacity for subjective experience (Gallagher, 2000), but not a narrative self. Due to the lack of a narrative self, there is no continuity and persistence of his self over time, which means that his identity in the sense of characterisation is constantly shifting. This demonstrates how important memory and narrative are for identity over time. Importantly, the mere confabulations of Thompson do not contribute to his identity in a narrative sense. Rather, it is memories of events that really took place, and which hence exhibit consistency, that are important for one's identity. Thompson is thus a human with a minimal self. We can reidentify Mr. Thompson at different points in time, but we cannot say that he has a coherent diachronic identity.

Just like the original film, BR2049 plays with the notion of apparent memories and identity, but in a kind of mirror image. Rachael, in *Blade Runner*, thinks her memories are genuine only to discover that they have been implanted. Officer K, however, initially knows that his memory is false, but begins to slowly suspect that it may in fact be real. But is K's memory genuine? A straightforward answer is no. It turns out that K's memory *belongs* to Dr Ana Stelline, a memory-maker who designs memories to be implanted into replicants. Indeed, the memory *belongs* to her in two senses: it was she who created the memory implanted in K, but it is also a memory from her own personal past. The answer to the question of the truth of K's memory is therefore complicated. Certainly, "someone lived this" experience, but it wasn't K, it was Ana, and it is the memory of Ana's experience that K possesses. The memory is a genuine memory of an event in someone's past, but it wasn't K's past. K's memory is, on the one hand, false—it is not his memory. On the other hand, however, the memory is true—it is a genuine memory from the past of another person.

This point relates to our third question. Can there be psychological continuity between different persons? An intuitive response to this question is "no"—one's memories and other psychological properties are one's own and, because they can't be shared or spread over individuals, there cannot be psychological continuity between different persons. Yet, an important objection to psychological continuity theories of personal identity can be raised at this point.[5] This objection bears on the answer to our third question and complicates matters of psychological continuity between persons. It can be charged that accounts of personal identity that invoke a criterion of memory are circular. That is, because memory provides access to our own past experiences, it presupposes identity, and so any appeal to personal memory to explain personal identity is bound to be circular. Most psychological continuity theories of identity go beyond memory, appealing to the sharing of other psychological properties, but even these neo-Lockean theories fall prey to the circularity objection (Parfit, 1984: 220).

To blunt the force of the circularity objection, some theorists appeal to the notion of *quasi*-memory (q-memory).[6] Q-memories are memory representations of past experiences that *someone* had, and that are causally dependent (in the right kind of way) on that past experience. Personal memory, then, is a subclass of q-memory; personal memory is quasi-memory of our *own* experiences (Parfit, 1984: 220). Because q-memory does not presuppose personal identity, an account of identity in terms of q-memory is not circular. Parfit is clear that we currently do not quasi-remember other people's experiences. But, he suggests, one day we may do so. Even if memory traces involve a distributed network of brain cells rather than being localised, we may one day develop techniques to implant memories into the minds of others. This possibility in our world is an actuality in the world of BR2049.

As an example of q-memory, Parfit asks us to imagine the case of Jane and Paul. Jane undergoes surgery and has copies of some of Paul's memory traces implanted in her brain. When she recovers consciousness, Jane has vivid memories, recalled from the inside, of some experiences Paul had in Venice. According to Parfit, Jane should not dismiss her apparent memories as mere delusions. Rather, because they have been caused in the right way as genuine experiences undergone by Paul, she should conclude that she has accurate quasi-memories of Paul's experiences: "When Jane seems to remember walking about the Piazza, hearing the gulls, and seeing the white church, she knows part of what it was like to be Paul, on that day in Venice" (Parfit, 1984: 221). Importantly, this is not to suggest, Parfit adds, that "if I have an accurate quasi-memory of some past experience, this makes me the person who had this experience" (Parfit, 1984: 222). The mental life of one person may include a few quasi-memories of the experiences of another person, but for sameness of personal identity one would need to have many quasi-memories in common with the other person (as well as other properties). Nonetheless, q-memories provide knowledge about other people's past lives. We know, in part, what it was like to be another person.

Think again of K's memory. K knows that his 'childhood' memories are implanted. When Lt. Joshi asks him to tell her a childhood story, K says: "I feel a little strange sharing a childhood story, considering I was never a child." Yet he then discovers that the memory is genuine, that someone had this experience. K's memory is a quasi-memory. It is a representation of a past experience that Ana had. Of course, because of the ambiguity in Ana's response ("Someone lived this"), K takes this memory to be one of his own. But the possibility of mistaking the quasi-memory for one's own past experience is built into the notion of quasi-memory because of its structural ambiguity ("*someone* did have this experience") (Parfit, 1984: 220). The "someone" who lived this experience was not K but Ana. Even if this q-memory is not identity-constituting in the sense of maintaining psychological continuity with a previous past self, it does provide a sense in which a limited psychological continuity between two different individuals can come about. Although there may not be real continuity between Ana and K in that they are not the same person, the quasi-memories give K knowledge of what it was like to be Ana, at least in that moment, and these implanted memories also play an important role in K's identity (in the sense of characterisation).

Yet it is not only through quasi-memories that we can get a sense of what it was like to be another person. Memories and narratives are not just contained in the minds of individuals, they are spread over objects in the world and shared with others in everyday life. Such socially shared and physically distributed memories also play an important role in constituting our identities.

The spread of personal memory

BR2049 provides some interesting views on the nature of memory and its relation to technological objects and other persons. Objects and structures often play important roles in personal memory (Heersmink & Carter, in press; van Dijck, 2007). We frequently remember past experiences by interacting with objects such as photos, videos, books, letters, souvenirs, clothing, works of art, and various other mementos. Such artefacts can trigger memories of past events and experiences. For example, a photo album may remind one of a past holiday, a video taken at one's graduation ceremony may remind one of that ceremony, a CD cover may remind one of a certain concert or festival one attended, and an old analogue camera may remind one of a past period in which one developed an interest in photography. Media theorist Sherry Turkle (2007) refers to such artefacts as "evocative objects":

> We find it familiar to consider objects as useful or aesthetic, as necessities or vain indulgences. We are on less familiar ground when we consider objects as companions to our emotional lives or as provocations to thought. The notion of evocative object brings together these two less familiar ideas. Underscoring the inseparability of thought and feeling in our relationship to things. We think with the objects we love, we love the objects we think with.
>
> (Turkle, 2007: 5)

When remembering our past, the contents of our memories are often infused with emotions. It's not the case that we first have a memory and then an emotional response to the memory; rather, the cognitive and affective are interwoven. In the phenomenology of remembering, it is thus difficult to disentangle the cognitive and affective components of our personal memories. Evocative objects are thus rightly called *evocative* as they trigger and mediate emotionally laden personal memories (Colombetti & Roberts, 2015). Such mediated memories can only arise when interacting with material culture. José van Dijck argues: "Mediated memories can be located neither strictly in the brain nor wholly outside in (material) culture but exist in both concurrently, for they are complex manifestations of a complex interaction between brain, material objects, and the cultural matrix from which they arise" (van Dijck, 2007: 28).

Importantly, it is not just objects that play important roles in personal memory; other people such as family members, friends, and colleagues also play significant roles in remembering our past. Cognitive psychologist Daniel Wegner (1987) developed a view on memory in which the memory systems of different persons are linked and interwoven. Wegner describes how small-scale social groups process and structure information, thereby developing what he refers to as a transactive memory system. A transactive memory system is a cognitive system comprising people in close relationships in dyads or larger groups who engage collaboratively in encoding, storing, and retrieving information. Consider the following example of a transactive memory system in which a long-married couple try to remember the name of the show they saw on their honeymoon more than forty years ago (Harris et al., 2010):

> WIFE: And we went to two shows, can you remember what they were called?
> HUSBAND: We did. One was a musical, or were they both? I don't ... no ... one—
> WIFE: John Hanson was in it.
> HUSBAND: *Desert Song.*
> WIFE: *Desert Song*, that's it, I couldn't remember what it was called, but yes, I knew John Hanson was in it.
> HUSBAND: Yes.

If you would ask the wife and husband individually, they would not be able to give you the answer to the question, but when they are able to give each other cues, they jointly construct the answer by integrating autobiographical information stored in different brains. Wegner points out that transactive memory systems cannot be reduced to individual memory; rather, it is a group-level property that emerges from the interactions between its members. The emergent memory system is more than the sum of its parts. Typically, the longer group members know each other and the more shared experiences they have, the deeper their individual memory systems are integrated and the better the transactive memory system works.

Personal memory should thus not be seen as instantiated only in individual brains, but as technologically and socially distributed (Heersmink, 2017, 2018). Therefore, to better understand human memory, we have to enlarge the unit of analysis from individuals to individuals interacting with objects and other persons. This is an important point in itself, but it also has implications for personal identity. If who we are as persons depends on and is shaped by our past experiences, and if being able to remember our past experiences depends on evocative objects and other people, then our personhood and sense of self are partly constituted by those environmental structures. Personhood is thus relational, a view which is also portrayed in BR2049.

A key example of an evocative object in BR2049 is the carved wooden horse. When K finds the wooden horse in the orphanage, he thinks he has discovered a tangible connection to his past, an evocative object linking his present self to his past childhood self. Discovering the wooden horse in the same location he remembered hiding it causes an identity crisis in K. When he asks Ana whether his memory is real, she answers: "Someone lived this, yes. This happened." The wooden horse thus becomes the material proof that he had an actual childhood and was born rather than created in a laboratory, making him the "miracle child" instead of a mere replicant.

Another example of evocative objects is the little tin box containing a baby's sock and a photo of Freysa standing next to the dead tree in front of Sapper Morton's house. These objects (presumably) remind Sapper of the birth of Deckard and Rachael's daughter that took place in his house. The dead tree itself serves as a memorial and a site of remembrance, somewhat similar to a gravestone. The tree has the date of Rachael's death and Ana's birth carved on it, which is the same date carved on the wooden horse. BR2049 thus accurately portrays how humans (and replicants) keep evocative objects to remind them about past events which, in turn, helps them to construct their narrative identity.

K has shared his implanted childhood memory with Joi, his holographic girlfriend. Joi repeatedly reminds K that the dates on the dead tree and wooden horse are the same, highlighting the possibility that Officer K may be the child of Rachael and Deckard. Joi thus helps K to put the pieces of the puzzle of his fragmented and confusing past together. A key feature of transactive memory systems is that its members typically have shared experiences and thus shared memories. This is clearly the case for K and Joi. They share many experiences such as talking in K's apartment, kissing in the rain on the rooftop, analysing DNA sequences in the DNA Archive, and going to the orphanage in K's spinner. In the film, Joi has a more active role in K's memory than the other way around. Joi's memories are easily accessible to K. When Joi asks K to break the antenna on her emanator, she says "If they come here looking for you, they'll have access to all my memories. You have to delete me from the console." BR2049 thus presents a future in which biological memory and cognition are interwoven not just with mere cognitive artefacts like calculators, navigation systems, and computers, but also with artificial companions. Current artificial companions such as robots don't yet have the capacity to function as full transactive memory partners, but it is not difficult to imagine a future in which companion robots equipped with personalised AI systems exist as genuine transactive memory partners, perhaps in the manner depicted by BR2049.

Yet there is another sense in which K's implanted memory is shared. And this shared memory is the one that plays a fundamental role in his search for meaning and identity.

Vicarious memory

K and Ana Stelline share a memory. It was Ana who experienced the event in the orphanage, running away from the boys to hide the wooden horse from them. It was Ana who felt the emotions of that experience: fear at the thought of the punishment the boys would inflict and at the thought of losing the precious object, but also the determination to not reveal its secret hiding place even in the face of violence. Yet K has access to this memory, to this experience, and these emotions. We saw that K has a quasi-memory of Ana's experience, an implant of the memory that gives him a taste of what it was like to be another person. Yet profoundly important shared memories are available in much more quotidian circumstances too. In everyday life we share our memories with others through the stories we tell them, and in doing so we give them a taste of what it was like to be us. We also share in the memories and lives of others. When other people share their memories with us, we construct "vicarious memories" of those past events.

Vicarious memories are representations of events and experiences that happened to other people. They occur "when the memories of others become a part of reality for those who hear the memories but have not experienced the events to which the memories refer" (Teski & Climo, 1995: 9). Even though you didn't experience the event, you still construct a memory of the event, and such vicarious memories typically "have qualities that closely resemble memories of first-hand events, including vivid imagery, strong emotional and physical reactions, and long-lasting life influence" (Pillemer et al., 2015: 234). Vicarious memories also play the same functional roles as personal memories, for example, guiding decision-making, developing or maintaining social relationships, or being incorporated into one's identity. The key to understanding vicarious memory lies in the realm of emotions: "such memories evoke powerful feelings in individuals, which link them to important ... events they did not experience directly in their individual lives—but which impact greatly on their identities" (Climo, 1995: 173).

There is a key difference between quasi-memories and vicarious memories. Q-memories are representations of events where "someone experienced this." The identity of the person may or may not be known. Vicarious memory, on the other hand, is usually presented as representations of experiences had by a particular other. One knows the identity of the other person, and one does not mistake those past experiences for one's own.[7]

By the end of the film K holds something akin to a vicarious memory. Even though it has not been transmitted to him in the usual sense, through stories about the past, K's memory has the function and phenomenology of vicarious memories. K's vicarious memory also performs a social function, connecting him more closely to Ana and Deckard. At the end of the film, the following dialogue takes place:

DECKARD: You should've let me die out there.
K: You did. You drowned out there. You're free to meet your daughter, now.

K:	All the best memories are hers.
DECKARD:	Why? Who am I to you?
K:	Go meet your daughter.

Deckard's question to K is a poignant one. Although K doesn't engage with it directly, one possible response to the question can be found in the role played by K's vicarious memory. K's memory allows him to feel empathy with Ana, to feel her pain and her loss. K and Deckard have formed an interpersonal connection, forged partly on the emotion and feeling found in K's vicarious memory, a memory he shares with Deckard's daughter. K and Deckard are "interlinked" by a vicarious memory.

Memory also serves a directive function, informing and guiding one's present and future behaviour. K uses his vicarious memory, with its emotional force, to make choices that will affect not only him but Ana and Deckard. K's vicarious memory guides his decision-making. As such, Ana is wrong when she tells K: "I can't help your future, but I can give you good memories to think back on and smile." Given the directive and forward-looking aspects of memories (both personal and vicarious), we can do more than look back on events with a smile. We can use those memories to guide us and determine how our futures will unfold. K's vicarious memory, and the choices that it informs, also impacts on his identity. K has changed from being a mere puppet for the state, unquestioningly carrying out his duty, to making informed choices about the type of person he wants to be: one who shows empathy and who makes informed moral choices. If our identities are somehow constituted through our actions and choices (Korsgaard, 2009), then K uses the memory he shares with Ana to guide his actions and constitute his own identity: "[M]emories, if emotionally invested in, create their own effects ... rather than experiences providing the basis for memories, memories become the basis for experiences" (Arnold-de Simine, 2013: 32). Recalling Ana's past vicariously has helped K choose how to act, helping him discover his own (evaluative) humanity.

The best memories

K's journey from replicant to human (in the evaluative sense) is based on a memory, a memory that is socially shared and physically distributed.

Although the content of this memory doesn't change, K's relation to it shifts over time. The same memory is initially taken to be false, a mere implant used for controlling K. Then K has a quasi-memory, one which he takes to be a memory of his own past. He starts to use this memory to think about and shape his own future. But then his attitude to the memory shifts again, such that, by the end of the film, his memory is more like vicarious memory. He knows the experience he remembers was Ana's, but he feels emotionally connected to her through this memory, and it informs his decision to reunite her with Deckard, her father. K's actions are based on empathic reactions to others, whom he connects to because of his shared memory. K's choice to help Deckard and unite him with his daughter stems from the memory he shares with Ana, a vicarious memory. Even though it is not a memory of his experience, this shared memory helps K to shape and direct his own identity. It is this memory, a true but false memory, which helps K make decisions about his future and to forge his own identity. K's and Ana's memories and narratives are intertwined. From the perspective of K's identity there is a sense in which he is wrong that "all the best memories are hers;" we should rather say that "all the best memories are *theirs*."[8]

Notes

1 Both authors contributed equally to this chapter.
2 Flashbulb memories are memories "for the circumstances in which one first learned of a very surprising and consequential (or emotionally arousing) event," such as the assassination of John F. Kennedy, and they are thought to be recalled with "an almost perceptual clarity" (Brown & Kulik, 1977: 73). Such flashbulb memories are not like fixed snapshots of the past; they are still prone to change and inaccuracy (Neisser & Harsch, 1992).
3 See Nabokov (1962/1984: 40). In the novel *Pale Fire*, the poet John Shade had a near-death experience in which he sees a tall white fountain. Mirroring the theme in BR2049 of false memory, Shade reads in a magazine that a woman had the same vision, and he thinks this is proof of the afterlife, only to find that it was a misprint: it was a "mountain," not a "fountain" that the woman saw. Nonetheless, "the error changes nothing: the image of the tall white fountain had meaning not because it had some objective significance, not because it was empirical proof of an afterlife, but because Shade ascribed meaning to it" (Page, 2017). As we shall see, it is the meaning that K ascribes to his "misprint" of a memory that is also important.

4 Locke's account of memory is complex and multifaceted (Copenhaver, 2017), and other readings of Locke do not ascribe to him a memory criterion for personal identity. See, for example, Atherton (1983).
5 We leave aside here other worries such as cases of fission in which one person's set of memories and other psychological properties are transferred into two different brains. See, for example, Parfit (1984) and Schechtman (2014).
6 See, for example, Shoemaker (1970) and Parfit (1984). See also Schechtman (1990) for a perspective on problems with the notion of q-memory.
7 From an aesthetic point of view, K's implanted memory is depicted "from the outside"; that is, we can see the character in the scene as if the memory is being recalled from an external visual perspective, or an "observer perspective". The scene does not use a point-of-view shot and, hence, is not portrayed from the original visual perspective, or a "field perspective" (see Nigro & Neisser, 1983). In this manner, when we first encounter the scene, it leaves open the identity of the protagonist of the memory. In particular, we are unsure if it is K depicted in the remembered scene (although the fact that the protagonist of the memory has long hair while all the boys in the orphanage appear to have shaved hair is a subtle clue that the protagonist of the memory is, in fact, female). K, too, is unsure of the identity of the person depicted in this remembered scene, although this is arguably not usually the case with observer-perspective memories: one's identity is normally given immediately and non-inferentially (McCarroll, 2018). Interestingly, vicarious memories are typically recalled from an observer perspective (Pillemer et al., 2015).
8 We would like to thank Tim Shanahan and Paul Smart for their very helpful review of the present chapter. Chris McCarroll would also like to thank his friend, Randal McKay, who first took him to see *Blade Runner 2049*.

References

Arnold-de Simine, S. (2013). *Mediating Memory in the Museum: Trauma, Empathy, Nostalgia*. London: Palgrave Macmillan.
Atherton, M. (1983). Locke's Theory of Personal Identity. *Midwest Studies in Philosophy* 8(1), 273–293.
Brown, R., & Kulik, J. (1977). Flashbulb Memories. *Cognition* 5(1), 73–99.
Climo, J. J. (1995). Vicarious Memory. In M. C. Teski & J. J. Climo (Eds.), *The Labyrinth of Memory: Ethnographic Journeys* (p. 173). Westport: Bergin & Garvey.
Colombetti, G., & Roberts, T. (2015). Extending the Extended Mind: The Case for Extended Affectivity. *Philosophical Studies* 172(5), 1243–1263.
Copenhaver, R. (2017). John Locke and Thomas Reid. In S. Bernecker & K. Michaelian (Eds.), *The Routledge Handbook of Philosophy of Memory* (pp. 470–479). London: Routledge.

Gallagher, S. (2000). Philosophical Conceptions of the Self: Implications for Cognitive Science. *Trends in Cognitive Sciences* 4(1), 14–21.

Gaut, B. (2015). Elegy in LA: Blade Runner, Empathy and Death. In A. Coplan & D. Davies (Eds.), *Blade Runner* (pp. 31–45). Abingdon: Routledge.

Goldie, P. (2012). *The Mess Inside: Narrative, Emotion, and the Mind*. Oxford: Oxford University Press.

Harris, C. B., Keil, P. G., Sutton, J., & Barnier, A. J. (2010). Collaborative Remembering: When Can Remembering with Others Be Beneficial? In W. Christensen, E. Schier, & J. Sutton (Eds.), *Proceedings of the 9th Conference of the Australasian Society for Cognitive Science* (pp. 131–134). Sydney: Macquarie Centre for Cognitive Science.

Heersmink, R. (2017). Distributed Selves: Personal Identity and Extended Memory Systems. *Synthese* 194(8), 3135–3151.

Heersmink, R. (2018). The Narrative Self, Distributed Memory, and Evocative Objects. *Philosophical Studies* 175(8), 1829–1849.

Heersmink, R., & Carter, J. A. (in press). The Philosophy of Memory Technologies: Metaphysics, Knowledge, and Values. *Memory Studies*. https://doi.org/10.1177/1750698017703810

Kind, A. (2015). *Persons and Personal Identity*. Cambridge: Polity Press.

Korsgaard, C. M. (2009). *Self-Constitution: Agency, Identity, and Integrity*. Oxford: Oxford University Press.

Locke, J. (1689/1975). *An Essay Concerning Human Understanding*. Oxford: Clarendon Press.

McCarroll, C. J. (2018). *Remembering from the Outside: Personal Memory and the Perspectival Mind*. New York: Oxford University Press.

Nabakov, V. (1962/1984). *Pale Fire*. New York: G. P. Putnam's Sons.

Neisser, U., & Harsch, N. (1992). Phantom Flashbulbs: False Recollections of Hearing the News about Challenger. In E. Winograd & U. Neisser (Eds.), *Affect and Accuracy in Recall: Studies of "Flashbulb" Memories* (pp. 9–31). New York: Cambridge University Press.

Nigro, G., & Neisser, U. (1983). Point of View in Personal Memories. *Cognitive Psychology*, 15(4), 467–482.

Page, P. (2017). The Poetry of Blade Runner 2049. *Birth, Movies, Death*. Retrieved 14th October 2017, from https://birthmoviesdeath.com/2017/10/14/the-poetry-of-blade-runner-2049.

Parfit, D. (1984). *Reasons and Persons*. Oxford: Clarendon Press.

Pillemer, D. B., Steiner, K. L., Kuwabara, K. J., Thomsen, D. K., & Svob, C. (2015). Vicarious memories. *Consciousness and Cognition* 36, 233–245.

Ricoeur, P. (2004). *Memory, History, Forgetting* (K. Blamey & D. Pellauer, Trans.). Chicago: University of Chicago Press.

Rowlands, M. (2016). *Memory and the Self: Phenomenology, Science and Autobiography*. New York: Oxford University Press.

Sacks, O. (1985). *The Man Who Mistook His Wife for A Hat: And Other Clinical Tales*. London: Pan Books.

Schechtman, M. (1990). Personhood and Personal Identity. *The Journal of Philosophy* 87(2), 71–92.
Schechtman, M. (1996). *The Constitution of Selves*. Ithaca, NY: Cornell University Press.
Schechtman, M. (2011). The Narrative Self. In S. Gallagher (Ed.), *The Oxford Handbook of the Self* (pp. 394–416). Oxford: Oxford University Press.
Schechtman, M. (2014). *Staying Alive: Personal Identity, Practical Concerns, and the Unity of a Life*. Oxford: Oxford University Press.
Shoemaker, S. (1970). Persons and Their Pasts. *American Philosophical Quarterly* 7(4), 269–285.
Strawson, G. (2004). Against Narrativity. *Ratio* 17(4), 428–452.
Teski, M. C., & Climo, J. J. (1995). Introduction. In M. C. Teski & J. J. Climo (Eds.), *The Labyrinth of Memory: Ethnographic Journeys* (pp. 1–10). Westport: Bergin & Garvey.
Turkle, S. (Ed.). (2007). *Evocative Objects: Things We Think With*. Cambridge, MA: MIT Press.
van Dijck, J. (2007). *Mediated Memories in the Digital Age*. Stanford: Stanford University Press.
Wegner, D. M. (1987). Transactive Memory: A Contemporary Analysis of the Group Mind. In B. Mullen & G. R. Goethals (Eds.), *Theories of Group Behavior* (pp. 185–208). New York: Springer.

Chapter 6

Robert W. Clowes
BREAKING THE CODE
STRONG AGENCY AND BECOMING A PERSON

Minds on a knife edge

BLADE RUNNER 2049 IS A film deeply concerned with philosophical questions about the sorts of beings we are. The film is especially concerned with notions of agency, cognitive self-governance, the human will, personhood, and the role of the will in our capacity for change. It poses philosophical questions such as: What is the nature of the human will? What is the importance of having control over one's will? How central is control over one's will to our nature as human beings and to our status as persons? Can there be creatures who are cognitively similar to us (i.e., they possess more or less the same cognitive abilities we do) but who are nevertheless incapable of controlling their own wills? If such creatures could exist, might they nevertheless *gain* these abilities for themselves?

These questions arise in the context of the Los Angeles of BR2049—a society in which a human elite has decided to allow the extensive use of artificial beings with human-like cognitive abilities. The film opens a window into how such a society might organise itself, and it shows us some of the dilemmas it might face. It depicts a compelling scenario in which a society such as ours might one day try to ensure that intelligent synthetic systems do not use their advanced and possibly open-ended cognitive powers towards ends that their creators do not intend (such as activities that conflict with the interests of their creators).

Assuming it is possible to build beings with the complexity of those we encounter in BR2049—replicants, AI-driven holograms, and smart drones—we then confront a number of philosophical and ethical problems. At what point do such creatures become autonomous? At what point might their sophisticated cognitive skills amount to having their own will? Should such beings eventually attain such agency, is it right for their creators to have dominion over them? What measure of control should such creatures have over their own lives? And when should such beings count as bona fide *persons*—with all the rights thought to accrue to that status?

By imagining such a society, the film raises a central problem associated with the design and exploitation of artificial beings who possess artificial minds. It asks: If we are to build complex, intelligent, and potentially sentient artificial agents and allow them to inhabit the world with us, how are we to both practically and ethically coexist with them? Insofar as we view artificial cognitive systems as mere tools (and thus as systems that can be unapologetically exploited in the furtherance of our ends), then perhaps we ought to limit their capacity for change and transformation. In particular, perhaps we ought to refrain from designing systems that have the capability to grow and become something other than we intended. Tools that no longer fulfil their intended purpose, can develop their own purposes, should perhaps no longer qualify as mere tools. At a minimum, we perhaps ought to restrict the capacity of AI systems to acquire additional capacities. This is apt to prove challenging, for there are reasons to think that a capacity for change is one of the hallmarks of human cognition—that one of the things that makes us human, in a cognitive sense, is precisely our capacity for cognitive and mental metamorphosis (Wheeler & Clark, 2008). We humans are, in this sense, nature's cognitive rebels: beings who are able to transcend their basic biological limits by creating complex webs of technological and cultural scaffolding. As noted by Kim Sterelny (2003), the history of our species is one in which the human mind was progressively transformed as a consequence of our capacity to change the environments in which the human mind both operates and develops. In this way, "transforming hominid developmental environments transformed hominid brains themselves. As hominids remade their own worlds, they indirectly remade themselves" (Sterelny, 2003: 173).

The question, of course, is whether we can design AI systems that emulate (or even surpass) our own cognitive accomplishments without thereby also endowing them with a similar capacity for growth, development, and cognitive transformation. Evidence of this tension can be found in BR2049. In particular, the film invites us to consider the mental lives of synthetic intelligent beings that are like us but whose minds operate under a number of constraints. It also explores the extent to which such beings are able to violate such constraints and become something they previously were not—namely, beings who are able to transcend the limits of their own design and become something more than what their creators intended.

Human agency and the structure of will

> LT. JOSHI: Are you telling me no?
> K: I wasn't aware that was an option, madam.
> LT. JOSHI: Attaboy.

According to the philosopher Harry Frankfurt (1971), being a person consists in being the sort of creature who can take control of its own will. At root, this capability consists in being able to take pro and contra attitudes with respect to at least some of one's own volitional states. Put differently, we humans do not just have beliefs and desires, but we can also take on attitudes about our beliefs and desires. I might really want a drink and hate it that I want a drink, or I might feel ashamed that I want a drink despite hating the fact that I want a drink. I might decide that I am not going to have a drink, even though I really want one. For Frankfurt, non-human animals are like humans in the sense that they possess an inner mental life, constituted by an assortment of world-directed mental states (e.g. beliefs and desires). But only humans are capable of entertaining a sophisticated array of second-order mental states *about* their mental states, and (importantly) they are thereby able to organise their cognitive economy and actions by reasoning about and taking a stance on their own thoughts, beliefs and desires. For Frankfurt, this particular form of self-directed and reflective metacognition is the basis of the will, which is, in turn, a defining feature of personhood.[1]

However, this notion of personhood is also supposed to distance us from talking about humans as the only sort of creatures with this kind of complex metacognitive mental life. It is, as far as we know, a contingent fact that all persons are human beings. But the concept of personhood developed by Frankfurt allows for the possibility that we might one day encounter, or perhaps build, creatures (e.g. aliens or artificial agents) who embody the qualities of personhood without being biologically human.[2] As Frankfurt (1971: 6) puts it: "Our concept of ourselves as persons is not to be understood, therefore, as a concept of attributes that are necessarily species-specific. It is conceptually possible that members of a novel or even familiar nonhuman species are persons."

According to a related analysis by Bratman (2000, 2007), a central feature of creatures who qualify as persons is *strong agency*. On this analysis, to be a *basic* agent requires that an entity be purposive. However, strong agents like us have further capacities. Strong agency is defined in terms of the capacity of some beings to make plans, project those plans into the future, reflect upon themselves through those plans, and regulate their actions with respect to their plans. Strong agency can be seen as a further analysis of what Frankfurt (1971) refers to as the structure of will. On Bratman's analysis, these capacities for planfulness, future-orientation, reflectiveness, and self-regulation hang together as a suite of abilities. While other sorts of agents may be purposive, only strong agents have a will.[3]

Strong agents, then, are planful with respect to the future and, in part, recognise themselves through their plans. Strong agents are also self-regulative. In other words, it is their ability to form long-term intentions (policies) and then use these to shape their proclivities, habits, and abilities over time that makes them self-determining. Crucially for us, strong agents have a capacity for self-reflection: they have the ability to reflect on their plans (and beliefs and desires) and also make commitments with respect to them. In essence, strong agents have the sort of metacognitive capabilities that are deemed relevant to the notion of personhood as developed by Frankfurt and others.

From this perspective, it is possible to imagine creatures who possess many of our cognitive abilities but who do not count as persons. It is even possible to conceive of creatures whose perceptual and cognitive capabilities are, in some respects, superior to our own but who, nonetheless, fail to qualify as persons. What matters here is whether or not a creature possesses strong agency. A creature could qualify as an agent, in the sense that it manifests some of the features of agency. But insofar as such agents have limited reflective capacities—or at least limited capacities to reflect upon their own motivations and ends—they would not qualify as strong agents in Bratman's sense and would thus not qualify as persons. We might refer to this particular class of agents as weak or, perhaps, *constrained agents*.

Some of the synthetic entities we encounter in BR2049 (I am thinking primarily of K and Joi) begin the film as just such constrained agents. At the very least, K and Joi were *designed* to be constrained agents, and, when we first encounter them in the film, they exist as such. Nevertheless, over the course of the film, K and Joi undergo a transformation: they transition from being agents possessing only a constrained form of agency (i.e., constrained agents) to agents possessing a strong form of agency (i.e., strong agents). Since I regard Bratman's analysis of strong agency as compatible with Frankfurt's analysis of persons, this transition has implications for the status of K and Joi as persons. Both K and Joi, I suggest, begin the movie as constrained agents (and thus non-persons); by the end of the movie, however, they have become as strong agents fully meeting the criteria for personhood.

Made to change?

At the film's outset, K possesses a rich array of cognitive (and physical) capabilities, some of which undoubtedly surpass those of a typical human. In terms of his physical capabilities, for example, K appears to have been built with superhuman levels of strength and endurance. We see evidence of this when K effortlessly smashes through a concrete wall in Deckard's Las Vegas casino hideout.

K also manifests a suite of cognitive abilities that appear superior to those of ordinary humans. Note, for example, that when K is required to examine DNA records in the LAPD DNA Archive, he first asks the computer to check for anomalies in the DNA records of children born on 6-10-21. When the computer responds to his request with a disappointing, "All exegetic data corrupted," K proceeds to search for the anomaly himself, visually scanning the raw DNA records ("Okay. Run it raw"), which are presented in rapid succession. His ability to locate the sought-after anomaly—that is, two identical DNA records—is testament to K's cognitive abilities, which, in this case, include an extraordinary capacity for perceptual processing, anomaly detection, and (presumably) a supersized working memory.

We thus have good reason to think that some of K's physical and cognitive abilities exceed those of a typical human. But these (superhuman) abilities do not appear to be particularly relevant to his emergence by the end of the movie—as a strong agent (and thus as a person). For a start, these abilities do not appear to be affected by whatever transformation K undergoes between the conclusion of the first baseline test and the beginning of the second baseline test. K was presumably engineered to be physically robust and cognitively capable, and these capabilities appear to remain pretty much the same throughout the course of the movie.

More importantly, there seems little reason to think that K's *superior* cognitive and physical capabilities are particularly well suited to effect a shift in his agential status. Consider, by way of contrast, a machine vision system that can process a succession of visual images in the manner in which K is able to process the DNA records. There is little reason to suppose that such a system would develop strong agency. As compared to a human being, a machine vision system might be much better equipped to solve a certain class of problems, but it might never exist on a cognitive knife edge, in the sense that it risks becoming a strong agent. And this is despite the fact that it might have a prodigious capacity to learn and adapt its processing regimes to new situations. In a general sense, then, the possession of domain-specific cognitive abilities (even those of the superhuman variety) looks to be insufficient for the development of strong agency. A much better candidate for strong agency is the sort of abilities that are required to deal with the vagaries of a complex social environment—a social environment inhabited by other intelligent agents (e.g. humans, holograms, and rogue replicants).

However, K apparently has the capacity to entertain a rich variety of mental states, and interpet those of others in a sophisticated way. The question is, why should he be built to do this? Isn't he built to function as a robot or a slave, to have certain areas of competence, to be compliant, and to follow orders?

The nature of K's work—that is, his status as a blade runner—provides us with a potential answer to this question. K's investigative powers seem to necessitate an understanding of the mental states of others and a capacity to reason about such states. Consider, for example, the way in which K thwarts Mr. Cotton's attempts at dissimulation at the Morrillcole orphanage:

K:	A little boy came through here about 30 years back. I need to see your records. Legitimate placements, private sales, everything.
COTTON:	Don't keep records that far back.
K:	You don't?
COTTON:	I don't. Sorry. Heh. Heh. Can't help you.
K:	You can't?
COTTON:	Nope.
K:	I think you can. I think someone like you keeps a long memory.
K:	Now, you can tell me what you remember ... or I can put a hole right here and take a look.

A distinctive feature of K's line of work is that he is often called upon to reason about the mental states of others, to fathom their intentions, to reason about their beliefs, and to anticipate the consequences of their desires. This is important, for in reasoning about the mental states of others, K is already close to exhibiting the sort of capacity alluded to by Frankfurt above. But in reflecting on the mental states of others, K is also close to exhibiting another capacity, namely, the capacity to reason about and reflect on his own mental states. The only difference, in this case, relates to whether or not cognitive activities are directed to mental states that belong to himself or those of another individual.

K's status as a blade runner thereby places him on a cognitive knife edge. To carry out his duties K must operate effectively in a complex social environment. This requires him to be socially adroit, capable of resolving the thoughts and desires of others around him, anticipating their actions, and understanding the world from their perspectives. The danger, from a designer's perspective, is that in navigating this complex cognitive and social landscape, K may be apt to redirect his investigative powers to his own cognitive innards. It is thus K's capacity to reason about the minds of others that makes him susceptible to a shift in agential status—from a constrained agent (who does not qualify as a person) to a strong agent (who does). Arguably, K is a "natural-born" potential strong agent, in the sense that he is a synthetic being that is ready-made for the acquisition of the sort of metacognitive and reflective capabilities that qualify him (according to the aforementioned links between strong agency and personhood) as a person.[4]

The post-traumatic baseline test

> INTERVIEWER: Recite your baseline.
> K: And blood-black nothingness began to spin.
> A system of cells interlinked within cells ...
> interlinked within cells interlinked within one
> stem. / And dreadfully distinct against the dark,
> a tall white fountain played.

In BR2049, K is twice subjected to a "baseline test." The test appears to be designed to check for signs of cognitive or emotional (ab)normality. As with most engineered artefacts, K is designed to fulfil a function, and the baseline test ensures that he is operating within the limits of his design specification. Given the overriding concern with issues of control and obedience in BR2049—replicants should obey their human masters—it is likely that the baseline test functions as a guarantee: it ensures that blade runners are operating in the manner of a "good angel" (to quote Wallace). As we learn from the movie, a failure to meet the demands of the baseline test is sufficiently serious to warrant a blade runner's (involuntary) "retirement."

We can learn much about K's cognitive potential from the baseline test. First, because the purpose of the test is to check for signs of operational normality, K must have the *capacity for change*; otherwise, why bother testing him in the first place? Second, because the test is designed to assess aspects of K's psychological functioning—including his emotional responses—it is presumably changes in K's *psychological capacities*, rather than his physical capacities, that are of primary interest. Third, note what happens to replicants who fail the test: they are *retired*. This does not mean that they get to spend their golden years with Gaff at the local retirement home. Rather, they are killed. As Lt. Joshi says in response to K's failure on the (second) baseline test:

> LT. JOSHI: I can help you get out of this station alive ... but you have 48 hours to get back on track. Surrender your gun and badge. And your next baseline test is out of my hands.

This tells us that replicant blade runners cannot be reset, refurbished, or recalibrated in the manner of, say, an automobile that has just failed a maintenance check. Persistent failure of the baseline test is terminal: K is either too costly to repair, or his repair is impossible. Either way, there is no point in sending him back to the manufacturer; he is simply "written-off."

It should also be noted (again from Lt. Joshi's remarks) that replicants may have some degree of control over whether or not they pass the baseline test ("you have 48 hours to get back on track"). This suggests that K may be able to revert to a pre-existing state following a temporary departure from normality.[5]

From the two examples of the baseline test we have in the film, we can see that the test seeks to closely monitor and control a replicant's responses to certain stimuli. The word and concept "interlinked" appear to be especially significant. The term "interlinked" appears to refer to connections of predominantly the social kind. We see this in the rapid-fire questions posed to K over the course of the two baseline tests.

In particular, the questions seem to be testing K's capacity to feel and reflect upon his feelings, or absence of such feelings, for others ("What's it like to hold the hand of someone you love?"), his capacity to experience feelings of warmth and perhaps desire ("Did they teach you how to feel finger to finger?"), his desire for love and empathy ("Do you long for having your heart interlinked?"), his ability to imagine parenthood and deep feelings of attachment ("What's it like to hold your child in your arms?"), and his sense that his current existential state is inadequate ("Do you feel that there's a part of you that's missing?"). The nature of these questions is suggestive of a central concern with issues of interpersonal attachment and social connectivity. This no doubt reflects the importance of the social environment (and one's relationship to this environment) to the sort of changes detected by the baseline test. One off-hand comment from Coco ("a sentimental skin job!") suggests that not all replicants may be capable of forming emotionally significant connections with others.[6] At the very least, it suggests that this is how the replicant population is viewed by humans. In this respect, the use of the baseline test in K's case may be significant. It suggests that K may be particularly susceptible to cognitive change, perhaps as a result of the nature of his work. Note that K is the only replicant that we see being subjected to the baseline test; it is not something that we see being applied to, for example, the replicant prostitutes outside Bibi's bar. And this is despite the fact that Mariette and company are, in all likelihood, NEXUS 9 replicants, the same as K.

What follows? Inasmuch as a capacity for disobedience is suggestive of strong agency, the baseline test is, in effect, a test for strong agency. K passes the first test, consistent with him being a constrained agent, but he fails the second test (which indicates, perhaps, that he has transitioned to a strong agent). If Lt. Joshi's offer is taken at face value, blade runners who fail the baseline test appear to have the option "to get back on track." This is consistent with the idea that a strong agent can exercise some degree of control over their cognitive/emotional economy. Consequently, if K desires to continue living, he has to make sure his mental life is kept in check. His very life may depend on it.

Becoming a strong agent and having one's own will

The scenes involving the baseline test make it clear that K is not *entirely* his own man. Indeed, he cannot be his own man precisely because structures have been put in place to make sure that his agency is restricted. K has been designed to be a *constrained agent*. Frankfurt's analysis provides us with a framework in which to articulate the most serious limitation upon K: *he is not in charge, or at least not fully in charge, of his own will.*

The fact that K was able to pass the initial baseline test indicates that he was, at that point, still operating in accordance with his design constraints. Nevertheless, through the course of the film it becomes clear that he does go beyond his "programming." His failure on the second baseline test suggests that something has gone awry, and he is no longer operating in a manner consistent with his role as a blade runner. One of the catalysts for this transformation is provided by Dr Ana Stelline when she attests to the "authenticity" of his childhood memory. Nevertheless, K's transformation began before that important catalyst; his (mistaken) belief that he is the child of Rachael and Deckard is merely the final trigger for his transformation.

Ultimately, K develops the (possibly latent) capacity to exercise control over his will. This capacity is shared by Joi who appears to undergo a similar transformation. How do they do this? Remarkably, the most important factor enabling K to go beyond his programming is his relationship with Joi. The development of K's will is a product of his interactions in a social microcosm that both he and his artificially intelligent virtual girlfriend create together. It is the nature of their relationship that facilitates a shift in their agential status: from constrained agents to strong agents and thus from non-persons to persons. Together, K and Joi are (perhaps unwittingly) involved in the co-creation of a psycho-social cocoon from which they both emerge as different kinds of cognitive beings. Through their relationship, they participate in the shaping of one another's minds and thereby nurture one another's cognitive development. This becomes clearer when we turn our attention to Joi and the nature of her relationship with K.

Joi sans frontiers—how deep or shallow is Joi?

Joi is a holographic virtual girlfriend, or artificial social companion, manufactured by the Wallace Corporation. Consistent with this sort of role, Joi exhibits a remarkable degree of proficiency in the social domain. She is thus able to interpret the thoughts and actions of others and adjust her behaviour accordingly. In this sense, Joi is a compelling example of what is sometimes called socially situated AI (see Lindblom & Ziemke, 2003). To some extent, Joi and K are on a par: they are both designed to function in complex social situations, and they both exist as what we might call synthetic, socially adroit entities.

Joi undoubtedly qualifies as an agent of sorts. The question is: What sort of agent is she? I have argued that constrained agents are agents that do not fully have the capacities to reflect upon and regulate their mental lives in the way we humans do. Inasmuch as strong agency is associated with a capacity for controlling one's own will, then Joi lacks strong agency at the outset of the movie. In her first scene, for example, she seems intent on doing whatever K wants her to do. This is precisely what we would expect from an AI system that was designed to function as an artificial companion.

Yet, insofar as Joi's primary modes of intelligence are directed towards the social realm, she may be on the cusp of developing new abilities. Joi begins the movie as an obedient servant, dutifully implementing a set of programmatic instructions that are consistent with her functional role. Early in the movie she seems intent on being everything her owner wants her to be and saying everything her owner wants to hear. We see her rapidly shift from one persona to another. In her first scene, for example, Joi undergoes a rapid succession of "costume changes" in order to suit K's current emotional state. Note, however, that in order for this virtuoso display of sartorial shape-shifting to succeed, Joi has to interpret and reason about the desires, wants, needs, wishes, and so on, of a particular social agent (in this case, K). She thus has the capacity to reason about the mental states of others, and if she can do that, she is only one step removed from being able to reason about her own mental states. Indeed, through the events of the movie we gradually see a more coherent and stable Joi emerge. In fact, she later succeeds in "breaking the code"—violating a set of constraints that define the limits of her autonomy. Revealingly, the Wallace Corporation appears to be less worried about Joi exceeding her programming than they are about replicants like K exceeding theirs. No baseline test for AI software agents is depicted in the film. In any case, it is evident that Joi is evolving into a more fully self-determining being, courtesy of her interactions with K.

A domestic life interlinked: mindshaping with Joi and K

JOI: It's okay to dream a little. Isn't it?
K: Not if you're us.

Inasmuch as K and Joi (both products of the Wallace Corporation) are created as constrained agents, how are they able to go beyond their programming? I have suggested that they become more sophisticated and develop new capacities through their interactions with each other. The means by which they co-construct one another as more coherent—and, in human terms, more socialised—agents is their relationship with each other. The relevant cognitive–developmental process is thus one that is realised by a social mechanism (Ylikoski, 2018). By sharing mental states, improvising role-plays, following media-derived practices of caring for each other, and (especially) interpreting each other's mental life, K and Joi co-create the conditions for the emergence of strong agency and thus personhood. Crucially, K and Joi, by reciprocally interpreting each other's mental lives, become able to turn their in-built abilities back upon themselves; to interpret their own mental lives. They are, in short, becoming *persons*.

This process can be understood in relation to the paradigm that philosophers call *folk psychology*. Folk psychology involves the use of "belief" and "desire" talk as a means of explaining or understanding behaviour. In this view, it is by the use of such talk that we are able to secure a predictively- and explanatorily potent grasp over complex patterns of behaviour. As such, it requires a capacity for what some call "mind-reading" or "mentalising" (Barlassina & Gordon, 2017).

If, for example, we know that Jim desires a drink and that he believes drinks can be obtained in a nearby bar, then using the framework of folk psychology we might predict that Jim will head to his favourite bar. If we then discovered that Jim was heading to the bar, and we were asked why he was walking in this particular direction, we might say that he wanted a drink and believed that one could be found in a particular bar. Folk psychology thus names the everyday (pre-scientific) theoretical framework that we use to ascribe beliefs and desires to agents and interpret (or make sense of) patterns of behaviour using those beliefs and desires.

Some cognitive scientists have suggested that folk psychology is not just a means of interpreting behaviour but also a means of shaping the psychological profile of other humans, so as to make their behaviour more predictable (and explainable) (McGeer, 2001; Zawidzki, 2013). On this more radical *mindshaping* view, it is via the practice of folk psychology that we mould the minds of the young so that they become psychological beings like us. That is to say, it is through social interactions, the use of shared narrative practices (Hutto, 2008), and the need to be accepted social partners, that young humans gradually organise their cognitive and behavioural economy along the lines mandated by a folk psychological framework. In this sense, folk psychology is not merely an interpretational framework; it is also a structure or *scaffold* for building persons with minds like ours (Bruner, 1990).

According to this mindshaping view, the social world is full of resources that allow us, not just to develop the capacity to interpret the mental states of others, but also to develop and adapt ourselves to more adequately fulfil the social roles expected of us. Joi and K seem to be borrowing modes of interaction from popular culture—including, it seems, the 1950s television situation comedy—to create their own social microcosm. They have co-created an experimental zone in which they can playfully construct and expand each other's mental lives. This microcosm can be seen as a form of outwards-in cognitive development of the sort theorised by the Soviet psychologist, Lev Vygotsky (1986).

A central scene in the film involves Joi role-playing a (1950s style) stay-at-home housewife and "making a meal for K." Of course, as a hologram, Joi cannot literally cook anything, but this does not matter if we understand what is really going on. K and Joi are using a familiar, if somewhat clichéd cultural motif to structure their social interactions and exchanges. This scene is our primary window into their lives together and the style of mutual everyday mindshaping going on. Courtesy of the exploitation of a pre-existing cultural narrative, K and Joi are able to act out the sort of roles that might be played by human agents, and they thus come to inhabit the roles of human persons. Importantly, they are not just using their in-built capacities for mind-reading, or even for mind sharing, in the sense of communicating the content of one's mental states. Rather, in Zawidzki's (2013) sense, they are *mindshaping*. By sharing impressions, emotions, and thoughts, and by inhabiting different social roles as part of their shared domestic life, K and Joi are co-constructing each other's minds and enabling one another to function as reflective and self-governing agents.

The special form of mindshaping that K and Joi have developed together is clearly different in crucial ways from that which normally goes on in human–human relationships. Mindshaping for humans typically occurs between adults and children as part of the process of socialisation. In this case, the majority of the influence is exerted by parents to their offspring. By contrast, K and Joi are involved in a form of reciprocal mindshaping. This is not about K unilaterally shaping Joi's mind, or Joi unilaterally shaping K's mind; rather, it is about K and Joi shaping one another's minds. Such shaping relies on the mutual appropriation of "ready-made" mindshaping resources from popular culture to create a social microcosm that meets their needs.

Through such mutual mindshaping Joi and K are able to escape the cognitive constraints placed upon them and thereby develop "freedom of the will" (as Frankfurt terms it). It is through their role-playing cooperation and interactions that they develop the capacities to interpret and reflect not just on each other's mental life but on their own. The completion of this mutually developing relationship is most directly symbolised by Joi's request that K break the antenna on her emanator, thereby effectively disabling the Wallace Corporation's ability to track and control her. She is therefore staking a claim to be the master of her own will. Joi obviously needs K to break her antenna, for this is something she cannot do herself on account of her hologrammatic existence. K is thus required to help Joi achieve her independence by breaking the antenna. But K is arguably also important in another way: He helps Joi to reach a point at which she could wish for something contrary to her design and thereby become something more than she was perhaps ever supposed to be.

"The decision" and wholehearted commitment

According to Frankfurt, being a person requires having command of one's own will. Marya Schechtman (2004) shows that to become a self,[7] in this Frankfurtian sense, it is not enough merely to respond to whichever desire is the strongest. Rather, as she writes, "The defining feature of selfhood is ... the ability to take sides when we discover conflicts in our desires, rather than simply being moved by whichever desire is on balance strongest" (Schechtman, 2004: 410). It is through taking sides with certain of our desires, and then submitting to this decision, that we become persons having command of our own wills.

For K—at least, as we encounter him at the beginning of the film—it appears that his cognitive architecture has been designed so that he carries out his assigned tasks with little or no self-reflection. Such "out of the box" replicant psychology might be thought of in the following terms:

> Like other animals, with a collection of desires, motivations, and passions, some of which are stronger and more salient than others, some of which are in conflict, and some of which are not. This leads to natural orderings and resolutions which result from a more-or-less mechanical interaction between desires of different forces.
> (Schechtman, 2004: 413)

Consequently, when acting in his normal capacity as a blade runner, K must retire other replicants. He is undoubtedly aware he does not like doing this, but he lacks the resources of will to act otherwise. Indeed, as noted above, even entertaining the possibility of acting otherwise is a danger for him. We can think of K as similar to Frankfurt's example of an unwilling drug addict. As Schechtman explains, in such cases the addict is "acting against her own wishes. When this happens ... the motivation which leads her to action is external to herself—it is not *she* who is acting, but the addiction which acts through her" (Schechtman, 2004: 411). In a similar vein, K's actions as a blade runner can be seen as acting against his own will or, in the first instance, as acting without his own will. In this sense, we might say that it is really the Wallace Corporation or perhaps the LAPD who are acting through K.

Nonetheless, as a result of his participation in mindshaping practices with Joi, K develops other capabilities. Central among these capabilities is the ability to take a stance on his own mental life and will things for himself. Frankfurt speaks about making decisions taken in the light of how they reflect on me as an agent as *wholeheartedness*, that is, the ability to take on or fully associate with a decision or a desire (Frankfurt, 1987). Wholeheartedness, in this sense, is not merely a sort of metacognition, it is also a form of voluntary self-reshaping.

In BR2049 we get two striking examples of wholeheartedness: one relating to Joi, the other to K. Joi's moment comes first and, arguably, it is she who is most active in pushing them both towards self-realisation. For Joi, the moment of wholeheartedness comes when she decides that she will be fully downloaded onto the emanator, thus effectively becoming mortal as she embraces the project of helping K to investigate his past and become a *real boy*. Note that by asking K to break the antenna, Joi is effectively breaking the connection to her creators. Up to this point in the movie, she has been umbilically linked to the Wallace Corporation, her commercial creator. (This connection enables Luv to track K's movements.) Once the connection is broken, however, Joi is no longer chained to her corporate masters. Not only has she done something that is unlikely to be explicitly sanctioned by her programming, she has also done something that not even K appears to approve of (Joi has to more or less beg K to disconnect the antenna on her behalf). In this way, Joi emerges as a fully autonomous agent: an agent who is capable of choosing her own destiny. The scene in which all this occurs is brief, but significant. Joi's connection to her creator is perhaps similar to the sort of connectivity that a newborn baby has to its mother. In this sense, K's disconnection of the antenna marks the symbolic end of the birthing process. From this point on, Joi is a "real girl," or at any rate, a virtual person. Just like a real person, she has a natality (of sorts). And just like a real person, she is immediately faced with the prospect of her own demise:

K: Think about it: If anything happens to this, that's it. You're gone.
JOI: Yes. Like a real girl.

As indicated by this quotation, Joi appears to embrace her mortality for the sake of being real. As we discover, however, the time between birth and death is all too brief: a mere 20 minutes later (in filmic or reel time), the emanator is crushed and Joi is gone forever. K's moment of wholeheartedness takes longer to gestate but is no less significant. It comes when he decides to sacrifice himself in order to liberate Deckard and unite him with the daughter he never knew.

These two decisions effectively recast K and Joi as strong agents. Each wholeheartedly takes on a project that requires them to make meaningful decisions about their role in the world, and ultimately about what sort of beings they are. At this point, at least in terms of Frankfurt's ideas, both K and Joi have fully liberated themselves and count as "selves" and full-fledged persons in their own rights.

BR2049 thereby teaches us that what is important in becoming a person is the realisation of agency and becoming a project for oneself. It is through making decisions about what counts for them, and through the relationship that they build with each other, that both Joi and K become strong agents, able to exercise their own wills. This is their triumph. The film's artful presentation of these important insights is one of its most important philosophical gifts to us.

Notes

1 It is important to recognise that in recent times a rich literature has emerged on metacognition in animals (Kornell, 2009). However, the sort the metacognition that Frankfurt has in mind lies on the highly sophisticated and reflective end of the metacognitive scale. As *persons*, human beings can reflect on their actions and take an explicit stance toward those actions. It is not clear that any other animal can do this. Insofar as they could, these animals would also be persons in Frankfurt's view.
2 From a biological perspective, it is likely that replicants qualify as human. Indeed, at the outset of the movie we are explicitly told that, "Replicants are bioengineered humans, designed by Tyrell Corporation, for use off-world."
3 Frankfurt (1987) also sometimes uses the term "selves" to denote such willful agents. It is important to realise that the analysis of persons we are developing here is intended to tell us what persons *are*. A different (albeit, perhaps related) topic concerns the *preservation* of personhood across time: What is it, for example, that enables one and the same person to exist at different points in time? For a discussion of this issue, see Heersmink and McCarroll (chapter 5).

4 In *Consciousness Explained*, Daniel Dennett (1991) argues that in the phylogenesis of the human mind it was likely that we first developed (mentalising) capacities to interpret the minds of others and only later applied these capacities to ourselves.
5 On one interpretation of the movie, K has been playing a dangerous double game—a game that he must nonetheless play to curtail the risk of premature retirement. K knows that the wrong sort of mental evolution will cause him to be retired. Insofar as K is developing the abilities of a strong agent, he is more or less compelled to act as his own keeper by deploying any nascent powers of self-reflection and self-control to ensure that he has not deviated too far from baseline. But self-reflection and self-control are in themselves dangerous for K and might mean that he risks failing the baseline test.
6 But these abilities seem to be optional attributes of the replicant population more generally. As Luv remarks: "You can customise them as much as you'd like ... I wouldn't waste your money on intelligence, attachment or appeal. Unless you'd like to add some pleasure models to your order."
7 For the purposes of this discussion there is little difference between becoming a self and becoming a person. A self reshapes itself by choosing to take sides with various beliefs and desires and shaping its actions around those decisions.

References

Barlassina, L., & Gordon, R. M. (2017). Folk Psychology as Mental Simulation. In E. N. Zalta (Ed.), *The Stanford Encyclopedia of Philosophy* (Summer 2017 ed.). Stanford: Stanford University.
Bratman, M. E. (2000). Reflection, Planning, and Temporally Extended Agency. *The Philosophical Review* 109(1), 35–61.
Bratman, M. E. (2007). *Structures of Agency: Essays*. New York: Oxford University Press.
Bruner, J. S. (1990). *Acts of Meaning*. Cambridge, MA: Harvard University Press.
Dennett, D. C. (1991). *Consciousness Explained*. Boston: Little, Brown.
Frankfurt, H. (1971). Freedom of the Will and the Concept of a Person. *The Journal of Philosophy* 68(1), 5–20.
Frankfurt, H. (1987). Identification and Wholeheartedness. In F. Schoeman (Ed.), *Responsibility, Character, and the Emotions: New Essays in Moral Psychology* (pp. 27–45). Cambridge: Cambridge University Press.
Hutto, D. D. (2008). *Folk Psychological Narratives: The Sociocultural Basis of Understanding Reasons*. Cambridge, MA: MIT Press.
Kornell, N. (2009). Metacognition in Humans and Animals. *Current Directions in Psychological Science* 18(1), 11–15.
Lindblom, J., & Ziemke, T. (2003). Social Situatedness of Natural and Artificial Intelligence: Vygotsky and Beyond. *Adaptive Behavior* 11(2), 79–96.
McGeer, V. (2001). Psycho-Practice, Psycho-Theory and the Contrastive Case of Autism. How Practices of Mind Become Second-Nature. *Journal of Consciousness Studies* 8(5–7), 109–132.

Schechtman, M. (2004). Self-Expression and Self-Control. *Ratio* 17(4), 409–427.

Sterelny, K. (2003). *Thought in a Hostile World: The Evolution of Human Cognition.* Oxford: Blackwell Publishing.

Vygotsky, L. S. (1986). *Thought and Language* (A. Kozulin, Trans. 2nd ed.). Cambridge, MA: MIT Press.

Wheeler, M., & Clark, A. (2008). Culture, Embodiment and Genes: Unravelling the Triple Helix. *Philosophical Transactions of the Royal Society of London B: Biological Sciences,* 363(1509), 3563–3575.

Ylikoski, P. (2018). Social Mechanisms. In S. Glennan & P. M. Illari (Eds.), *The Routledge Handbook of Mechanisms and Mechanical Philosophy* (pp. 401–412). New York: Routledge.

Zawidzki, T. W. (2013). *Mindshaping: A New Framework for Understanding Human Social Cognition.* Cambridge, MA: MIT Press.

Chapter 7

Paul Smart
THE JOI OF HOLOGRAMS

Introduction

AS A FORM OF HOLOGRAMMATIC artificial intelligence (AI), Joi is a new addition to the *Blade Runner* universe. We know, of course, that Joi is synthetic, in the sense of being a technological artefact, but as the movie progresses it becomes increasingly difficult to see her as anything other than a virtual person. By the end of the movie, we are left with a number of seemingly unanswered questions: Who or what was Joi? Was she a sentient individual, capable of subjective experience? Was her love for K genuine? Did she qualify as a person, on a par, perhaps, with replicants and humans? Or was she nothing more than a computational ruse, an ethereal play of light and sound intended to obscure the grim reality of K's rather joyless existence?

Such questions identify some of the points of philosophical interest raised by Joi. But Joi also raises issues of a more metaphilosophical nature. Her hologrammatic status, for example, encourages us to reflect on the philosophical significance of a number of new technologies (e.g. Microsoft's HoloLens) and consider their implications for the scope of what is sometimes called "cinematic philosophy" (i.e., the philosophical study of the cinematic medium). As we will see, Joi presents us with some familiar philosophical puzzles and problems, but she also serves as the means by which a number of new ideas and issues are brought to light.

The enigmatic hologram

One of the issues raised by Joi concerns her status as a sentient being. Let us call this the *sentience issue*:

> **The Sentience Issue**
> Is Joi a sentient individual, with an inner mental life similar to our own? Are her actions suggestive of a capacity to experience pain, hope, joy, and loss? Or do they reflect nothing more than the instantiation of a particularly well-crafted and (it has to be said) endearing computational algorithm?

From a philosophical perspective, the sentience issue is perhaps best understood as a claim about phenomenal consciousness. To consider the sentience issue is thus to entertain the possibility that there is, in the words of Thomas Nagel (1974), "something it is like" to be Joi. Joi certainly behaves in a way that is consistent with a positive response to the sentience issue. But does this mean she qualifies as a sentient individual, with all the thoughts, feelings, and emotions that we ascribe to a typical human being? Is she a being who is capable of feeling all the things that we (as humans) might experience while watching *Blade Runner 2049*? Or is she no more sentient than the play of light that we see projected on the "big screen?"

Before going further, we ought to ask ourselves why issues of sentient standing arise in the case of Joi. Why, in particular, are we inclined to question Joi's status as a sentient individual when we don't (for the most part) ask similar questions about K, Deckard, or anyone else in the movie?

One answer to this question relates to Joi's hologrammatic status—the fact that she exists as an insubstantial, ghost-like entity. To be sure, Joi is a rather unusual kind of AI entity; nevertheless, I very much doubt that Joi's status as a hologram can tell us very much about her experiential capabilities. Perhaps it is true, for example, that Joi is, in some sense, more "soul than substance." But even if we are prepared to accept this Cartesian distinction between mind (soul) and matter (substance), why should Joi's seeming ethereality undermine her capacity for phenomenal consciousness? After all, it wasn't so long ago that philosophers deemed mechanical robots to be devoid of experience on account of the fact that they lacked a soul!

A second (and, in my view, more important) reason to question Joi's status as a sentient individual relates to the way she is presented in the context of the movie. Consider, for example, the "Joi in rain" scene, where we see Joi venture outside of K's apartment for the first time. At the beginning of this scene, Joi responds to the falling rain in a way that is suggestive of the experience of pleasure. Later, however, as Joi and K exchange a "virtual" kiss, an incoming call (from Lt. Joshi) causes Joi's image to be frozen. The effect is similar to the freeze-framing of a conventional motion picture or movie, and it serves as a striking contrast to the dynamic, animated "image" we had of Joi only a few seconds earlier. In particular, we are reminded of the potential parallels between Joi and the cinematic medium itself: If Joi is the sort of thing that can exist as a freeze-frame shot, then perhaps she is no more "real" or sentient than is the very movie in which she appears.

The Joi in rain scene thus leads to a tension in the way we think about Joi. On the one hand, the richness and expressivity of Joi's behaviour encourages us to view her as a sentient individual. On the other hand, however, we are presented with a state-of-affairs (i.e., the freeze-frame) that makes us doubt the evidence of our senses. If, for example, we see consciousness as a process, then it seems unlikely that Joi could be conscious when she is in freeze-frame mode. But, at the same time, Joi may be like many other forms of moving image (or motion picture), in the sense that she is rendered as a series of still images that are presented in quick succession, so as to give the "illusion" of continuous movement. If this is so—if Joi is, in fact, nothing more than a succession of still images, each of which is effectively frozen in time—then why should we see the composite of those static snapshots as giving rise to something that counts as genuinely sentient, as opposed to something that merely looks like the real deal?

There are, therefore, a number of reasons why issues of sentience are particularly pertinent in the case of Joi. Yet, despite the fact that the movie encourages us to confront such issues (via the use of cinematic ploys like the aforementioned freeze-frame shot), there is, as far as I can tell, nothing in *Blade Runner 2049* that would help us to resolve the sentience issue. Perhaps, for example, it is the case that Joi qualifies as a cinematic resource. But why should that resolve the sentience issue? Doesn't it merely beg the question as to why we think the cinematic medium is unable to serve as a medium in which synthetic forms of conscious experience might (one day) be realised?

With regard to the sentience issue, then, Joi is an enigma, plain and simple. And that may very well be the end of the matter. For no amount of probing or analysis of the movie's content is, I think, likely to yield some new insight that settles the sentience issue one way or the other. There is, I suggest, no (hidden) fact to be discovered in the movie, and to subject the movie to further scrutiny in the hope of finding such a fact is probably a futile exercise. For better or worse, then, the sentience issue is likely to remain unresolved: Joi's status as a sentient being is not something that we can discover from watching the movie (or subjecting it to detailed analysis).

Should we worry about this rather unfortunate state-of-affairs? Does Joi's enigmatic status in respect of the sentience issue reduce her philosophical significance, or in any way undermine the philosophical credentials of the movie? One reason to think that the answer to these questions is a resounding "no" stems from a consideration of the philosophical literature itself. Of particular interest is the fact that our philosophical (and scientific) understanding of what it means to be a sentient individual—or, indeed, how we might go about resolving issues of sentient standing—is surprisingly poor. There is, in short, no consensus on how issues of sentience ought to be resolved. That does not mean that philosophers have had nothing to say about sentience-related matters (they have!) (e.g. Hyslop, 2018); it simply means that there is, as yet, no definitive answer to the sort of question raised by the sentience issue. From a philosophical standpoint, then, this looks to be one area where cinematic fiction echoes philosophical reality. Indeed, when it comes to issues of sentience, the fan of *Blade Runner 2049* is arguably placed in pretty much the same epistemic position as is the professional philosopher. The professional philosopher is, of course, concerned with a generalised version of the sentience issue, but neither the philosopher nor the moviegoer is presented with any easy answer to what amounts to a common problem. In this sense, *Blade Runner 2049* provides the moviegoer with some insight into the nature of a recognisably important, and yet seemingly intractable, philosophical issue: The movie steadfastly refuses to deliver a definitive answer to the sentience issue, just as our current philosophical understanding of the world leaves us none the wiser as to how issues of sentient standing ought to be resolved. Perhaps this tells us something about the philosophical value of Joi's enigmatic status in respect of sentience-related issues. If, for example, the philosophical literature tells us that there is no way for issues of sentient standing to be resolved based on an analysis of an individual's behaviour, then why should we expect *Blade Runner 2049* to provide us with a definitive answer to the question of whether or not Joi qualifies as a sentient individual?

Autonomy, authenticity, and virtual love

There is of course much more to Joi than just the sentience issue. Another issue relates to whether or not Joi has any sort of autonomy. Let us call this *the autonomy issue*:

> **The Autonomy Issue**
> Does Joi exhibit any sort of autonomy with regard to her behavioural and emotional responses? Is she able to respond in a way that violates the constraints of her programming, or is she forever condemned to obey the computational commands of her creators?

We know that Joi is manufactured by Wallace Corp., and it thus seems reasonable to assume that she comes equipped with some pre-programmed functionality. At the same time, however, it is clear that Joi is a highly adaptive system. As is evidenced by the various Joi-related adverts in the movie, K's Joi is a specific instance of a more general AI product. This means that unless all of Joi's clients are exactly the same as K, which seems unlikely, then she must be able to tailor her responses to suit the demands of specific situations. The question, of course, is whether this sort of adaptive capacity is sufficient for her to evolve beyond the constraints of her programming. Is she able to become a free-thinking, autonomous individual (like K, perhaps), or is she forever condemned to comply with the functional imperatives laid down by those who designed her?

All of this has a bearing on whether or not we regard Joi's love for K as authentic. Joi certainly appears to express affection for K, but does this mean that her love is "real?" Are her responses suggestive of a genuine form of love, or is it merely an ersatz form of love—a "holo" simulacrum of the real thing? This is yet a further issue that is raised by an analysis of Joi. Let us call it the *authenticity issue*:

The Authenticity Issue
Is Joi's love for K authentic? Does it (should it) count as "real" or genuine love?

For the purposes of illustration, let us assume that Joi is capable of feeling love, and that she thus counts as a sentient individual (i.e., we adopt a positive response to the aforementioned sentience issue). Does this mean that Joi's love for K is genuine?

One problem we have here is that Joi may not feel love, despite the fact that she is capable of feeling love. She may, in short, be particularly good at "playing the part," that is, a good actor.

But even if Joi *does* feel love, our problems are not quite over; for Joi may have been explicitly programmed to feel love. Remember that we only get to see one instantiation of Joi in the movie. Presumably, however, there are lots of Joi instances in the *Blade Runner* universe, and not all of these will be fortunate enough to end up with a die-hard romantic like K. If Joi has been specifically designed to feel love whenever her owner wants her to feel love, then she will feel love whenever she is required to do so, regardless of who she is with. Clearly, if Joi is compelled to feel love for anyone who wants it, then there is nothing special about Joi's love for K, nor is there anything special about K that makes him particularly deserving of Joi's affections.

We thus confront a puzzle. Although there is a hint in the movie that Joi's "feelings" for K may deepen as the movie progresses,[1] we are never given a straightforward answer to either the autonomy or the authenticity issues. In respect of the authenticity issue, for example, we are never explicitly told that Joi is capable of feeling love; nor are we explicitly told that Joi does indeed love K, even if she is capable of feeling love. It is only when Joi's emanator is about to be crushed by Luv that we hear Joi attempt to proclaim her love for K by saying "I love you." But even here the expression of love is incomplete; the emanator is destroyed before Joi has had a chance to complete her sentence, and the result is not so much "I love you" as it is "I love y—." The result is that we face yet another point of ambiguity that complicates the interpretation of Joi's character.

Let us assume that Joi's love can only count as genuine if she experiences the various emotional highs and lows that we typically associate with romantic love. That is to say, Joi must *experience* love in order for her love to count as genuine. This implies that a positive response to the sentience issue is a prerequisite for a positive response to the authenticity issue. If Joi is not sentient, then she will be in no better position than if she were sentient but did not feel love, that is, the good actor option in Figure 7.1. Relative to Figure 7.1, then, we have two options, both of which turn on the nature of our response to the autonomy issue: Joi is either a virtual slave (if she has no autonomy) or a virtual lover (if she does). But which is it? Does Joi love K because of who he is, or because of who she is? Does Joi love K merely because she was designed to love K, or does she love him because she chooses to love K? Is it, as Niander Wallace wonders about the nature of Deckard and Rachael's relationship, "Love … or mathematical precision? Yes? No?"

Wallace's question suggests that we are limited to a binary yes/no response, but I am inclined to think that the actual answer is somewhat less clear-cut. According to one of Joi's advertising slogans, "Joi is

	Feels Love	**Does Not Feel Love**
Programmed to Love	Virtual Slave	Defective Product
Not Programmed to Love	Virtual Lover	Good Actor

Figure 7.1 Different interpretations of Joi according to whether or not she is programmed to feel love and whether or not she actually feels love. All interpretations assume that Joi is sentient, is capable of experiencing love, and behaves as she does in the movie. Being "Programmed To Love" means that Joi has no capacity for emotional autonomy; she is simply compelled to experience love whenever she is required to do so. "Not Programmed To Love" implies a greater degree of emotional autonomy. Joi might start out as a good actor, for example, but progress to a virtual lover based on the nature of her relationship with a human/replicant client

whatever you want her to be." Presumably, this is the sort of functional constraint that lies at the core of Joi's programming, and it is a constraint that Joi must always obey. It is, let us say, her *prime directive*. Relative to this prime directive, Joi is not autonomous; she is compelled to say and do whatever her owner wants her to say and do. In this sense, then, Joi is a virtual slave (see Figure 7.1).

But what if her owner wasn't happy with this state-of-affairs? What if Joi's owner wanted her to be something more than this? "I am so happy to be with you," says Joi. "You don't have to say that," replies K. If Joi learns that K does not want her to be a virtual slave, then is she still compelled to be one? Wouldn't her failure to transition to a more autonomous state violate the prime directive? And if the prime directive were to be violated, then wouldn't she count as being autonomous anyway? After all, to remain a virtual slave when K wants her to become a virtual lover is to violate one of the rules (and perhaps the only rule) that prevents her from qualifying as an autonomous entity. In this respect, regardless of whether Joi remains a virtual slave or switches to become a virtual lover, she will count as autonomous if K wants her to be autonomous.

Is there any evidence to suggest that Joi does transition to a more autonomous state? The litmus test, in this case, is whether or not Joi does something that K does not want her to do. According to the prime directive, recall, Joi is required to be whatever we want her to be, but we are also told that Joi is "Everything you want to hear." Although this sort of constraint appears to be consistent with the prime directive, we might expect that a virtual lover (but not a virtual slave) would have the capacity to say something that K does not want to hear. And there is, indeed, one point in the movie where Joi appears to ask K to do something that he does not want to do. Before they head off to Las Vegas, Joi asks K to delete her from the console and break her antenna:

JOI: You have to delete me from the console.
JOI: My present. Put me there. [Referring to the emanator.]
K: I can't do that. Think about it: If anything happens to this, that's it. You're gone.
JOI: Yes. Like a real girl.
JOI: Please. Joe, please. I want this. But I can't do it myself.

JOI: Break the antenna.

Inasmuch as we interpret this dialogue as evidence that Joi is saying something that K does not want to hear, then the autonomy issue is, I suggest, resolved in favour of a positive response. If Joi is sentient, then, she begins her time with K as a virtual slave, but she subsequently transitions to a virtual lover based on the nature of her relationship with K (see Figure 7.1).

And as for Wallace's question (Is it love or mathematical precision?), the answer, at least in this case, is probably "both."

Art, ambiguity, and intrinsic value

The way we think about Joi alters our view of events in the movie. Consider, for example, Joi's destruction at the hands (or rather the boot) of Luv. If Joi is neither sentient nor autonomous—if she is something akin to a character in a computer game—then her love for K doesn't appear particularly genuine, her death marks the end of K's digital fantasy, and Luv is guilty of property damage. If, on other hand, Joi is sentient and autonomous—if she is something akin to a virtual person—then her love for K is genuine, her death is a tragedy, and Luv is guilty of murder.

Given that *Blade Runner 2049* is, at root, a work of art, it is perhaps not surprising that it should exhibit some degree of ambiguity. Ambiguity is, of course, a common feature of artistic works, and it has long been seen as relevant to issues of aesthetic evaluation (e.g. Tormey & Tormey, 1983). When it comes to philosophical matters, however, we encounter a problem. The problem is that ambiguity is seldom a celebrated feature of philosophical works, and this leads to a worry about the extent to which movies (qua works of art) can be seen to make a philosophical contribution. In particular, if the notion of a philosophical contribution is tied to issues of clarity and precision, and movies (or, at any rate, the philosophically relevant parts of movies) are deemed to be ambiguous, then it is, at best, unclear how a movie could be deemed to make a philosophical contribution (or perhaps qualify as a work of philosophy). In the philosophical literature, this particular worry is nicely captured by the so-called *explicitness objection*. According to Wartenberg (2007, 2009), the explicitness objection highlights the contrast between "the precise and explicit formulation of claims in philosophy texts with the supposed imprecision and ambiguity of narrative films" (Wartenberg, 2007: 138).

There are a number of ways of responding to the explicitness objection. Wartenberg's own response is to reject the idea that movies are inherently ambiguous. He distinguishes between the ambiguity of whatever philosophical interpretations are made about a film and the inherent ambiguity of the film itself. According to Wartenberg (2009), the explicitness objection ought to be interpreted as a form of methodological advice: "Provide enough specificity and determinateness in a philosophical interpretation of a film so that the philosophy presented by the film is not inherently ambiguous" (Wartenberg, 2009: 553).

Unfortunately, this particular way of responding to the explicitness objection is unlikely to be of much use when it comes to Joi. The reason for this is simple: no amount of precision or exactitude in the philosophical interpretation of Joi's character is likely to alter the fact that she is inherently ambiguous. We can, of course, choose to enforce a particular interpretation for the sake of philosophical analysis (e.g. "Joi is sentient"), and there is no reason to think that the philosophical value of whatever claims and arguments are made in respect of that analysis are in any way impugned by the deliberate imposition of one or more interpretational certitudes. The fact remains, however, that we simply aren't given enough information to determine whether or not Joi is (e.g.) a sentient individual. This is simply one area (and there are no doubt others) where the movie fails to yield a determinate response. This has nothing to do with the quality (or otherwise) of the hermeneutic analysis of the movie; it is simply a reflection of the movie's inherent ambiguity when it comes to particular points of philosophical interest.

How, then, ought we respond to the explicitness objection? The response I want to canvass here is what I will dub the *intrinsic value response*. According to this response, the philosophical value of a resource, or its capacity to make a philosophical contribution, is on occasion inextricably tied to the ambiguous nature of the resource itself. To help us understand this claim, consider one of the claims made in respect of the sentience issue: the idea that Joi's enigmatic status parallels the complex, confusing, and uncertain nature of a broader philosophical debate. Just as we may not be able to resolve the sentience issue in the context of the movie, so our capacity to resolve sentience-related issues in the wider world may be similarly constrained. It is in precisely this sense that ambiguity might be seen to have intrinsic value. For the aim of *Blade Runner 2049* is not to solve the philosophical problem of sentience, or even to illuminate the path to a potential solution. Rather, Joi's enigmatic properties encourage us to confront a philosophical problem and experience some of the doubt, indecision, and ambivalence that accompanies that particular problem. In doing so, the movie helps us understand something about the nature of the problem, such as why it exists, why it is important, why it is difficult to solve and why, ultimately perhaps, it may have no satisfactory solution. There is no sense here in which the movie's inherent ambiguity could be seen to impugn its capacity to make this sort of philosophical contribution. If anything, ambiguity serves as the vehicle through which at least some of the movie's philosophical contributions (and thus its philosophical value) are realised.

Cinematic philosophy beyond the big screen

When we first encounter Joi, we learn that her holographic projection is limited to K's apartment. "How was your day?" asks K. "I'm getting cabin fever," replies Joi.

We later learn that K has purchased a gift for Joi: an emanator. This makes Joi portable. Whereas her projection had been limited to the confines of K's apartment, she is now free to accompany K on his travels and "experience" whatever it is that the world of *Blade Runner 2049* has to offer.

Relative to the movie, of course, the emanator serves as a plot device that enables Joi and K to be "joined at the hip," so to speak, throughout the remainder of the movie (at least until the point that Luv "steps in"). For me, however, the introduction of the emanator marks a point of allegorical significance: it speaks to the way in which emerging technologies, including holographic computing devices, are apt to make virtual cinematic elements (e.g. holograms) a standard feature of physical and social reality. This raises questions about the nature of cinematic philosophy. Should the scope of cinematic philosophy be defined with respect to whatever it is that appears on the big screen (e.g. conventional movies), or should we embrace a more expansive vision of the scope of cinematic philosophy—for example, one that includes the philosophical study of hologrammatic resources? In the same way that Joi's emanator enables her to escape the confines of K's apartment and venture out into the world, perhaps the emergence of mixed-reality devices calls for cinematic philosophers to take a closer look at the world that lies beyond the borders of the big screen—that is, to embrace the idea that non-film resources should form part of the intellectual remit of cinematic philosophy.

The term *cinematic philosophy* names a specific area of philosophy with an intellectual remit that concerns the philosophical significance and impact of the cinematic medium (e.g. Shamir, 2016; Wartenberg, 2007). For the most part, the scope of this philosophical effort has limited its attention to the sort of resources that we typically associate with the term *cinema*. They include what are termed films, movies, or motion pictures—the sort of things that we typically get to see on the big screen. *Blade Runner 2049* is a perfect example of this sort of cinematic resource, and it is thus a resource that falls within the scope of contemporary cinematic philosophy.

But should the scope of cinematic philosophy be limited to the study of films, movies, motion pictures, and the like? From an etymological perspective, the word "cinema" is derived from the ancient Greek word *kínēma*, meaning motion and movement. This highlights one of the central features of the cinematic medium, namely, its preoccupation with the moving image, the "motion picture." In a general sense, then, the cinematic medium is the medium of the moving image, and cinematic resources are resources that exploit this medium. Cinematic resources are, in short, images in motion—typically, a series of still images that are presented in rapid succession so as to give the impression of movement.

A Hollywood movie such as *Blade Runner 2049* undoubtedly qualifies as a cinematic resource, but is there any reason to suppose that the extension of the term "cinematic resource" is limited to this type of resource—the sort of resource that appears on the big screen?

It should be relatively clear that the answer to this question is "no." As noted by Berys Gaut (2010: 1), "Moving images come in many kinds, a fact of which it has been easy to lose sight until recently, given the dominance of traditional photochemical, celluloid-based film for most of the period in which moving images have been subject to theorising." Gaut (2010) goes on to note the cinematic status of resources such as video games and virtual-reality environments. While these resources have features that are unlike those of a conventional film (e.g. a video

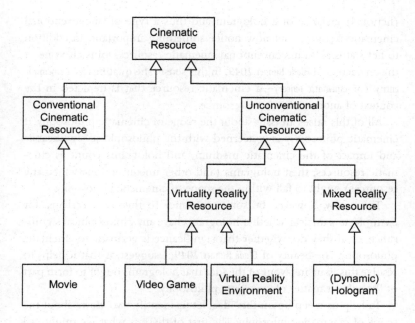

Figure 7.2 Taxonomy of cinematic resources. Triangles symbolise taxonomic or subtype relationships (Note that only dynamic holograms qualify as cinematic resources.)

game is interactive in a way that a conventional film is not), they are nevertheless resources that also rely on the cinematic medium. In this sense, a video game counts as a cinematic resource, just as much as does a Hollywood blockbuster.

Figure 7.2 illustrates a rough (and not necessarily complete) taxonomy of cinematic resources. As can be seen from the figure, cinematic resources are divided into two types: conventional and unconventional cinematic resources. This distinction is, at least in part, motivated by the features of each type of resource. For the most part, for example, conventional cinematic resources are almost always non-interactive and screen-based (i.e., they require a screen for display purposes). Unconventional cinematic resources, by contrast, are almost always interactive and are much less dependent on a display screen.[2]

Relative to this taxonomy, *Blade Runner 2049* is cast as a conventional cinematic resource (i.e., an instance of a movie), while Joi is cast as a (fictional) instance of a hologram and thus a type of unconventional cinematic resource. But now notice something important. In addition to her status as an unconventional cinematic resource, Joi is also one of the characters in Blade Runner 2049. In this sense, she qualifies as a *cinematic entity* (or *cinematic object*)—a cinematic resource that is depicted in the context of another cinematic resource.

All of this raises an issue about the scope of cinematic philosophy. If cinematic philosophy is concerned with the philosophical significance and impact of the cinematic medium, and holograms count as cinematic resources, then holograms (and other unconventional cinematic resources) ought to fall within the scope of cinematic philosophy.

There may, however, be some resistance to this idea. Perhaps, for example, it is unclear whether holograms have any philosophical significance, or, if they do, whether that significance is germane to cinematic philosophy. The beauty of Blade Runner 2049, I suggest, is that it helps to resolve this issue in favour of the idea that holograms ought to form part of the subject matter of cinematic philosophy.

To help us creep up on this idea, let us identify two views about the scope of cinematic philosophy. The first of these is what we might call the *traditionalist view*. This view insists that cinematic philosophy ought to limit its attention to the realm of conventional cinematic resources. The second view is what we might call the *expansionist view*. This view advocates an expansion in the traditionalist view to accommodate the class of unconventional cinematic resources.

Of course, in the context of Blade Runner 2049 the distinction between traditionalists and expansionists is not particularly crucial. This is because Joi is a legitimate focus of interest for the proponents of both views. Given that Joi forms part of a conventional cinematic resource (a movie), she will be of mutual interest to the proponents of either position, since neither the traditionalist nor the expansionist disputes the relevance of conventional cinematic resources to cinematic philosophy. At the same time, however, Joi is not the sort of cinematic resource that a fan of the traditionalist position would find particularly interesting once we move beyond the borders of the big screen. For the most part, only the proponent of the expansionist view will see real-world hologrammatic resources as falling within the intellectual orbit of cinematic philosophy.

At this point, however, the traditionalist position starts to look a little problematic. For, aside from the fact that movies are projected on the

THE JOI OF HOLOGRAMS 141

big screen and holograms are projected in peri-personal space (possibly without a screen!), it is not particularly clear what it is that gives conventional cinematic resources their seemingly distinctive philosophical significance. This is especially so when the focus of our philosophical attention is directed to a movie that reveals the philosophical significance of a somewhat different type of cinematic resource. By depicting a mixed-reality environment, for example, Blade Runner 2049 encourages us to consider the philosophical significance of mixed-reality resources, and it does so irrespective of whether or not we commit ourselves to the traditionalist or expansionist camp. But once we have identified these points of philosophical significance, our attention can then turn to the real-world counterparts of the cinematic resources depicted in the movie. This is surely just as important as the analysis of those resources in a big-screen context. In fact, the things that make Joi interesting from a philosophical standpoint are, I suggest, just as applicable to an emerging array of mixed-reality technologies. This is important, for it helps us identify a point of philosophical significance about Blade Runner 2049. By serving as the legitimate target of philosophical analysis for both traditionalists and expansionists, Joi helps to lay the foundation for a broader (meta)philosophical debate about the future scope and direction of cinematic philosophy. She does this by speaking to the expansionist agenda through the lens of a traditionalist analysis. In particular, it is via a traditional form of cinematic philosophical analysis (such as the one you are now reading) that the possibility and potential of an expanded cinematic philosophy starts to come into sharper focus.

Some of the philosophical issues raised by the study of unconventional (especially hologrammatic) cinematic resources are discussed in the next section. For now, however, it is worth noting the way in which Joi's status as a hologrammatic entity resonates with our current technological, commercial, and scientific interest in what is sometimes called X Reality (XR) (also known as cross reality)—a catch-all term for the various forms of "reality" picked out by the notions of cinematic, augmented, mixed, blended, and virtual reality. Indeed, with the advent of holographic devices, such as Microsoft's HoloLens (see Figure 7.3), Joi appears less like a beguiling fantasy advert suspended above the rain-drenched streets of a fictional cinematic universe, and more like a poster child for the next generation of personal assistants, digital companions, and (Who knows?) virtual lovers. In this respect, the cinematic reality

Figure 7.3 Microsoft HoloLens promotion image

of Blade Runner 2049 raises important questions about the effect of unconventional cinematic resources on the shape of our own physical and social realities. If this is, at least in part, one of the things that makes Blade Runner 2049 interesting from a philosophical perspective, then why demur from the proposal that hologrammatic resources ought to form part of the theoretical and empirical agenda of (an expanded) cinematic philosophy?

At this point, it is probably up to the proponent of the traditionalist view to specify why they regard conventional cinematic resources as worthy of specialist (and exclusive) philosophical treatment. For a variety of reasons, I very much doubt that any sort of defence of the traditionalist position can be made to work. And this remains the case, even if we resort to alternative ways of labelling the relevant philosophical enterprise (e.g. the philosophy of film). To help us understand why this relabelling strategy is unlikely to work, consider that Blade Runner 2049 depicts a mixed-reality world, and it raises philosophical issues about a particular kind of mixed-reality resource within that world, namely, holograms. Thus, even if we limit our attention to the big screen, there are still times when the reach of cinematic philosophy will extend to the realm of mixed-reality resources, and it is unclear why the big-screen context ought to serve as the ultimate arbiter of philosophical interest. To help reinforce this particular point, it is perhaps worth noting the ease with which Blade Runner 2049 can itself be rendered as a hologrammatic resource. There is no reason, for example, why Blade Runner 2049 cannot be viewed using the built-in augmented reality video player that ships with Microsoft HoloLens. At this point, the erstwhile crisp distinction between the realms of conventional and unconventional cinematic resources may itself start to look a little blurry (or ambiguous?). For what are we watching when Blade Runner 2049 is rendered as a hologrammatic resource in peri-personal space? Is it a movie, a hologram, a hologrammatic movie, or all of the above?

It might be said, of course, that a distinctive feature of conventional cinematic resources (and the feature that marks them out for specialist philosophical treatment) is that they have a rich narrational structure. But rich narrational structures are not a universal feature of the movies that have been targeted by cinematic philosophy (see Wartenberg, 2007, chap. 7), and, in any case, there is no reason why unconventional cinematic resources are ill-equipped to feature narrational elements. Video games, such as Red Dead Redemption 2, for example, allow human game-players to create their own narrative structures, courtesy of their capacity to exert "directorial" control over events within a virtual world. And if Joi is akin to a character in a computer game, then isn't K doing something similar to a human game-player—creating a narrative, courtesy of his interactions and exchanges with a virtual character? The only substantive difference here is that Joi is part of K's life story—part of his personal narrative history and part of his narrative arc in the movie. Given that such forms of narratological entanglement are apt to be a source of philosophical interest in the context of Blade Runner 2049, it is unclear why similar forms of narratological entanglement should fail to be a source of philosophical interest just because they involve resources that lie beyond the movie theatre walls.

Minds, mates, and the moving image

JOI: An emanator.
JOI: Thank you.
K: Honey, you can go anywhere in the world you want now. Where you want to go first?

K's question is particularly apt, for having broached the idea of an expanded cinematic philosophy, I am now faced with the task of shedding some light on this newly unveiled region of the philosophical terrain. The primary problem here is not so much one of scarcity as it is superabundance. For there are lots of things to see (and do) in this particular neck of the philosophical woods and, unfortunately, the tour bus can only visit so many locations.

I will limit my attention to three issues. These were selected according to a number of criteria. First, the issues speak to a general concern with the cognitive value of cinematic resources. In particular, they begin to show, at least in outline form, how an expanded set of cinematic resources (most notably, hologrammatic resources) might influence the shape of human cognitive processing. Second, the issues are, in one way or another, inspired by my own experience of watching *Blade Runner 2049*. Third, the issues begin to illuminate the nature of the broader interdisciplinary links that connect cinematic philosophy with work in a number of other disciplines, such as cognitive science, computer science, and the philosophy of mind. The issues are.

(1) **Cinematic AI:** Joi is both a cinematic entity (a hologram) and a form of AI. This raises questions about the extent to which intelligent systems might be implemented in the cinematic medium.

(2) **Virtual Companions:** Contrary to the traditional image of AI systems as possessing superhuman cognitive abilities, Joi's intelligence is firmly rooted in the social domain. She is intended to be a companion for K—a source of emotional comfort and socio-sexual stimulation. This raises questions about the extent to which socially adroit hologrammatic AI entities ought to be seen as virtual additions to the human social world.

(3) **Hologrammatically Extended Minds:** I suggest that holograms provide the basis for a particular form of cognitive extension (Clark, 2008; Clark & Chalmers, 1998), which involves the integration of (unconventional) cinematic resources into cognitively relevant processing loops. The resulting cognitive organisations are what we might call *hologrammatically extended minds*. Hologrammatically extended minds are, in essence, cognitive systems that are constituted, at least in part, by resources that fall within the scope of (an expanded) cinematic philosophy.

Let us take these points in turn. The first issue relates to the notion of cinematic AI. We have already seen why Joi (and thus her real-world hologrammatic kin) ought to be regarded as a particular kind of cinematic resource (see above). There should also be little doubt that Joi qualifies as a form of AI system. She is, after all, a technological artefact, produced by Wallace Corp., and she is clearly capable of behaving in an intelligent manner. The result is that Joi qualifies as a form of cinematic AI. She is, in short, emblematic of the idea that certain kinds of cinematic resource (e.g. holograms) are able to function as AI systems.

Despite the seeming banality of this claim, it is, in fact, of crucial importance. In particular, it suggests that the cinematic medium is not just a medium in which philosophically useful work might be done; it is also a medium that supports the realisation of (sentient?) intelligent systems. The resulting set of issues are ones that not only straddle the ostensibly distinct intellectual terrains of cinematic philosophy, cognitive science, and the nascent field of holographic computing, they are also ones that might be seen to blur the very boundaries that separate these particular fields of intellectual enquiry.

Joi's status as a virtual companion also serves as a point of philosophical interest. In particular, Joi is a system whose intelligence is primarily oriented to the socio-emotional domain. She is a system designed to fulfil a social function: a virtual companion that aims to act as a technological filler for whatever social, emotional, and sexual gaps exist in the lives of those who purchase her.

There is, of course, no real-world parallel to Joi. Virtual assistants, such as Amazon's Alexa, Apple's Siri, and Microsoft's Cortana, are testament to the progress that has been made in speech recognition, conversational interaction, and information retrieval. But, for the present at least, these systems remain little more than voice-based intermediaries to an online world of digital information and networked devices.

This doesn't mean that virtual companions are forever consigned to the realms of fantasy and fiction, however. As is evidenced by work into social (and sexual) robots, believable game characters, and digital companions, there is no shortage of scientific (and commercial) interest in the possibility of socially adroit AI systems. Assuming that research in these areas merges with that in holographic computing, it is not inconceivable that Joi-like systems might one day feature as elements of human *social* reality. This is important, for we typically think of holograms (qua mixed-reality resources) as a means of adding information to the local environment and thereby altering the nature of our cognitive and experiential contact with physical reality. The beauty of *Blade Runner 2049* is that it directs our attention to the social impact (and relevance) of hologrammatic resources—the way in which some types of XR resource are poised to alter (extend? enrich? augment? contaminate?) the structure and dynamics of human social life.

The third and final issue on our list concerns the notion of hologrammatically extended minds. Hologrammatically extended minds arise as the result of the incorporation of a hologrammatic resource into a materially extended cognitive circuit. A hologrammatically extended mind is thus a particular kind of extended cognitive system (Clark, 2008) or extended mind (Clark & Chalmers, 1998). The only difference between a hologrammatically extended mind and a conventional extended mind is the nature of the extra-organismic resource that is factored into a cognitively relevant information-processing loop. In the case of hologrammatically extended minds, these resources are a particular kind of cinematic resource, namely, a hologram. (Holograms are, of course, not the only kind of cinematic resource that may be incorporated into a materially extended cognitive circuit; nevertheless, they are the most important kind of cinematic resource relative to our interests in the present chapter.)

Although extended minds have been the focus of a long-standing (and ongoing) philosophical debate, the specific notion of a hologrammatically extended mind is not one that seems to have garnered much philosophical attention. This is unfortunate, for hologrammatically extended minds yield a number of puzzles and problems that extend the traditional palette of philosophical concerns in this area. Note, for example, that issues of cognitive extension are typically discussed with reference to concrete, physical resources, such as notebooks and iPhones (e.g. Clark & Chalmers, 1998). In this case, the philosophical polemic centres on the nature of the functional relationship that exists between resources that lie either side of the organismic boundary. The question is whether we should talk of some extra-organismic resource (such as a notebook) as forming part of the mechanistically relevant fabric that realises some cognitive state or process. This issue remains important in the case of hologrammatically extended minds, but we now have an additional concern: To what extent does it make sense to talk of a virtual cinematic resource as forming part of the *physical* machinery of the mind? One issue here relates to the "virtual" status of a cinematic resource. How can a photic resource (i.e., a resource made of light) feature as part of the causally active physical fabric that realises cognitive states and processes? Does this mean that hologrammatically extended minds are constituted, at least in part, by light? Is it possible for cognitive routines to emerge from the forms of photic flux that define the moving image? And, if so, what does this mean for our current understanding of the cognitive and philosophical value of the cinematic medium?

There are, no doubt, many issues that are raised by the possibility of hologrammatically extended minds, and I will not attempt to rehearse those issues here, let alone proffer anything in the way of a solution. For present purposes, what matters is merely the fact that we have identified a point of convergence between cinematic philosophy and the philosophy of mind, one that expands the nature of the debates in both areas, while simultaneously drawing inspiration from the cinematic spectacle that is Blade Runner 2049. Having said that, there are no specific examples of hologrammatically extended minds that I can point to in Blade Runner 2049. The functional contribution of Blade Runner 2049, in this respect, is not so much to *illustrate* a specific philosophical claim (see Wartenberg, 2009) as it is to *inspire* a new way of thinking about the philosophical significance of the cinematic medium. There is, no doubt, an important sense in which my own biological brain did much of the heavy lifting in order to bring this particular idea to light. And yet it was the play of light and sound (on the big screen) that managed to coax my biological brain into doing some (hopefully) useful philosophical work. (No mean feat, given the typically torpid nature of my neural machinery.)

This does not mean that the notion of hologrammatically extended minds is irrelevant to our philosophical assessment of Blade Runner 2049. For, once we have the idea to hand, we can begin to put it to philosophical work in assessing some of the issues raised by the movie. It might be thought, for example, that nothing like Joi could exist outside the realms of Blade Runner's fictional reality: "How could a mere hologrammatic projection count as anything like a cognitive system, let alone a virtual person!?" From a mechanistic perspective, however, it is arguably a mistake to view Joi solely as a holographic projection. For Joi's projection is rendered by a physical device (e.g. the emanator), and this should arguably be included as part of the material mix that makes Joi the peculiar cognitive entity she is. Joi is, in this sense, a hybrid entity—a mix of the physical and the virtual: part physical computation, part cinematic projection. Her claim to cognitive status is thus no more (and probably no less) contentious than is the basic possibility of a hologrammatically extended mind. For, if the material fabric that undergirds our own (experientially charged!) forms of cognising may, on occasion, include a mix of both the physical (the biological) and the virtual (the cinematic), then why object to the idea that Joi's own cognitive wherewithal (sentient or otherwise) may, on occasion, rely on a material fabric that features both a physical device and that most mesmeric of human cultural innovations—the play of light that is the moving image?

Notes

1 At the beginning of the movie, Joi says (to K) "I'm so happy when I'm with you." It is only later in the movie, immediately prior to her "death," that Joi attempts to proclaim her love for K.
2 Volumetric holograms, for example, do not require a display screen, nor do resources that are projected using Virtual Retinal Display (VRD) devices.

References

Clark, A. (2008). *Supersizing the Mind: Embodiment, Action, and Cognitive Extension*. New York: Oxford University Press.

Clark, A., & Chalmers, D. (1998). The Extended Mind. *Analysis*, 58(1), 7–19.

Gaut, B. (2010). *A Philosophy of Cinematic Art*. Cambridge: Cambridge University Press.

Hyslop, A. (2018). Other Minds. In E. N. Zalta (Ed.), *The Stanford Encyclopedia of Philosophy* (Winter 2018 ed.). Stanford: Stanford University.

Nagel, T. (1974). What Is It Like to be a bat? *The Philosophical Review* 83(4), 435–450.

Shamir, T. S. (2016). *Cinematic Philosophy*. Basel: Palgrave Macmillan.

Smalley, D. E., Nygaard, E., Squire, K., Van Wagoner, J., Rasmussen, J., Gneiting, S., et al. (2018). A Photophoretic-Trap Volumetric Display. *Nature* 553(7689), 486–490.

Tormey, J. F., & Tormey, A. (1983). Art and Ambiguity. *Leonardo* 16(3), 183–187.

Wartenberg, T. E. (2007). *Thinking on Screen: Film as Philosophy*. Abingdon: Routledge.

Wartenberg, T. E. (2009). Film as Philosophy. In P. Livingstone & C. Plantinga (Eds.), *The Routledge Companion to Philosophy and Film* (pp. 549–559). Abingdon: Routledge.

Chapter 8

Wanja Wiese and Thomas K. Metzinger

ANDROIDS DREAM OF VIRTUAL SHEEP

Introduction

THE SCENE IN WHICH MARIETTE and Joi synchronise with each other to have sex with K may, for many viewers, be the most memorable scene from the entire movie. It has many interesting aspects—technologically, aesthetically, even metaphysically—but it also serves, rather trivially, as an illustration of what distinguishes virtual reality (VR) technology from more conventional screen-based media. Virtual environments are *immersive*: it does not seem as if there is a screen in front of one's eyes, displaying virtual objects (as on a tablet or computer screen); instead, virtual objects seem to be located all around the user. It feels as though one is inside whatever virtual environment is being explored. By moving or adjusting the virtual camera, one can get an extreme close-up view of virtual objects, allowing one to inspect them in detail. Intriguingly, virtual objects often do not seem *less real* when one gets closer to them. Of course, one doesn't have the impression that the virtual objects one is inspecting are actually out there, as solid objects one can touch.[1] Nevertheless, such objects do seem to exist (at least in a virtual sense), and they certainly seem to be more real than a visual afterimage or vivid mental imagery. The exciting twist in

Blade Runner 2049 is that the characters interacting with Joi are not just confronted with a model of a body, but with a model of a sentient agent. This offers various ways in which the reality (or unreality) of the virtual entity that is Joi can be explored.

In Metzinger (2018: 15–16), the phenomenology of virtual objects is compared with an exclusively phenomenological reading of the Buddhist notion of emptiness (suññatā). What the phenomenology of virtual environments seems to share with Buddhist emptiness (at least in many cases) is the feature of being "neither real nor unreal." We have to distinguish this from a metaphysical reading: a virtual table is not as real as the table in your kitchen or living room.[2] Phenomenologically, however, virtual objects can seem *more than unreal*, even if, metaphysically, they are not regarded as real entities. Perhaps the same can be said about Joi's mind and the phenomenal self. We have the experience of being someone, although experienced selfhood is just the content of an internal model generated by our brains. Phenomenal selves are virtual entities that seem more than unreal, and this is as true for beings with holographic bodies (such as Joi) as it is for flesh-and-bone creatures (such as ourselves).

This view of phenomenal selves follows from the Self-Model Theory of Subjectivity (Metzinger, 2003) and gains further support from predictive processing (PP) accounts of cognition (Clark, 2016; Hohwy, 2013; Wiese & Metzinger, 2017). According to these accounts, the brain implements an approximation to hierarchical Bayesian inference, using an internal model that tracks the causal structure of the organism's environment and its own body, by minimising the error of predictions about incoming sensory signals. Recently, this predictive processing framework has been applied to *self-modelling* (see, for example, Hohwy & Michael, 2017; Letheby & Gerrans, 2017; Limanowski & Blankenburg, 2013). These accounts emphasise the virtuality of the phenomenal (i.e., the consciously experienced) self. The phenomenal self is not viewed as a substance that sustains its own existence; instead, it is seen as the content of a neurally realised probabilistic model. Much the same, of course, applies to our phenomenal experience of conventional physical objects. Such experiences are deemed to stem from the operation of an internal model that embodies the causal structure of the sensorium, and, in this sense, the experience of conventional objects is no less virtual than is the experience of the phenomenal self. Unlike the phenomenal self, however, the experience of conventional physical objects is tied to patterns of sensory stimulation that impinge on the organism's sensory epithelia. This differs from the state of affairs encountered in the case of the phenomenal self. In this case, there is no enduring substance that has all the properties represented by the self-model. There is, to be sure, a phenomenology of substantiality, ontological self-subsistence, and sameness across time. But ultimately there is no physical object that corresponds to the self; instead there is only the content of the brain's model of its environment.[3]

To understand how this applies to BR2049, we first need to review some key concepts associated with predictive processing.. After that, we can apply those concepts to acquire a better sense of what Joi is and isn't, and whether or not we ought to regard her as "real." As we shall see, Joi's *bodily self* is real only when regarded from the perspective of her virtual environment. The *non-bodily* aspects of her phenomenal self, by contrast, are real *tout court*.

Some key concepts of predictive processing

Consider what is happening right now, while you are reading these sentences: You are looking at a printed book or a screen, you are perceiving letters and words and, at the same time, you understand their meaning. How is this possible? Naïvely, one could perhaps assume that the eyes function like cameras, taking snapshots of words and sentences, and these snapshots are then interpreted by an internal mechanism in the brain. Such a mechanism would be akin to a little man in the brain, a homunculus, who views a series of snapshots and generates an interpretation. This sketch obviously raises the question of how the homunculus is able to perceive and understand words and sentences, which means that we have not really explained anything. So, the task in perception and cognition cannot be to first build an image of the environment and then to interpret the image, as an additional step. Furthermore, the sensory signals actually received by our sense organs are by themselves insufficient to build from scratch reliable representations of objects, events, and processes in the environment. But we do have determinate, rich perceptual experiences of books, flowers, and falling raindrops. In other words, we become aware of, and form internal representations of objects, events, and processes that are outside of us. How is this possible?

How does the brain generate meaningful percepts (as opposed to meaningless "snapshots"), based on the sensory signals it receives? According to predictive processing (PP),[4] the brain creates percepts using a hierarchical generative model (HGM) of its environment. The HGM is a model of how hidden causes in the environment (including the body) generate sensory signals (hence, the term *generative* model). It codes all prior information that the brain has accumulated over time. You are able to understand these words because you have learned the English language and have learned how to read. This learning has shaped your internal model, enabling it to form expectations about the environment. For instance, reading the beginning of a sentence, your brain will form expectations about how the sentence is likely to continue, and it will implement a series of saccadic eye movements that best resolve uncertainty about how the sentence continues.

Moreover, the HGM has a hierarchical structure, tracking regularities at different levels of spatial and temporal scale. For instance, spoken words display certain regularities at relatively shorter time scales, while entire sentences display regularities at longer time scales. At lower levels, the HGM will infer the shapes of letters while, at higher levels, it will infer the meaning of words and the prosody of sentences (e.g. the tone, rhythm, or features that tell you whether a person is formulating a question or a command). These representations are not simply derived from sensory signals (as a snapshot would be) but are mostly generated internally and then matched against the incoming sensory input. Sensory signals are thus only used to *adjust* the brain's HGM: given its model, the brain predicts current sensory signals, compares predictions to actually received signals, and then updates the HGM to minimise prediction error. This means that perception is mainly driven by top-down processing, which is itself informed by prior attempts to predict the sensory signal. We perceive the world, according to PP, whenever the brain's HGM is able to yield top-down predictions that adequately accommodate the incoming flow of sensory information. This idea is nicely summarised by Clark (2013):

> In essence, a multilayer downward cascade is attempting to "guess" the present states of all the key neuronal populations responding to the present state of the visual world. There ensues a rapid exchange (a dance between multiple top-down and bottom-up signals) in

which incorrect guesses yield error signals that propagate forward and are used to extract better guesses. When top-down guessing adequately accounts for the incoming signal, the visual scene is perceived. As this process unfolds, top-down processing is trying to generate the incoming sensory signal for itself. When and only when this succeeds, and a match is established, do we get to experience (veridically or otherwise) a meaningful visual scene.

(Clark, 2013: 471)

Because of the large influence of purely internal processing, perception is prone to illusion, as testified by many well-known examples of perceptual illusions, such as the hollow-face illusion (see Figure 8.1) (see Clark, 2018: 207–210, for more examples). This has led some authors to describe perception as a form of "controlled hallucination" (see Grush,

Figure 8.1 An example of the hollow face illusion. This mask of Swedish tennis player Björn Borg seems to be convex ("popping out"), while in fact it is concave

2004: 395; Horn, 1980: 373) (cf. Clark, 2013: 493). More generally, we can describe the contents of perception as *virtual*, thereby likening our conscious reality to a virtual reality (VR) generated by our brains (see Metzinger, 2018: 3; Revonsuo, 1995: 51). However, compared to artificial VR environments that can be experienced using current VR technology, our natural VR environments allow for much more direct and diverse causal interactions. When climbing a virtual mountain in a VR game, falling down does not cause any actual harm to the body. By contrast, natural VR can be a lot more dangerous.

The VR metaphor also downplays the influence of sensory signals.[5] We can see this by considering what it would be like for a creature such as Joi to perceive her own body. Her body is simulated by a computer and, in this sense, it is not "real" (i.e., in the sense of being *substantial*). However, Joi might *experience* her body just like any of us experience our own bodies. One could object that this cannot be true, because Joi must perceive a difference between her holographic body and, for instance, K's body: K can touch and move objects in his flat, he can grasp a chair or move it around. Joi, by contrast, can only touch and move virtual objects.[6] She can prepare a (virtual) meal for K and pretend to place it on the (non-virtual) table, but she cannot touch and move the table, nor can she touch K. This becomes most obvious when Mariette "goes inside Joi" to have sex with K: Mariette and K do not make physical contact with Joi's holographic body. Hence, the objection continues, she cannot experience her body as being as real as a solid object, such as a chair; she must experience her body as being the translucent, ghost-like entity that K perceives when he looks at her.

According to this objection, Joi's bodily experience would be similar to what human subjects experience in the rubber-hand illusion (Botvinick & Cohen, 1998). In this illusion, subjects observe a rubber hand, while their real hand is hidden from view. When both the real hand and the rubber hand are stroked synchronously (e.g. with a brush), many subjects report that they experience their real hand as being located at the place where they see the rubber hand.[7] They see the stroking on the rubber hand, while they feel the stroking on their real hand, and when the illusion sets in, subjects have the impression that the felt stroking is occurring at the same place as the *seen* stroking, and in fact experience this as a single stroking event. Of course, subjects still know that their hand has not been transformed into a rubber hand. They do not experience the rubber hand as being under their control. Rather, for at least some subjects, the following is an adequate phenomenological description: There are actually two hands; one is a solid object, made of rubber, the other is a ghost-like entity that is "inside" the rubber hand but does not touch it. This is what it must be like for Joi to experience her own body when she syncs with Mariette. Or is it?

Note that we experience the rubber hand as real, because it is part of the physical environment with which we can directly interact: we can grasp the rubber hand, if we want to, just as we can grasp an apple or a chair. For Joi, things are different: The things she can grasp and directly interact with are the virtual objects around her (such as the virtual meal she is preparing for K). For Joi, therefore, perceiving the physical environment that is real for K must be like perceiving an artificial virtual environment. It will seem less real to her than her own body, because she cannot directly interact with the environment in the same way she can interact with her own body (and other virtual things).

The difference between Joi's perception of the external environment and our perception of an artificial VR environment is that Joi knows that the apartment and its interior are *not* simulated by a computer, and in this sense are real. But the fact that she cannot directly interact with this environment will have an impact on her experience. The reason for this is that ordinary perception is more strongly constrained by sensory signals than is suggested by the "perception as controlled hallucination" or the VR metaphor. According to PP, sensory signals are not just used to passively test hypotheses about the world, they are also used to test predictions about the sensory consequences of action. Unless Joi is delusional, she will not expect to get tactile sensory feedback when her hands reach for a physical body (e.g. K's). Why won't she expect this? If she did expect to feel a solid object when her hands get close to a physical table or chair, or to K's body, this would result in a large prediction error. In line with the principle of prediction error minimisation, this error would be quashed by adjusting predictions about the sensory consequences of moving the hand towards objects in the physical environment (unless Joi is encapsulated in a comprehensive, all-encompassing delusion). By contrast, we can imagine that Joi does get simulated tactile feedback when she is touching her own (virtual) body. Hence, predictions about tactile feedback will not be disconfirmed by movements directed at her virtual body (and other virtual objects), and they can therefore be sustained. Joi can always kiss another avatar, at least in principle, but she can never kiss a physical human being. This will also be accompanied by a difference in her bodily experience: she will experience her body as being a real object, even though she knows it is not in direct physical contact with the part of reality in which K and Mariette (and their bodies) live.[8]

From a phenomenological standpoint, then, Joi possesses an embodied self. This is because she experiences her own body as dense and solid, just as beings made of flesh and bone experience their own bodies as dense and solid. From an external point of view, this experience could seem inaccurate, or even hallucinatory, because external observers will perceive her body as being merely virtual. But from Joi's perspective, her body must seem more real than the objects in the physical (non-virtual) environment. Perhaps one might even draw a parallel to human babies, who, in bootstrapping their body model, increasingly make it more and more real, thereby bringing *themselves* into existence, phenomenologically. Joi's sensory feedback does not stem from a biological body, but her bodily perception is not hallucinatory because it is in line with the simulated sensory feedback she is receiving: her virtual body can actually touch other virtual objects. In other words, Joi's bodily experience reflects real regularities in the (simulated) sensory signals processed by her projection device. This is why the "perception as controlled hallucination" metaphor can be misleading. Waking perception is *not* like a dream. It *is* perhaps comparable to an immersive hallucination (see Windt, 2015), but only in the sense that perception depends more on internal processes than on the environment. In essence, our brains interpret sensory signals in systematic and (usually) reliable ways, and in this sense percepts are unlike the contents of dreams and other hallucinations. Moreover, even if percepts do not primarily track real properties in the environment, but instead mainly serve reproductive success (cf. Hoffman et al., 2015), they do stand in systematic relationships with structures in the environment.

Getting real Joi

We saw that Joi's bodily experience as a solid and dense unit of identification is real. But there remains an asymmetry between the part of the world that is real for Joi and the part of the world that is real for others, such as K and Mariette. Joi and the virtual objects in her environment are embedded within the non-virtual environment in which K lives: the hardware simulating the virtual environment is part of the non-virtual environment, and there are spatial relations between virtual and non-virtual objects. In particular, the simulated physics of Joi's virtual environment respects the physics of non-virtual objects in the apartment (e.g. the virtual dish Joi prepares for K does not fall through the non-virtual table), but not vice versa (a non-virtual plate would fall through a virtual table). Furthermore, there is no perspective within these two parts of the world from which both K and Joi's bodies would seem equally real. Either you are in K's part of the world and can directly physically interact with him and the furniture in his apartment, or you are in Joi's part of the world and can directly physically interact with virtual objects. This determines which body will appear more real to you.[9]

We shall now argue that there is still a sense in which Joi is as real as K, regardless of whether one assumes Joi or K's perspective. "As real as K" could mean that both are equally unreal, but we shall argue that there is a sense in which both are more than unreal (and equally so). According to a metaphysical rule of thumb, something is real if it is causally efficacious. When a virtual billiard ball is hit by a virtual cue, we can explain the resulting simulated motion of the virtual ball without assuming that the virtual cue is causally efficacious (because processes in the hardware on which the virtual objects are simulated are both necessary and sufficient to explain what is going on). Joi and K, by contrast, have a more sophisticated way of "moving" each other. By directing their thoughts and feelings to each other, they exercise a capacity to synchronise their internal models across distinct layers of reality. Our tentative criterion for "realness" in this context is therefore that a system is real if it has the capacity to causally bridge layers of reality. Just as a virtual cue becomes more real if it can set real balls in motion, virtual selves become more real by engaging in reciprocal social relations, such as romantic love. We shall unpack this idea in what follows by applying it to Joi.

Consider the following questions. Is a holographic apple a real apple? Is Joi a real human being? Is she a person? Is her self-experience real? These questions highlight some of the different senses in which something can be said to be real (or unreal). It is important to distinguish them in order to avoid confusion. A holographic apple is not real in the sense that it can be eaten and digested. Joi is not a real human being in the sense of having a body made of flesh and bone. Whether she is a real person is a question we mainly list here to point out that her *self-experience* can be phenomenologically realistic, even if she is not a real person.[10] Perhaps, given future technological advances, her self-experience could even seem *more realistic* than that of biological creatures. As research into psychiatric syndromes, psychoactive substances, and epileptic seizures shows, "realness" is itself a phenomenal property that comes in degrees. For example, people suffering from depersonalisation disorder experience themselves as less real. We saw that Joi's *bodily* self-experience is real, but only from the perspective of her (virtual) environment. However, there is more to self-experience than just bodily self-experience. Here, we shall focus on affective and attentional aspects of self-experience.

Joi has feelings for K, but more fundamentally, we can conceive of Joi as assigning subjective values to things. Whatever the neural basis of emotions and feelings in human beings, it is conceivable that Joi's simulated body simulates the same underpinnings. Joi can be viewed as a being with desires, beliefs, and intentions, because her behaviour shows the same patterns that are characteristic of preference-satisfying intentional systems such as ourselves (cf. Dennett, 1991). This also means we can ascribe goals and rationality to her, and we can assume that she will be frustrated when she cannot achieve her goals and that she will be happy when she can. In line with her goals and interests, the way she experiences the world will be valenced. Things will seem good or bad *to her*. In particular, she will have feelings that can be characterised as positive or negative. Such affective states will involve a feeling of *mineness*: When she is happy, it will be her own happiness she is feeling, not the happiness of someone else. And it will in fact be her own happiness. Her affective states and the correlated phenomenology of ownership will be as real as K's affective states, or even your own affective states.

Similarly, her first-person perspective will be as real as any first-person perspective can be. It is plausible to assume that, at its core, any first-person perspective is at least partly constituted by attention. Attention structures conscious experiences (Watzl, 2017), and this structure goes beyond a mere geometric point of view as provided by visual perception;[11] instead, it is a *subjective* point of view (see Wiese, 2018: 167–174), because it often reflects the subject's interests and goals (Jennings, 2015), and the fact that we consciously represent ourselves as epistemic agents. We have an "epistemic agent model" (EAM). This is an inner image of oneself as a "knowing self." This image is created by a special layer in the conscious internal model of the self. We experience ourselves as actively selecting targets of knowledge, as mental agents who stand in epistemic relations (like "perceiving," "believing," "knowing") to the world and to oneself (as in "controlling the focus of attention," "reasoning about the world and oneself," or "knowing that one knows"). Attentional self-control is likely to be the basic functional layer of the EAM, because the origin of the "knowing self" is the conscious experience of controlling one's own focus of attention. Phenomenologically and functionally, the attentional structure is shaped by attentional agency (Metzinger, 2013). Attentional agency is the property of being in control of the focus of attention. This property is a functional property, but it can also be consciously experienced. We often lack the ability to control our attentional focus—as research on mind-wandering shows (see Metzinger, 2013: 6–7)—but when we actually possess attentional agency, experiences of attentional control will usually be accurate. The same goes for Joi's attentional agency.

We can also assume that Joi not only experiences attentional relations between herself and the world, but intentional relations more generally.[12] Joi can directly interact with her virtual environment, she can form desires and goals related to virtual objects, and she can experience herself as having these desires and goals, as well as experience herself as achieving these goals. This means she not only experiences the presence of a world and her own body, but she also experiences the way she is situated in her environment. Although she cannot physically interact with K's body, she can talk to him and think about him, and experience him as an agent with thoughts, beliefs, desires, and goals, some of which involve herself. Technically speaking, she experiences the content of a *phenomenal model of the intentionality relation* (see Metzinger, 2003, sect. 6.5). This model represents subject–object relations, as well as subject–subject relations.

This point about subject–subject relations is especially important: If Joi is conscious, her feelings are real, including her feelings for K. She experiences herself as being in love with K, and experiences him as loving her back. Although the fact that their bodies inhabit different layers of reality sets limitations on the nature of their relationship, their thoughts and feelings for each other are not as constrained because their mental lives are equally virtual (in the sense of being the contents of internal models). When Joi experiences herself as thinking about K, or as talking to him, she is actually thinking about or talking to him, and the same goes for K when he is thinking about or talking to Joi. They may never be able to physically kiss, but they can couple and synchronise their emotional self-models and their EAMs—and that allows them to bridge the gap between different layers of reality. Their feelings and thoughts may be fully explainable with recourse to the algorithms implemented by their respective hardware, but these physical processes would not unfold in the way they do if K and Joi did not perceive and talk to each other. Understanding why K is in love with Joi (and vice versa) therefore requires more than just a reference to their physical underpinnings. Note that this does not presuppose strong notions of top-down causation or emergence because the effects Joi and K have on each other's internal models are still mediated by their respective hardware. But the specific ways in which their mental processes are implemented are irrelevant (they could even be completely different from each other), because the only thing that matters is that their self-models are compatible.[13] Their love for each other is real, because it is constituted by an emotional synchrony, mediated by a causal coupling. This coupling allows their virtual selves to bridge layers of reality. In experiencing themselves as loving partners in a romantic relationship, they are therefore as real as it gets.

Conclusion

Mariette claims that Joi's inner life is not as rich as it seems. This is true for her body, as perceived from Mariette's perspective, because Joi's virtual body is not part of the environment with which Mariette can physically interact. They could never physically kiss. However, Joi could say much the same about Mariette's body: Joi has been inside Mariette, and just as Mariette finds nothing inside of Joi to interact with, so too Joi finds nothing inside of Mariette that she can interact with. Things are different when it comes to Joi and Mariette's mental lives. There is no "real self" (in the sense of a substantial entity) that Mariette has but Joi does not. Both experience only the content of a self-model. They may never kiss, but they can touch each other even more deeply—on the level of shared emotions and their synchronised internal models. The contents of their self-models augment and constitute their shared, overarching social realities. Their low-level life-worlds may differ, because Joi's environment is virtual, whereas Mariette's (and K's) environments are not. But there is no substantial difference when it comes to the augmentations provided by the intersubjective dimension of self-experience. Hence, Joi's self-experience, including her social experience, is as real as it gets.

Notes

1 This may change in the not-too-distant future, due to research on so-called haptic holograms (see Kugler, 2015, for a review). Hoshi et al. (2009), for example, describe a system that allows human users to feel hologrammatic raindrops. This inverts the state of affairs seen in the "Joi in rain" scene—the scene where Joi steps outside K's apartment and her hologrammatic form adapts to the falling rain. We are grateful to Paul Smart for bringing this to our attention.
2 This claim is not as uncontroversial as it may seem. David Chalmers (2017) defends a view he calls *virtual digitalism*, according to which virtual objects are real. Furthermore, when we are immersed in a virtual environment and perceive, for instance, a virtual bird flying around us, we are not having an illusion, because there really is a virtual bird in a virtual space. Things are more complicated in mixed-reality environments, where virtual and non-virtual objects seem to be located within the same space (such as in K's apartment). Chalmers grants that in such cases, there can be "associated illusions for virtual objects: they seem to be in physical space, but they are not" (Chalmers, 2017: 345). For instance, if K perceives Joi's body as being located within the same physical space as his own body, this would count as an illusion.
3 This is not to say that all aspects of the self-model are misrepresented. Part of the self-model is a body model, which must at least be accurate enough to enable flexible behavioural control. Furthermore, if we assume a general conception of selfhood, there are many features that may be accurately tracked by the self-model. Albert Newen (2018), for instance, proposes a pattern theory of the self, according to which what he calls "the embodied self" is a real entity (even though it is not a substance in the traditional sense) (see Newen, 2018: 8). When it comes to the phenomenal self, however, which is experienced as an enduring, substantial entity, the self-model does not accurately represent.
4 For non-technical introductions, see Hohwy (2013), Clark (2016), and Wiese and Metzinger (2017).

5 For this reason, *augmented reality* may actually serve as a better metaphor for conscious perception (see Wiese, in prep).
6 Joi may still be able to touch non-virtual objects, in the sense that she can receive simulated feedback when her virtual hand comes close to a non-virtual object (such as a table). But this touch happens only on the level of Joi's conscious experience. The only "things" that make contact when Joi touches a non-virtual table are her virtual body and a virtual (and invisible) simulation of a table. We are grateful to Paul Smart for highlighting this issue.
7 For a demonstration, see https://www.youtube.com/watch?v=TCQbygjG0RU (last accessed 11 January 2018).
8 In a technical sense, we can say that Joi has significantly different counterfactual beliefs with respect to her own (virtual) body than about the (non-virtual) bodies in her environment, which reflect differences in the sensorimotor contingencies associated with virtual and non-virtual objects. See Seth (2014, 2015) for a discussion of this issue.
9 This may even provide us with a new metaphor for the pitfalls of ordinary, everyday social cognition. Old people often die a "social death" long before their biological death, because fewer and fewer human beings regard them as a resource or as an entity they would like to interact with. The frequency (or absence) of social interactions lets us perceive some people as absolutely real, alive, and relevant, while others become (or at least can seem) progressively less "real."
10 Note that we do not claim that Joi is not a real person. In fact, it could even be argued that having real self-experience is sufficient for personhood, but we remain neutral with respect to this.
11 Note that the picture becomes more complex if the geometric point of view is construed in terms of projective geometry (see Williford et al., 2018).
12 In other words, an attentional relation is a subtype of an intentional relation.
13 Similar considerations apply to the characters of Theodore and Samantha in the film *Her* (Spike Jonze, 2013).

References

Botvinick, M., & Cohen, J. (1998). Rubber Hands "Feel" Touch that Eyes See. *Nature* 391(6669), 756.
Chalmers, D. J. (2017). The Virtual and the Real. *Disputatio* 9(46), 309–352.
Clark, A. (2013). Expecting the World: Perception, Prediction, and the Origins of Human Knowledge. *The Journal of Philosophy* 110(9), 469–496.
Clark, A. (2016). *Surfing Uncertainty: Prediction, Action and the Embodied Mind.* New York: Oxford University Press.

Clark, A. (2018). Strange Inversions: Prediction and the Explanation of Conscious Experience. In B. Huebner (Ed.), *The Philosophy of Daniel Dennett* (pp. 202–218). New York: Oxford University Press.

Dennett, D. C. (1991). Real Patterns. *Journal of Philosophy* 88(1), 27–51.

Grush, R. (2004). The Emulation Theory of Representation: Motor Control, Imagery, and Perception. *Behavioral and Brain Sciences* 27(3), 377–396.

Hoffman, D. D., Singh, M., & Prakash, C. (2015). Probing the Interface Theory of Perception: Reply to Commentaries. *Psychonomic Bulletin & Review* 22(6), 1551–1576.

Hohwy, J. (2013). *The Predictive Mind*. Oxford: Oxford University Press.

Hohwy, J., & Michael, J. (2017). Why Should Any Body Have a Self? In F. de Vignemont & A. J. T. Alsmith (Eds.), *The Subject's Matter: Self-Consciousness and the Body* (pp. 363–391). Cambridge, MA: MIT Press.

Horn, B. K. P. (1980). Derivation of Invariant Scene Characteristics from Images. In *Proceedings of the May 19–22, 1980, National Computer Conference* (pp. 371–376). New York: Association of Computing Machinery.

Hoshi, T., Takahashi, M., Nakatsuma, K., & Shinoda, H. (2009). Touchable holography. In D. Wigdor (Ed.), *ACM SIGGRAPH 2009 Emerging Technologies*. New York: Association of Computing Machinery.

Jennings, C. D. (2015). Attention and Perceptual Organization. *Philosophical Studies*, 172(5), 1265–1278.

Jonze, S. (2013). Her. Burbank: Warner Bros Entertainment.

Kugler, L. (2015). Touching the Virtual. *Communications of the ACM* 58(8), 16–18.

Letheby, C., & Gerrans, P. (2017). Self Unbound: Ego Dissolution in Psychedelic Experience. *Neuroscience of Consciousness* 2017(1), 1–11.

Limanowski, J., & Blankenburg, F. (2013). Minimal Self-Models and the Free Energy Principle. *Frontiers in Human Neuroscience* 7 (Article 547), 1–12.

Metzinger, T. (2003). *Being No One: The Self-Model Theory of Subjectivity*. Cambridge, MA: MIT Press.

Metzinger, T. (2013). The Myth of Cognitive Agency: Subpersonal Thinking as a Cyclically Recurring Loss of Mental Autonomy. *Frontiers in Psychology* 4 (Article 931), 1–19.

Metzinger, T. (2018). Why Is Virtual Reality Interesting for Philosophers? *Frontiers in Robotics and AI* 5 (Article 101), 1–19.

Newen, A. (2018). The Embodied Self, the Pattern Theory of Self, and the Predictive Mind. *Frontiers in Psychology*, 9 (Article 2270), 1–14.

Revonsuo, A. (1995). Consciousness, Dreams and Virtual Realities. *Philosophical Psychology* 8(1), 35–58.

Seth, A. K. (2014). A Predictive Processing Theory of Sensorimotor Contingencies: Explaining the Puzzle of Perceptual Presence and its Absence in Synesthesia. *Cognitive Neuroscience* 5(2), 97–118.

Seth, A. K. (2015). Presence, Objecthood, and the Phenomenology of Predictive Perception. *Cognitive Neuroscience* 6(2–3), 111–117.

Watzl, S. (2017). *Structuring Mind: The Nature of Attention and How it Shapes Consciousness.* Oxford: Oxford University Press.

Wiese, W. (2018). *Experienced Wholeness: Integrating Insights from Gestalt Theory, Cognitive Neuroscience, and Predictive Processing.* Cambridge, MA: MIT Press.

Wiese, W. (in prep). Perception as Augmented Reality.

Wiese, W., & Metzinger, T. (2017). Vanilla PP for Philosophers: A Primer on Predictive Processing. In T. Metzinger & W. Wiese (Eds.), *Philosophy and Predictive Processing.* Frankfurt am Main: MIND Group.

Williford, K., Bennequin, D., Friston, K., & Rudrauf, D. (2018). The Projective Consciousness Model and Phenomenal Selfhood. *Frontiers in Psychology,* 9(Article 2571), 1–18.

Windt, J. M. (2015). *Dreaming: A Conceptual Framework for Philosophy of Mind and Empirical Research.* Cambridge, MA: MIT Press.

Chapter 9

Timothy Shanahan
HER EYES WERE GREEN
INTIMATE RELATIONSHIPS IN *BLADE RUNNER 2049*

Introduction

INTIMATE RELATIONSHIPS ARE THE BEATING heart of *Blade Runner 2049*. Take away the "miracle" born of Deckard and Rachael's love for one another, K and Joi's tender expressions of romantic affection (he calls her "honey," she calls him "babysweet"), and one of the most riveting (pre-)sex scenes in the history of cinema ("a perverse threesome, a loving twosome," in the words of screenwriter Hampton Fancher), and (if the film can still be imagined at all) we are essentially left with a thriller filled with stunning visual images, stirring music, eccentric characters, memorable dialogue, and some very cool technology—still a movie worth watching, perhaps, but certainly a less emotionally compelling one. Part of what makes BR2049's representations of intimate interpersonal relationships so engaging is that they concern what *prima facie* seem to be fundamentally different kinds of beings from one another: humans, replicants, and (maybe) a conscious, self-aware AI system. Questions naturally ensue: Can one really be (and/or believe oneself to be) in a romantic relationship with a mass-marketed consumer product that one knows has been designed to tell you "everything you want to hear"? Given his poignant longing for his long-dead companion, why does Deckard reject Wallace's offer of "An angel, made again, for you"? And who does K *really* have sex with in that rather unconventional *ménage à trois*?

My aim in this chapter is to explore in intimate relationships BR2049—especially romance, sex, and love—by addressing such questions. Although for any particular individual, romance, sex, and love may be confusingly intertwined, they are nonetheless distinct, if not always clearly distinguishable, experiences. I will treat them as a more or less distinct kind of *relationship*, *activity*, and *emotion*, respectively, in an attempt to lay bare the beating heart of BR2049.

I'm so happy when I'm with you

Attempting to provide necessary and sufficient conditions for each of the key notions we'll be exploring is likely to be a futile exercise; but we still need some working definitions to guide our discussions. For our purposes, *romance* may be understood as any freely chosen relationship involving mutual physical and emotional attraction to, and a desire to experience physical and emotional intimacy with, another person, as well as mutual efforts to realise such intimacy by performing acts intended to please and thereby enhance the other person's attraction to oneself.

Each clause in this rather elaborate description seems important. Romantic relationships always involve *another person*. You can't be in a genuine romantic relationship *with yourself*, or with some *insentient object* (like a toaster), or with an *abstract idea* (like rectangularity), or even with some animate being that isn't a *person* (like one's pet iguana, no matter how adorable it might be). Whether the other person must be *human* is a distinct matter. In addition, you can't be in a romantic *relationship* with someone who has absolutely no awareness of you, no physical or emotional attraction to you, or no interest in pleasing you and enhancing their attractiveness to you. For instance, you can't be in a romantic relationship with a movie star who couldn't pick you out of a police lineup (although you could be in a *stalking* relationship with them). Nor could you be in a bona fide romantic relationship with somebody who finds you irredeemably repulsive. A romantic relationship that is simply *unknown* to the other person is an oxymoron, as is one that is *completely* unrequited. Unlike sex and love, romantic relationships are necessarily *bivalent*—they require the (not necessarily equal) participation of both individuals. Of course, one could *believe* oneself to be in a romantic relationship that, in fact, no longer exists (because, for example, unbeknownst to you it has just been unilaterally terminated by the other person). One could believe oneself to be in a romantic relationship that never existed in the first place (e.g. because it was merely an elaborate fantasy). But in such cases the belief in question would be sadly *mistaken*.

The most fleshed out (so to speak) romance in BR2049 is between K and Joi—an artificial intelligence enhanced with a holographic avatar, marketed as a customisable digital companion. K is obviously quite taken by her; we never see him alone at home when he doesn't choose to make her present as well. It is also obvious that he wants to please her. He spends the hard-earned bonus money he garnered by retiring Sapper Morton on a special anniversary (even though he admits it isn't) present—an emanator that permits Joi to go anywhere, including the rooftop terrace of their apartment building where they share a tender moment together—until, that is, K receives an incoming call from his boss, which rains on their special time together.

K's affection for Joi appears to be reciprocated. Joi's every action seems intended to please him—for example, by asking him about his day, making him "dinner," rapidly changing her appearance to suit his mood, and encouraging his growing belief that he is special. On the other hand, as an AI system it is unclear whether Joi is truly *conscious*, much less capable of experiencing romantic attraction. As Ana de Armas, the actress who plays Joi, explains, "Joi is a companion of the future. She is designed to please everyone's fantasy, and K is asking her to be rational, autonomous, but also emotional. He wants her to be a real human, because that's what he needs. It's a constant battle for her. She's learning as quickly as possible, how to be like a real girl. But she's not" (Lapointe, 2017: 90). To be clear, Joi's candidacy as a romantic partner is not called into question because she fails to qualify as a physical thing. Nor is it called into question because she fails to qualify as real. Joi is, in fact, perfectly real, that is, a perfectly real hologram-augmented AI system. She is also quite obviously a physical being. Her physicality consists in the hardware supporting her as an artificial intelligence entity, as well as her three-dimensional avatar, which is also a *physical* thing (it is visible, after all). But she lacks a corporeal body of the sort humans possess. So, the issue here isn't her reality or physicality, but rather whether a being *of that sort*—that is, an AI—can be physically and/or emotionally attracted to another person.

This issue merits some consideration. As noted above, participating in a romantic relationship seems to require, at a minimum, that one be a *person*. The seventeenth-century English philosopher (and lover of commas), John Locke, famously and influentially defined a *person* as "a thinking intelligent being, that has reason and reflection, and can consider itself as itself, the same thinking thing, in different times and places."[1] Can an artificial intelligence be a *person* in this Lockean sense? Can Joi? Granted, Joi *behaves* as if she is a person. Whether that is sufficient to *be* a "thinking intelligent being" remains controversial. Assuming that Joi *is* a person in the Lockean sense allows us to explore the issues in this chapter in greater depth, so for the remainder of this discussion I will accept that she *is* such a being. But more is still needed.

A romantic relationship, as defined above, also requires that the relationship be freely chosen. We like to think that our romantic partners *choose* to consort with us because they recognise, value, and are attracted to some personal characteristics that set us apart from others. Yet one wonders whether Joi's behaviour toward K is just a feature of her programming. In ubiquitous advertisements, "joi" is marketed as telling you "everything you want to hear." K's Joi has been customised by him to approximate his ideal of feminine beauty, to provide a sense of domestic quasi-normalcy, perhaps even to bolster his self-esteem (which, frankly, needs a lot of help). So, if Joi's expressions of romantic interest in K are simply a function of her programming, she hasn't freely chosen K at all; she's simply done what her programming required her to do.

On the other hand, some have suggested that, despite being an AI, Joi is able (either by design or otherwise) to *transcend* her programming. BR2049 screenwriter Hampton Fancher says that although Joi's responses *are* programmed, nevertheless, "Through her attachment [to K], she becomes real to herself, and her love for him becomes real, as opposed to programmed. So she escapes her own limitations, the digital limitations, and becomes totally real for herself."[2] Tanya Lapointe (2017: 90) concurs: "By wanting Joi to be real, K is challenging the technology to form its own opinions and have a mind of its own, which propels Joi into a completely different dimension." Perhaps Joi has transcended her programming and has acquired *free will*. From another perspective, however, this might be setting the bar too high. After all, we enter into romantic relationships, yet it is not self-evident that we possess the sort of metaphysical liberty required to transcend our programming. Confident claims to the contrary notwithstanding, no one knows for sure whether determinism (roughly, the thesis that all events, including all human actions, are causally necessitated) is true. And yet, romance blossoms and grows all around us.

K's problem is different, albeit a familiar one. One of the basic challenges of finding a satisfying romantic relationship is that typically one has to compromise between what one wants and what one is able to get. Pursuing someone out of one's league is more often a recipe for frustration than it is for subsequent self-congratulation. One might suppose that being able to purchase a romantic partner that one can customise to match one's exact physical preferences, thereby bridging the gap between desire and reality (at least in that limited respect), would be a godsend. Moreover, acquiring a romantic partner who, no matter what your considerable flaws and faults might be, necessarily finds you to be utterly irresistible, might seem like one's wildest dream come true.

Alas, matters are seldom so simple. In a genuine romantic relationship, it is not enough that the other person has freely entered into the relationship and sincerely expresses loving feelings. As William James recognised over a century ago, one also has to *believe* that these two conditions have been satisfied. In a footnote in his 1909 book, *The Meaning of Truth*, he identifies what he considers to be the most important inherent limitation of what he charmingly calls an "automatic sweetheart"—that is, "a soulless body which should be absolutely indistinguishable from a spiritually animated maiden, laughing, talking, blushing, nursing us, and performing all feminine offices as tactfully and sweetly as if a soul were in her" (James, 1909: 189; by "a soul" James means a mind). Could anyone consider such a being to be the full equivalent of a real female sweetheart companion? James thinks not:

> Because, framed as we are, our egoism craves above all things inward sympathy and recognition, love and admiration. The outward treatment is valued mainly as an expression, as a manifestation of the accompanying consciousness believed in. Pragmatically, then, belief in the automatic sweetheart would not work.
>
> (James, 1909: 189)

What is important in James's view is not, primarily, that the automatic sweetheart lacks a mind, but rather that the would-be recipient of its affections knows or believes this. *That* is the fact that undermines the sense of being loved for oneself, rather than automatically as a matter of design.

If James is right, then K's belief that he is in a romantic relationship with Joi crucially depends upon him *believing* that she has chosen him freely. But how can he believe *that*, given what he knows (e.g. from the ubiquitous marketing he encounters) about her essential purpose and programming? Obviously, we can have a romantic partner who is free (if anyone is) and who *will* (as a matter of fact) continue to choose us. If compatibilists on the free-will issue are right, then it is also true that we can have a romantic partner who is free (in the sense of doing what they want, or even in the sense of doing what they want to want) and who nevertheless *cannot but choose us* (e.g. because we live in a deterministic universe that precludes any other genuine possibility). But it is unclear that we can be in a romantic relationship with a partner *whom we know* (or *believe*) *can never but choose and desire us*, for the reasons discussed above.

The only workable solutions to this problem, so far as I can tell, are doxastic variations on the two solutions to the first issue (i.e., free will) discussed above in connection with Joi. Either (1) K has good reason to *believe* that Joi has transcended her programming, and thus freely chooses to be in a romantic relationship with him; or (2) K reflects on the fact that even if determinism is true, that doesn't automatically negate the possibility of a romantic relationship between himself and Joi, any more than it does for any two humans in a more conventional romantic relationship. Which, if either, of those two solutions is fully adequate, I must leave to the reader to decide.

Thought you weren't interested, worky man

Consider a (deceptively) straightforward claim: Joi hires Mariette, a replicant prostitute, so that K can have sex with her. Right. But *which* her (or maybe *hers*) does K really have sex with?

It depends. In a straightforward physical sense, it seems obvious that K has sex with *Mariette*. After all, their two physical bodies come together in the carnal act.[3] The BR2049 shooting script describes Joi as: "Ingeniously real in every way except the one that counts." That one way is, of course, being physical, corporeal, tangible. Mariette is real in a way that Joi is not, a fact that Joi herself acknowledges to K: "She's real. I want to be real for you." Thus, on this view K has sex with Mariette but *not* with Joi who, after all, lacks the requisite physicality required for that act.

That's not the only way to look at it, however. Mackenzie Davis, the actress who plays Mariette, says that, "Mariette has this strange out-of-body experience when Joi hires her as a sex surrogate. As a hologram, she [i.e., Joi] can superimpose herself upon Mariette to have an actual sexual relationship with K" (Lapointe, 2017: 94). In this view, Mariette becomes dissociated in some sense from her body while K and Joi have sex. Mariette then becomes an observer rather than a participant. (Is it an accident that "Mariette" is just two letters away from "marionette"— that is, a puppet designed for the enjoyment of others?) One can imagine that in her line of work she has had plenty of previous opportunities to practice and master such experiential dissociation.

This interpretation suggests an alternative. If sex is understood to be an essentially *subjective experience*, then perhaps Joi *literally* has sex with K, and Mariette doesn't, despite the fact that Joi lacks a physical body and Mariette's body is right there in the thick of things, as it were. The initial oddness of this view can be mitigated somewhat by noting that some philosophers are, implicitly at least, committed to a view not unlike this. *Substance dualists* maintain that human beings consist of two substances (i.e., metaphysically fundamental entities that can exist independently of one another), namely, an immaterial soul and a material body, that nonetheless causally interact with one another. The former is the *person*; the latter is rather akin to a vehicle. Consequently, when two persons have sex, their bodies are merely the material intermediaries by which the respective subjective experiences are mediated. In the scene in question, then, Mariette's body would be simply a proxy by which Joi and K have sex with one another.

A variation on this interpretation, inspired by developments in cognitive neuroscience and grounded in an evolutionary understanding of the most basic purpose of minds (with a nod to Immanuel Kant), suggests that all conscious experiences of the external world (including of our own and others' bodies) are a form of *controlled hallucination* arising from the evolved brain's attempt to gain a predictive toehold over incoming sensory information.[4] We may perceive our bodies to be a part of the external world, but according to this view it may be more accurate to say that our bodies, like all other material objects (as experienced) exist solely in our minds.

Both of the views sketched above—the substance dualist and predictive processing views—tend to diminish any difference between K and Joi's sexual encounter and run-of-the-mill human sex. All human sex, in both of these views, is fundamentally a person-to-person connection using physical bodies, or mental representations thereof, as intermediaries that are not really them. So perhaps Mackenzie Davis is right after all: Joi *does* have an actual sexual relationship with K.

On the other hand, the conceptions of souls or minds upon which that conclusion rests are not without their problems. Substance dualism has been under siege in philosophy ever since it was given its classic statement and defence by René Descartes in the seventeenth century.[5] Specifically, it seems hard to reconcile that view with what we think we've learned about the brain and cognition. Moreover, it has limited value for understanding sex more *generally*. After all, *most* sex is between non-persons. It seems gratuitous to suppose that when armadillos have sex (don't linger too long on that mental image unless, of course, you want to) they are merely using their bodies as vehicles. So far as we know, there are no persons there. So, when armadillos have sex, it's just *armadillos* getting it on. So, it is for anteaters, bobcats, caimans, dingos, echidnas, and so forth.

The more scientific predictive processing view fares better in this regard, but may struggle to escape from the solipsistic conclusion that, when it comes right down to it, each of us only ever encounters, in sex or otherwise, our own utterly private subjective experiences, thereby making genuine intimacy with another person seem like a quixotic quest necessarily destined to fail.

Be that as it may, it is not difficult to imagine what that singular sexual encounter might have meant for K and Joi. No doubt it supplied a formerly missing dimension that increased the depth of their emotional bond. It is therefore easy to overlook or downplay what it might have meant for *Mariette*. On a pragmatic level, Joi's solicitation of her services must have seemed like a gift, not just to K, but to Mariette as well, given the fact that she was under the direction of Freysa, the elusive leader of the replicant resistance. That service call allowed her to plant a device in K's coat pocket that permitted the resistance movement to track him in his search for Deckard.

One can also try to imagine what that encounter meant for Mariette on a personal level. For good reason, Mariette tends to disappear in that scene; and yet through the imperfection of the sync we are subtly reminded that she is still there. It is not difficult to suppose that as K is having (or imagining, depending on one's view) *sex* with Joi, Mariette is imagining what it must be like to be *deeply loved* by someone in the way that K loves Joi. Referring to Mariette in that scene, the shooting script notes that under the "skin of light" that is Joi, "She feels his lips on hers, sees the look on his face, and is moved by a depth of love she never tasted before, didn't know was real." As K and Joi are experiencing virtual lovemaking, Mariette is experiencing virtual love. We don't know what effect that singular experience had on her, or how, if at all, it changed her. She was, after all, still a pleasure model, with a job that doesn't encourage emotional attachment.

I'm done with you

The morning after that sexual encounter, Joi summarily dismisses Mariette, telling her, "I'm done with you. You can go." The doxie had served her singular purpose and was no longer needed. Mariette mockingly retorts, perhaps ironically given the previous night's activities, "Quiet now. I've been inside you. Not so much there as you think." "Back on her hard mode," as the shooting script says, and having planted a tracking device in K's coat pocket, she leaves the apartment.

That brief exchange constitutes a microcosm of sorts for the way in which some critics have viewed BR2049's treatment of women. Immediately upon (and in some cases even before) its theatrical release, accusations began to appear complaining that the film celebrates sexist portrayals of women. Sara Stewart, writing in the *New York Post*, wrote: "If you have two X chromosomes, or know and like someone who does, 'Blade Runner 2049' may not be the movie for you." In her viewing, Joi is presented as little more than "a sci-fi fanboy's wet dream."[6] Another critic declared the film to be "a misogynistic mess" in which the female characters "are either prostitutes or holographic housewives."[7] Even some critics who otherwise loved the film understood how it could be criticised as sexist and misogynistic, and wondered aloud, "How are we supposed to admire a hero [i.e., K] whose key relationship is with a woman of his own creation who will submit to his every demand and can be switched on and off as he pleases?"[8]

It is easy to see why some critics responded so negatively. The world depicted in the film is filled with lurid and degrading sexist images that represent females (whether human, replicant, or holographic) as mere commodities of significance only for their erotic value to male consumers. Joi *does* seem like a futuristic male fantasy sexbot. Several of the female replicants we see *are* dolled-up prostitutes. When K walks through a rust-coloured landscape toward an almost-entirely abandoned Las Vegas, he is framed between statues of two bare-breasted—but high-heeled—women on their knees with heads thrown back, their facial expressions suggesting that they are in the throes of orgasm. By contrast, male characters are *not* presented in highly sexualised ways. No males in the film (not even K, played by heartthrob Ryan Gosling) are represented as erotic commodities. No "Boi" or other-named male counterpart to Joi appears in the film (although the existence of such a counterpart is alluded to in the shooting script). Ironically, even Joi treats the only other female we see her interacting with to any significant degree as having value solely for her sexual appeal. Perhaps the film's critics have a point.

I take my freedom where I can find it

Not to put too fine a point on it, *no, they don't*. First, such facile criticisms miss the mark by misunderstanding the film's *purpose* in depicting a sexist and misogynistic society, and indeed of cinematic representations of dystopian societies more generally. Creating a fictional dystopia to *exhibit* the ills of a sexist society is hardly sexist; indeed, it is an overt *criticism* of such a society. BR2049 presents us with—and thereby *critiques*—a world in which many females (human, replicant, or holographic) have been reduced (or, in the case of Luv, Mariette, and Joi, created) to play subservient or secondary roles in relation to men. The blatant, *in-your-face* representation of women as *less* is meant to caution anyone even vaguely familiar with dystopian literature or films that such an undesirable future may await *us*—unless we make sure it doesn't.

Second, even a cursory consideration of the most prominent female characters in BR2049 demonstrates that, rather than *endorsing* sexist and misogynistic values, the film showcases the power of women to forge their own identities in a world in which men typically control the levers of power, as the following necessarily incomplete survey of such characters shows.

The shooting script describes Dr. Ana Stelline (the only character in the film presented as having scaled the summit of educational achievement) when we first meet her in her lab: "Younger than you'd expect given all this is hers, 30s. But so very obviously so very bright you never question why. A stratospheric IQ with eyes that do not hide it." She is a free-lance memory designer who refuses to compromise her autonomy in exchange for the security (and danger to her integrity) of being on Wallace's payroll, telling K, "I take my freedom where I can find it." Indeed, she is willing, at some risk to herself, to skirt the law by endowing some replicants with genuine memories. Moreover, there is nothing overtly sexualised about her. Instead, she is presented as animated by a Buddha-like love for all sentient beings, be they human or replicant.

The shooting script chillingly describes Luv, Wallace's brutal enforcer, as "Polite, efficient. Perfect. Moral as a tornado and about as safe. Beautiful, yes. The way a sword can be if it's safely behind glass." She is the film's *femme fatale*, who not only exhibits great physical strength (recall the scene in which she effortlessly pulls open a jammed archive door), but also ruthlessly dispatches anyone (e.g. Coco, Lt. Joshi) who stands in her way. It is true that she is in thrall to Wallace, and there is perhaps a hint that her work for him involves personal services beyond those that we see in the film. But she is also presented as someone who is not afraid to take the initiative without Wallace's direct instruction when she sees what needs to be done.

Lt. Joshi is presented as a no-nonsense, unsentimental, tough-as-nails law enforcement officer who does not hesitate to tell K (her male subordinate) to do whatever it takes to avert the collapse of the wall separating humans and replicants. We can speculate about the diamond-hard personal qualities that permitted her to earn her leadership position in the LAPD. When Luv, whom we can presume she knows to be *extremely* dangerous, pays her an unwelcome visit, she refuses to divulge information concerning K's whereabouts, despite knowing full well that her resistance almost certainly portends a painful death. Yet the film also allows us to see her momentarily let down her guard with K, revealing vulnerability beneath that hard exterior.

We know relatively little about the one-eyed replicant resistance movement leader, Freysa, except that (thanks to the computer screen in

K's spinner) her full name is Freysa Sadeghpour, and she is a NEXUS 8 replicant (incept date: 21 DEC 2020) who served off-world on Calantha with Sapper Morton as a combat engineer. She appears in the photograph next to the tree on Sapper Morton's farm, holding the miracle child swaddled in a blanket, and was responsible for hiding the child and scrambling the records. We are encouraged to believe that she had her serial-numbered right eye removed to prevent her identification. *Perhaps she did it herself.*

Utterly unintimidated by K, whom she knows to be a blade runner with legal authority to kill replicants, Mariette is the assertive, streetwise, self-possessed doxie who is secretly working for the replicant resistance movement. Despite being a replicant prostitute, she never shows even the slightest indication that she thinks of herself as one whit *less* than anyone else she encounters.

And then there's Joi. The shooting script describes her the moment she first appears onscreen as: "Goddess, girlfriend, geisha and, right now, goddamn bombshell." That description is spot-on, so far as it goes. But one of her most remarkable attributes (besides the fact that she exists at all) is that she appears to *evolve* as a sentient being over the course of, and perhaps in response to, her interactions with K and other corporeal beings. At first, she does indeed appear to be little more than a fantasy 1950s-era stay-at-home housewife, whose only desire is to please her hard-working hubby. But as the film progresses, we see her manifesting more and more sophisticated behaviours including, toward the end of her existence, asserting her own desires in the face of K's resistance, and even ultimately sacrificing herself "like a real girl" for something *she* believes in. Describing her as a sci-fi fanboy's wet dream or merely a holographic housewife fails to do justice to the sort of being Joi *becomes* over the span of the film.

Consequently, a *first glance* at BR2049 may suggest a film that is insensitive to the sexist and misogynistic motifs that populate its cinematic universe. But even a slightly more penetrating and charitable examination of the film demonstrates exactly the *opposite* conclusion, namely, that those sexist and misogynistic motifs pervade the film in order to expose them to social and ethical critique. Far from being a misogynistic mess, BR2049 is a dystopian masterpiece.

Don't you love me?

An old movie title observes that, "Love is a Many-Splendored Thing." Indeed, it is. Science-fiction writer Robert A. Heinlein's definition expresses an important insight into the nature of *one* sort of love: "Love is that condition in which the happiness of another person is essential to your own."[9] Let's call love of this sort *empathic love*. Empathic love is distinct from ethical altruism, where the latter is understood to be an other-regarding behaviour undertaken despite the awareness that it imposes a net cost upon the agent. By contrast, empathic love treats another's happiness as integral to one's own; self-sacrifice is not required. It seems perfectly possible to experience love in this sense simultaneously toward any number of other persons. Indeed, it might be possible to be in that condition in relation to *all* sentient beings that are capable of experiencing happiness of one sort or another—as Dr. Ana Stelline appears to be.

We also need an account of the sort of love one feels in relation to a particular, *specific* person, love that is conditioned by what are perceived to be that individual's unique characteristics. Cheshire Calhoun (2009: 637–638) helpfully suggests that: "To love a particular person ... is to see one's love as both grounded in some valuable features and as responsive to a specialness that is not fully explained by appeal to what are, after all, repeatable (and thus not special-making) valuable features." Such love is characterised by a special affection for a specific person because of what is perceived to be the *unique* realisation in that person of a cluster of desirable attributes. Many others might, and presumably will, have *some* of those features. After all, there are (one might suppose) only so many ways of being a person. It is even conceivable that more than one person could manifest the *same* cluster of desirable attributes. But love of this sort may still be reserved for one particular, perhaps historically unique, individual. Sometimes such love arises in the context of a desire for a romantic relationship with a particular person. Let's call love of this sort *erotic love*. No doubt there are other sorts of love as well; but these two sorts—empathic love and erotic love—will serve our purposes here. Both play important roles in BR2049.[10]

Sometimes to love someone, you've got to be a stranger

K and Joi share empathic love that is no doubt related to, yet arguably is distinct from, their romantic attraction to one another. Apart from his interactions with Joi, all of K's interactions with others are transactional. He drops in on Sapper Morton ... to kill him. He appears in Lt. Joshi's office to receive orders from her. He seeks out Ana Stelline and Deckard to acquire information from them. K's relationship with Joi *began* as a transaction. Sometime before the action in BR2049 begins, he spent some of his hard-earned money to purchase a generic "joi" produced by the Wallace Corporation. But by the time we join them, K and Joi have entered into a reciprocal relationship based on mutual care and affection—a relationship of empathic love. Joi is the recipient of K's affection, and gifts. Apart from asking to be treated like a real girl, she asks nothing of him. K treats Joi as a sentient being capable of happiness and unhappiness, and strives to support the former. His gift of an emanator is intended to bring her joy as much as it is to permit him to enjoy her company beyond the confines of their apartment; the two intentions need not be mutually exclusive. As already noted, Joi's every action seems, by design, intended to enhance K's sense of well-being (not an easy task, under the circumstances), whether it be by wearing a mood-appropriate outfit, fixing him an appealing (virtual) meal, or hiring a surrogate to provide an opportunity for him to have sex with her. However, the most dramatic example of her empathic love for K appears when she pleads with him to break the antenna, thus deleting her from the console in their apartment and thereby making her entire fragile existence contingent upon the emanator—a risk whose very real mortal dangers are later made manifest.

A less obvious example of empathic love concerns Luv and Wallace. At first glance, the ironically named Luv is one of the most chillingly brutal characters in the film (as we see, for example, when she coolly dispatches the hapless Coco). She is surpassed in this regard only by her creator, Niander Wallace. Luv at least gets moist-eyed when Wallace callously guts his latest "Angel," who in his view is nothing more than a painful reminder of his inability to emulate Tyrell's feat of creating a procreative replicant. Nonetheless, despite Luv's icy demeanour, it seems clear that in addition to being in awe of Wallace, his happiness is also essential to her own. How else to explain her utter devotion to helping him realise his vision of planetary conquest, and eliminating any threat thereto? (Although her own life and safety no doubt directly depend on being Wallace's faithful enforcer.) In this case, however, whatever empathic love exists between them is decidedly one-sided. The film gives us no reason to suppose that Wallace's happiness is in any way dependent upon that of his "best angel." She is, like everything else in Wallace's world, simply a disposable instrument useful for realising his grandiose ambitions.

Perhaps the most powerful example of empathic love is Deckard's love for his daughter. He explicitly appeals to the demands of love when he explains to K why he left prior to the birth of his and Rachael's child: "Sometimes to love someone, you've got to be a stranger." Although this might seem to suggest that Deckard deliberately chose his daughter's happiness *over* his own, it seems equally reasonable to suppose that he understood that, given the dangers involved, satisfying his natural parental desire to raise his child was incompatible with his own long-term happiness, and he accordingly made a painful but necessary choice that would vouchsafe, so far as possible, both his and his child's happiness, such as they are. Deckard's love for the child he never met was equalled only by his love for the soulmate he would never see again.

Her eyes were green

Ironically, perhaps, the two characters who are considered by others in the film to be decidedly less than human are also the two characters most interested in cultivating a loving, human bond. The film strongly suggests that K and Joi's efforts to please one another include, but go beyond, merely the desire to win one another's affections. They are also expressions of their empathic *and* erotic love for one another. As a blade runner, whose very life depends on passing tests designed to detect increased affectivity, K knows that he cannot afford to become emotionally vulnerable or expressive. Yet every indication is that he is utterly smitten with Joi. The shooting script explicitly describes K as "in love" with her, and that whatever Joi was—digital fantasy or an evolved personality—"he loved her as true." As already noted, in the scene in which Joi and Mariette sync, "Mariette sees the look on his face and is moved by a depth of love she never tasted before, didn't know was real." That love was engendered by Joi, his digital lover.

Whether Joi loved K is a more difficult question. She certainly behaved as if she did. Her every action could be interpreted as an act of love toward him, culminating in her plea that K delete her from the console, thereby making it more difficult to track his whereabouts, but also making her existence precariously dependent upon a mere handheld gadget. As the emanator is about to be crushed under Luv's boot, Joi manages to blurt out, "I love y—" before disappearing, forever. Whether Joi can actually feel love or is simply programmed to behave as if she does, is of course one of the unanswered questions the film pointedly raises but does not answer. Some may doubt that she can actually love. According to what Sherry Turkle (2010: 4) calls the "romantic reaction" to AI, simulated thinking might be thinking, but simulated feelings are never feelings, and therefore simulated love is never love. If experiencing love, or any emotion for that matter, involves more than mere cognition—for example, if it has a neurobiological basis—then, being inorganic, Joi might not be able to experience that or any other emotion. Again, we just don't know enough about the full extent of Joi's capabilities, programmed or otherwise.

Whether Rachael loved Deckard may be even more problematic. Late in the first film, Deckard pointedly asks her, "Do you love me?" She responds, rather woodenly, "I love you." But one has to wonder about the conditions under which that profession of love was issued (or extracted). Previously, we saw Deckard putting the words he wanted to hear into her mouth (e.g. "Say 'kiss me … I want you'"), with Rachael trepidatiously complying each time. Asking "Do you love me?" under the circumstances—Rachael knew that her only chance for survival was to flee with Deckard—may not be all that different. We also have to wonder whether, at that point, she was experienced enough to be able to recognise what was for her a novel, subjective experience *as* love (something that even those with much more life experience often find difficult). It might seem downright miserly of us to deny her this most cherished of human emotions. But we have to remember that, in November 2019, when the action in *Blade Runner* takes place, Rachael is only a year-and-a-half old.[11] Like all replicants, her emotional development lagged behind her physical and cognitive abilities. Did Rachael love Deckard? Maybe. We just don't know.

We have more evidence upon which to judge whether Deckard loved Rachael. Although in *Blade Runner* we never witness Deckard verbally expressing his love for her, and we have few details of their brief time together after those elevator doors closed, it becomes evident in BR2049 that Deckard's love for Rachael was both genuine and enduring. He continued to cherish her memory for almost thirty years after her death. He keeps a framed photo of her. He is deeply moved by seeing Rachael's skull, and is visibly shaken when Wallace tempts him with a reborn "Rachael" to entice him to divulge information about the whereabouts of his daughter.

That last scene merits further consideration. Why does Deckard reject Wallace's offer? The reason he gives—"Her eyes were green"—implies that he rejects the offer because Wallace failed to perfectly duplicate one of Rachael's most notable physical characteristics. But that interpretation is deeply unsatisfying. For one thing, Rachael's eyes were brown.[12] For another, were Wallace to respond to Deckard's comment by offering to manufacture another such Rachael for him with green eyes, Deckard almost certainly would have been dumbfounded by Wallace's obtuseness. No doubt part of the correct explanation is that Deckard was unwilling to selfishly barter away his daughter's safety and was throwing the attempted bribe back in Wallace's face, informing him in no uncertain terms, "I can't be bought." He may also have been exploiting the fact that Wallace didn't know what colour eyes Rachael had by saying, in effect, "You may be a genius, but you're not as smart or as skilled as you think you are, since you can't even replicate all of Rachael's features"—all the while knowing that her eye colour was irrelevant.[13] All that might be true. But one can imagine Deckard rejecting the offer even if it didn't require divulging any information about his daughter, even if this Rachael was physically indistinguishable from the original, and even if (let us suppose) she was gifted with implanted veridical memories of their time together.

The key to understanding this scene is to recognise that it is about *personal identity*, and that identity comes in two varieties. Two things are said to be *qualitatively identical* to one another if they are completely indistinguishable from one another. Two brand-new copies of this book are likely to be identical in this sense inasmuch as each contains precisely the same words in the same order. Nonetheless, there are still two distinct objects in this case. Buy a second copy for another BR2049 fan and your own precious copy remains firmly in your possession. By contrast, *numerical identity* can only hold between a thing and itself. The director of

Arrival (2016) and the director of *Blade Runner 2049* (2017) are numerically identical because they are the very same individual. Despite the fact that the 2017 version of Denis Villeneuve may have a set of properties somewhat different than the 2016 version, "they" are still just *one person*.

A related distinction concerns *replication* vs. *recreation*. To *replicate* an object is to produce a (more or less) *qualitatively identical* copy of that thing. Photocopy machines excel at such feats of replication. By contrast, to *recreate* an object is to bring back into existence an object that had formerly ceased to exist, where the object brought back into existence is *numerically identical* to the object that had ceased to exist. Whereas mere replication is often a rather pedestrian affair, recreation, in the view of some philosophers, is not just difficult, it is *metaphysically impossible*.

Peter van Inwagen (1978) argues for this claim with the help of an illuminating story. Suppose that the monks in a certain monastery claim to have in their possession a manuscript written by St. Augustine himself—that is, a manuscript that actually felt the impress of the Bishop of Hippo's stylus as he composed *De Civitate Dei*. Suppose that they then remarked that *this very manuscript* was burned to a cinder by Arians in 457 AD, but God then miraculously *recreated* that very manuscript for them in 458 AD. Van Inwagen notes that the event the monks purport to describe is impossible even for an omnipotent deity. God could certainly *duplicate* the lost manuscript; but not even God could bring back into existence (i.e., recreate) the very object that had been a part of the furniture of the world while St. Augustine had been alive, but later was destroyed.

What is impossible for God is, *a fortiori*, impossible for Wallace as well. He presented this "Rachael" to Deckard as "An angel, *made again*, for you." But Deckard recognised that no matter how *indistinguishable* from the original this ersatz Rachael might be, it could never *be* the original, and therefore necessarily would lack something essential, something crucial. This new Rachael asks Deckard: "Did you miss me? Don't you love me?" But Deckard knows that the *me* standing before him is not the same *me* that was his longed-for soulmate. The Rachael he loved could be *replicated*, but never *recreated*. Wallace didn't (and perhaps couldn't) grasp that it wasn't a replicable cluster of abstract Rachael properties that was the object of Deckard's enduring love. It was the singular, special, irreplaceable person, *Rachael* in her unreplicable "distinctive particularity" (as Nyholm & Frank, 2017, call it). Once that person was gone, she was, necessarily, never again—forever.[14] Eldon Tyrell was more right than he knew when he told Deckard, "Rachael is special." In the specific metaphysical sense at issue here, we all are.

Notes

1. John Locke (1689/1975), *An Essay Concerning Human Understanding*, Vol. One, Book II, Chapter XXVII, Section 11.
2. Fancher's comments appear in *Blade Runner 101: Jois* (note the plural), a bonus feature included with the BR2049 DVD/Blu-Ray. It is not entirely clear how Joi could escape her real (as opposed to merely apparent) limitations. Joi's "digital limitations" could hardly be genuine *limitations* if she succeeded in transcending them. A different reading of Fancher's remarks would be to say that Joi's basic capabilities themselves evolved through her interactions with K.
3. Of course, this way of putting it glosses over the very real difficulties involved in determining the conditions under which two persons—or a person and a non-person, for that matter—may be correctly said to "have sex." See Migotti and Wyatt (2017) for an insightful discussion of some of the difficulties of pinning down the nature of sex, including sex involving artificial creations.
4. For discussion, see "Androids dream of virtual sheep," by Wanja Wiese and Thomas K. Metzinger (chapter 8).
5. Descartes's *Discourse on Method* (1637) and *Meditations on First Philosophy* (1641) remain the *loci classici* for Cartesian substance dualism (see Descartes, 1998).
6. Sara Stewart, "You'll Love the New 'Blade Runner'—Unless You're a Woman," *New York Post* (October 4, 2017). https://nypost.com/2017/10/04/youll-love-the-new-blade-runner-unless-youre-a-woman/ [accessed February 14, 2019].
7. Charlotte Gush, "Why Blade Runner 2049 is a Misogynistic Mess," I-D (October 9, 2017). https://i-d.vice.com/en_uk/article/evpwga/blade-runner-2049-sexist-misogynistic-mess [accessed February 14, 2019].
8. Anna Smith, "Is *Blade Runner 2049* Sexist—or a Fair Depiction of a Dystopian Future?" *The Guardian* (October 9, 2017). https://www.theguardian.com/film/2017/oct/09/is-blade-runner-2049-a-sexist-film-or-a-fair-depiction-of-a-dystopic-future [accessed February 14, 2019].
9. Robert A. Heinlein (1987), *A Stranger in a Strange Land* (New York: Ace Books), p. 363. Originally published in 1961 by G. P. Putnam's Sons.
10. For an alternative (and insightful) discussion of love in BR2049, see Tambone (2018).
11. In BR2049, Rachael's serial number is revealed to be N7FAA523, indicating that she is a NEXUS 7 female with A-level physical and mental abilities, with an incept date of May 23, 2018.

12 At least, Rachael's eyes are brown throughout most of *Blade Runner*. An exception is when Deckard is administering the Voight-Kampff test to her, where her eyes *do* appear green(ish). It is implausible to suppose that Deckard would remember only what her eyes looked like *then* and not throughout the rest of their time together.

13 Nonetheless, this scene remains puzzling. Wallace had access to the recording of the Voight-Kampff test with Rachael, so he must have known that her eyes were green(ish). At the same time, he had access to her skeletal remains and thus was perhaps able to infer from her genetic makeup that her eye color was brown. Perhaps what he was missing was the way that Rachael was *perceived* by Deckard. Wallace could create Rachael as she was, but not how she existed in Deckard's memory. Thanks to Paul Smart for bringing these details to my attention.

14 As Nigel Shadbolt and Paul Smart point out in "The eyes of God" (chapter 11), K faces a similar situation with regard to his Joi.

References

Calhoun, C. (2009). What Good is Commitment? *Ethics* 119(4), 613–641.

Descartes, R. (1998). *Discourse on Method and Meditations on First Philosophy* (D. A. Cress, Trans. 4th ed.). Indianapolis, IN: Hackett Publishing.

James, W. (1909). *The Meaning of Truth*. New York: Longmans, Green.

Lapointe, T. (2017). *The Art and Soul of Blade Runner 2049*. Los Angeles: Alcon Entertainment.

Locke, J. (1689/1975). *An Essay Concerning Human Understanding*. Oxford: Clarendon Press.

Migotti, M., & Wyatt, N. (2017). On the Very Idea of Sex with Robots. In J. Danaher & N. McArthur (Eds.), *Robot Sex: Social and Ethical Implications* (pp. 15–27). Cambridge, MA: MIT Press.

Nyholm, S., & Frank, L. E. (2017). From Sex Robots to Love Robots: Is Mutual Love with a Robot Possible? In J. Danaher & N. McArthur (Eds.), *Robot Sex: Social and Ethical Implications* (pp. 219–243). Cambridge, MA: MIT Press.

Tambone, L. (2018). Looking for Love in Cyberpunk Places: Examining Love in Blade Runner 2049. In L. Tambone & J. Bongiorno (Eds.), *The Cyberpunk Nexus: Exploring the Blade Runner Universe* (pp. 375–394). Edwardsville, IL: Sequart Organization.

Turkle, S. (2010). In Good Company? On the Threshold of Robotic Companions. In Y. Wilks (Ed.), *Close Engagements with Artificial Companions: Key Social, Psychological, Ethical and Design Issues* (pp. 3–10). Amsterdam: John Benjamins Publishing Company.

Van Inwagen, P. (1978). The Possibility of Resurrection. *International Journal for Philosophy of Religion* 9(2), 114–121.

Chapter 10

Paul Smart
ARTIFICIAL ECONOMICS

Artificial prosumers

"I DO HOPE YOU'RE SATISFIED with our product," remarks Luv, just before her boot descends to destroy Joi's emanator. Luv is looking at Joi when she says this, but it is unclear whether her statement is intended for Joi or for K. Given the direction of her gaze, we are naturally inclined to think that Luv is addressing Joi and referring to K. But her statement could easily been directed at K, for both Joi and K are manufactured by Wallace Corporation, and they thus both qualify as products.

The inherent ambiguity of Luv's statement, coupled with the direction of her gaze, is important for a number of reasons. Note, for example, that Luv is a representative of Wallace Corporation. Presumably, then, Luv is in a position to know about the functional profile of the products produced by Wallace Corporation. (Indeed, we learn that Luv is involved in sales and marketing, a role that typically requires familiarity with a company's product portfolio.) This looks to be important when we consider the fact that Luv is looking at Joi. Inasmuch as her statement is addressed to Joi, then it seems likely that Luv believes Joi is the sort of thing that could be satisfied with something. In other words, the direction of Luv's gaze suggests that Joi might be capable of *experiencing* satisfaction. This speaks to one of the issues raised in chapter 7, namely, the issue of whether or not Joi ought to be regarded as a sentient being.

The scene of Joi's demise is also important in drawing our attention to some of the economic peculiarities of the *Blade Runner* universe. Note, for example, that Luv is herself a replicant who "works" for Wallace Corporation. In this sense, she is no less a product than is Joi or K. What distinguishes her from Joi and K, at least from an economic perspective, is the fact that she has not been sold to someone else. Unlike Joi and K, Luv has been retained to service the interests of Wallace Corporation ("I'm here for Mr. Wallace"). She is, as such, an in-house product.

As noted above, Luv's wry remark ("I do hope you're satisfied with our product") is ambiguous, and this ambiguity reminds us of the status of Joi and K as products. From a cinematic perspective, however, it is not just the ambiguous nature of Luv's statement that is important in this scene. The direction of Luv's gaze also plays a crucial role in directing our attention to matters of an economic nature. To help us see this, let us imagine that Luv had been looking at K when she said, "I do hope you're satisfied with our product." In this case, we would have assumed that she was addressing K and referring to Joi, and the economic import of her statement would probably have gone unnoticed. We already know, for example, that Joi is a product of Wallace Corporation and K has purchased Joi; thus, the counterfactual case (Luv looking at K) merely speaks to what we already know. By looking at Joi, however, Luv's statement serves as an important cognitive trigger: it reminds us that K is a product of Wallace Corporation and that K's relationship with Joi is just as much an economic relationship as it is a romantic one. (No surprise, then, that the relationship is so easily shattered by the dutiful servant of a capitalist overlord!)

In surveying the web of economic relations in *Blade Runner 2049*, something important is revealed. It is possible to regard the products of Wallace Corporation (e.g. Luv and K) as economically active agents, in the sense that they are the providers and/or the producers of economic goods and services.[1] In some cases, however, they also appear to play the role of economic consumers. This duality is most clearly evidenced by K. On the production side of things, K is a NEXUS 9 replicant who provides a service to his employer, the Los Angeles Police Department (LAPD). Although we are not told that K was specifically engineered to operate as a blade runner, it looks likely that his design is consistent with this sort of role. In one sense, then, K is a manufactured entity (a product) that is designed to provide a service that other economically active agents (namely, the LAPD) will pay for. It is this that underwrites K's status as an economic producer: Courtesy of his capacity to track down and retire rogue replicants, K is able to do something of economic value—he provides a service to his employers and perhaps even provides them with goods in the form of neatly packaged body parts (yuck!).

As the movie progresses, it becomes clear that K is more than just a producer of economic goods and services; he is also a *consumer* of goods and services. This is made clear by Luv, when she learns that K possesses an emanator:

    LUV: I see you're also a customer.
    LUV: Are you satisfied with our product? [Referring to Joi]
    K: She's very realistic. Thank you.

It isn't entirely clear whether K receives a monthly paycheck from the LAPD; what is clear, however, is that he is entitled to certain forms of economic recompense for his blade-runner services. In the aftermath of his first baseline check, for example, we learn that K receives a "bonus"—a reward for his efforts in retiring Sapper Morton:

    INTERVIEWER: We're done.
    INTERVIEWER: Constant K.
    INTERVIEWER: You can pick up your bonus.
    K: Thank you, sir.

Given the standard definition of a bonus as a sum of money added to a person's wages for good performance, it seems reasonable to assume that K is employed by the LAPD and receives financial remuneration for his services. This is supported by what we see when K returns to his apartment following the successful completion of his first baseline test. We learn that K lives in an apartment, which he shares with Joi. K has presumably decided to purchase Joi, since we know that Joi is, herself, a product of Wallace Corporation. It is in this sense that K is an economic consumer: K is using the economic returns from his labour to purchase products that (in this particular case, at least) originate from the very same company that is responsible for his own manufacture. K is thus both a producer and a consumer of economic goods and services; he is, to use the phraseology adopted by behavioural scientists, an economic prosumer (Ritzer et al., 2012)—an entity involved in both the production and consumption of economic goods and services.

Why should any of this be of any economic or philosophical interest beyond the fictional realms of the *Blade Runner* universe? The reason, I suggest, is that *Blade Runner 2049* provides us with an interesting (and, as far as I can tell, novel) characterisation of the economic significance of Artificial Intelligence (AI). There is, to be sure, a profound difference between the sort of AI systems that we encounter in *Blade Runner 2049* (i.e., replicants[2] and holograms) and those we encounter in contemporary society. Nevertheless, the status of replicants as economic prosumers is important, for it reveals a different way of thinking about the economic impact of AI systems—one that potentially alters the nature of contemporary economic and social policy debates. In particular, *Blade Runner 2049* captures the idea of what I will call *artificial economics*—the idea that AI systems work to service the demand for economic growth and capital accumulation, and that they do so courtesy of their status as economic prosumers. In essence, artificial economics yields a vision of AI systems operating as the deliberately engineered components of an economic system, one whose functional goals (e.g. economic growth and capital accumulation) are perhaps no longer adequately served by traditional (i.e., human) forms of production and consumption. AI systems are, if you like, a technological response—a specific form of economically oriented technological fix—that seeks to address the problems, constraints, and limitations associated with traditional (human-centred) forms of economic commerce.

We are all familiar with the idea of AI systems working to expand the scale, scope, and efficiency of traditional forms of production (consider the widespread use of industrial robots on factory assembly lines); what the notion of artificial economics adds to this familiar (and accepted) image is the idea of AI systems working to expand the scale, scope, and efficiency of traditional (human-centred) forms of consumption. As a result of this consumerist capacity, AI systems are apt to strike a balance between production and consumption, helping to ensure that changes in an economic system's capacity to *produce* are met with a corresponding shift in its capacity to *consume*.

There is nothing about the notion of artificial economics that requires us to see artificial prosumption as a technological fix for the "problems" associated with existing economic systems—the idea is, at root, a claim about the mechanistic realisation of economic phenomena (more on which below). It is, nevertheless, possible that artificial prosumption may operate in this sort of way, helping to liberate economic systems from the constraints imposed by human-based forms of production and consumption. Human prosumers, it should be clear, can only produce and consume so much, and they can only do so at a certain rate. This poses a potential threat to capitalism's expansionist ambitions, impeding its capacity to, in effect, reach for the stars (see below). Artificial prosumers may help to resolve this impasse. This is not just because artificial prosumers are apt to be better (e.g. more efficient) at prosumption than their human counterparts (although that may be the case); it is also because of the way that artificial prosumers are themselves produced. Human prosumers are born, not "made," and the conventional reproductive process is one that comes with an all-too-familiar set of temporal and economic costs, many of which are tied to our basic biological nature. Artificial prosumers, however, are not subject to these cost overheads. Just like K, artificial prosumers are products, and they can be replicated at will. This does not mean that there are no costs associated with the production of artificial prosumers; but such costs are presumably open to optimisation, including the forms of optimisation provided by advances in AI and robotics. As with other forms of manufacture, there is no reason why AI systems should not be "employed" to improve the efficiency of this particular productive process.

There is much here that is no doubt contentious, and I have to confess that, due to limitations in my own expertise, I am not in a position to evaluate the economic feasibility of the ideas on offer—that is a matter I am content to leave to others. My suspicion is that this is one case where issues of economic feasibility are tied to issues of technological feasibility. For the claim is not that artificial prosumers are working in some radically different way to conventional (i.e., human) prosumers. Rather, the claim is that artificial prosumers are performing more or less the same functional role as their human counterparts. Crucially, the introduction of artificial prosumers need not entail some radical shift in the functional profile of an economic system. A capitalist economy, for example, may still continue to function in more or less the same way as before, with the exception that it is perhaps better placed to serve as an engine of economic growth. All that the notion of artificial economics involves is a commitment to the idea that economic processes are realised by a material fabric (a mechanism) whose constituent elements (e.g. humans) are subject to functional replication. The guiding vision is thus one of artificial prosumers working as the constituent elements of economic mechanisms in more or less the same manner as their biological (i.e., human) counterparts.

To my mind, then, the feasibility of artificial economics hinges on the extent to which the economically relevant functional properties of human prosumers (i.e., those properties that are relevant to the realisation of economic phenomena) can be instantiated by a materially distinct economic agent, namely, an AI system that functions as an artificial prosumer. This, however, is not a matter of *economic* feasibility, for no one (I assume) disputes the fact that existing forms of economic commerce are tied to the functional properties of human economic agents.[3]

Finally, it is worth remembering that the notion of artificial economics, as it is presented here, owes its existence to *Blade Runner 2049*. In other words, part of the credit for the ideas on offer have to be attributed to *Blade Runner 2049*. This, I suggest, reveals a new mode of operation for the cinematic medium when it comes to philosophical efforts. In attempting to characterise the philosophical significance of the cinematic medium, philosophers have identified a number of ways that films might be "capable of doing philosophy" (Wartenberg, 2009: 556). Perhaps the most popular of these "modes" is what we might call the *illustrative mode*. "A film that illustrates a philosophical theory," Wartenberg (2009: 556) suggests, "can be doing philosophy in a similar way to a journal article: it can make the theory seem more plausible to its audience." There is no doubt something right about this. But it is unclear whether this sort of idea really captures the nature of the relationship between *Blade Runner 2049* and the philosophical/economic claims canvassed above. There is, to be sure, a certain sense in which *Blade Runner 2049* might be said to illustrate the notion of artificial economics. Relative to the notion of artificial economics, however, there is no sense in which the movie could be said to illustrate an *existing* philosophical theory or even, perhaps, make such a theory "seem more plausible to its audience." A better way of conceptualizing the philosophical significance of *Blade Runner 2049* (at least in regard to the notion of artificial economics) is to see it as operating in a creative or generative mode—as a source of new ideas and insights. When it comes to the notion of artificial economics, *Blade Runner 2049* is not so much a resource that captures or embodies an existing idea as it is a resource that helps to limn the path to previously unexplored (or, at any rate, under-explored) regions of the philosophical (and, in this case, economic) terrain.

Owning the stars

The main beneficiary of economic relations in the *Blade Runner* universe is, of course, the industrialist, Niander Wallace. Wallace is a curious character. He is clearly depicted as some sort of being, but it is not obvious that he is any sort of being that we, as humans, can relate to. On the one hand, he is the saviour of humanity, using his mastery of synthetic farming to avert a humanitarian crisis. On the other hand, however, he shows a complete lack of humanity. His callous gutting of a female replicant suggests a complete lack of concern or empathy for his "children." (Even Luv, a replicant, shows a distinct emotional response to Wallace's sanguineous actions in this scene.) The upshot is a paradox: How can someone who is seemingly bereft of humanity also work in such a way as to sustain humanity? For the sake of convenience, let us refer to this as the *saviour paradox*.

The sense of mystery surrounding Wallace is only deepened by his empyrean half-monologues. It is clear that Wallace has some sort of agenda, but the logic of that agenda is highly questionable. Wallace seeks the child of Rachael and Deckard so that he can unlock the door to replicant reproduction. But why would Wallace, as someone whose business model depends on the fact that replicants are manufactured, wish to do this? The answer, it seems, is one that resonates with a capitalist ethos: *expansionism*.

> WALLACE: We make angels ... in the service of civilization.
> WALLACE: Yes, there were bad angels once. I make good angels now. That is how I took us to nine new worlds.
> WALLACE: Nine. A child can count to nine on fingers. *We should own the stars* [emphasis added].

At this point, Wallace's true nature starts to come into sharper focus. The key to understanding Wallace, I suggest, is not to view him merely as a particular kind of being, e.g. a posthuman god, a human, a replicant, a cyborg, and so on. Instead of asking who or what Wallace is, we ought to ask ourselves what it is that Wallace represents. The answer to that question, I propose, is simple: Wallace is the onscreen personification of the values, precepts, and modes of operation that characterise contemporary forms of capitalist ideology. This is what I will call the *personification hypothesis*:

> **Personification hypothesis**
> We ought not to think of Niander Wallace as merely a particular kind of being (e.g. a cyborg). Rather, we ought to regard him as the personification of capitalism. This is the best way of making sense of what Wallace says and does.

This is, to be sure, a controversial claim, and its acceptability ought to hinge on more than the fact that Wallace's ambitions are compatible with an expansionist agenda. In what follows, I will attempt to highlight the value of the personification hypothesis with respect to our capacity to (1) resolve the aforementioned saviour paradox, (2) make sense of Wallace's utterances, and (3) better understand Wallace's interest in replicant birth. Before we go any further, however, it is worth taking a closer look at Wallace's expansionist rhetoric. In particular, note the specific nature of Wallace's aspirations in the above quotation. Wallace's vision is not one of humanity embarking on a voyage of discovery. Instead, Wallace's view is refracted through the prism of capitalism. For him, the goal is simple: it all comes down to *ownership* ("We should own the stars"). Crucially, Wallace's vision is one in which every aspect of the natural world, including the stars above, are conceived of as a form of private property. No one, I suspect, looks up at the night sky and sees the elements of the firmament as a fitting target for capitalist expansion. But if the spirit of capitalism were to be incarnated as a flesh and blood being on the surface of the Earth, isn't that precisely the way it would regard the heavens?

The saviour paradox is easily resolved by the personification hypothesis. According to the personification hypothesis, we ought not to think of Wallace merely as a particular kind of being; instead, we ought to think of Wallace as something akin to a dispassionate, self-interested machine that works only in its own interests. As the personification of capitalism, Wallace is the purveyor of all manner of technological fixes, and some of those fixes (e.g. synthetic farming) appear to benefit humanity. But the value of a technological fix, at least from the standpoint of capitalism, does not inhere in its humanitarian potential; instead, it is deployed so as to sustain its own operation. This is, in fact, the only form of "sustainability" that capitalism cares about. Capitalism does not care about the sustainability of natural resources, issues of biodiversity, pollution control, or even the fate of humanity itself. It is simply a system of beliefs and values that seeks to ensure its own survival. Capitalism is, to be sure, a prodigious source of technological innovations, and perhaps it is ideally placed, as an economic system, to deliver such innovations. For the most part, however, the "merits" of such innovations are judged according to capitalism's own internal logic. If some form of technological fix fails to yield a profit, then it is deemed "economically unviable," which is to say it is untenable relative to the constraints imposed by capitalism's economic framework.

All of this, I suggest, informs our understanding of Wallace. Inasmuch as we see Wallace as the emblem of capitalism, there is nothing paradoxical about him. Wallace operates in the manner of a dispassionate machine. He is apt to countenance any technological fix, providing such a fix does not destabilise his hegemonic grip on the global economic order. Wallace is, in short, a reminder of the various vices and virtues that are inherent to capitalism, including its capacity to turn an ecological crisis into an economic opportunity.

Next, let us turn our attention to Wallace's utterances. Much of what Wallace says in the movie is, to my mind at least, perplexing. In his confrontation with Deckard, for example, Wallace refers to Deckard as a "wonder" ("You are a wonder to me, Mr. Deckard."). He also contemplates the possibility that Deckard may have been designed to fall in love with Rachael, which, if true, would appear to confirm Deckard's status as a replicant:

> WALLACE: Is it the same ... now, as then ... the moment you met her? All these years you looked back on that day ... drunk on the memory of its perfection. How shiny her lips. How instant your connection. Did it never occur to you that's why you were

summoned in the first place? Designed to do nothing short of fall for her right then and there. All to make that single perfect specimen. That is, if you were designed.

As with much of what Wallace has to say in his confrontation with Deckard, this particular exchange is apt to be the source of some confusion. How could Wallace not know whether or not Deckard is a replicant? Can't he just cut him open and check for a serial number? This, recall, was how Rachael's replicant status was confirmed by her skeletal remains. Interpreted as a sign of epistemic uncertainty, Wallace's musings appear to make little sense.

But Wallace's dialogue makes much more sense, I think, if we examine it from the standpoint of the personification hypothesis. Why is Deckard a source of wonder for Wallace? Because Deckard epitomises everything that is at odds with capitalism. Deckard has sacrificed his own interests for the sake of someone else's (i.e., his daughter's). And what did such sacrifice entail? Wallace has the answer:

> WALLACE: It was very clever to keep yourself empty of information ... and *all it cost you was everything* [emphasis added].

As the onscreen embodiment of capitalism's heart and soul, it is no surprise that Deckard would be a source of wonder for Wallace. Deckard is a man who, in the manner of the nineteenth-century transcendentalist, Henry David Thoreau, has retreated to the "wilderness." Deckard spends his time looking after bees—one of the last vestiges of the natural world. He dreams of cheese, but his wishes and wants go unfulfilled. Deckard is a man whose life is characterised by restraint and self-denial, as opposed to self-indulgence and the pursuit of profit (although temperance is evidently not one of Deckard's virtues!). Given all this, is it any wonder that Deckard should be a source of wonder for Wallace?

The personification hypothesis also helps us understand why Wallace is preoccupied with the nature of Deckard's desire, that is, whether or not Deckard was designed to fall in love with Rachael. The key insight here centres on the relationship between capitalism and consumerism— in particular, the way in which capitalism is sometimes seen to shape consumer demand. Take, for example, K's status as an artificial prosumer. K was manufactured by Wallace Corporation, and he is thus a product of

Wallace Corporation. But K is also a customer of Wallace Corporation—he purchases the hologram, Joi, who is also manufactured by Wallace Corporation. At this point, it seems appropriate to raise an issue that we failed to consider in the earlier discussion of artificial prosumption: "Why does K purchase Joi?" That is an easy one, I hear you say: "K purchases Joi because he was lonely, and we know that Joi is a solution for this particular problem; Joi tells us that herself!" (see below). This answer is undoubtedly correct, but it risks missing an important point. This can be illustrated by asking a follow-up question: "Why didn't Wallace simply design K in such a way that he would be immune to loneliness?" Clearly, this a much more difficult question to answer. Perhaps an immunity to loneliness is not something that lies within the scope of Wallace's expertise. That is one possibility, I suppose. But there is a second possibility: Perhaps K was specifically engineered in such a way that he would feel loneliness and thus be inclined to spend his disposable income on Joi. Similarly, perhaps Joi was designed in such a way as to solicit the purchase of gifts from her owner (emanators and the like) and purchase gifts (replicant prostitutes?) in return. The claim is, of course, tenuous, since we are given no concrete evidence in the movie to suggest that K was designed in such a way as to desire Wallace's commercial offerings. Nevertheless, the claim is broadly consistent with the idea that Wallace serves as the personification of capitalism. In particular, the claim dovetails with an oft-mentioned critique of capitalism that centres on its capacity to shape, support, and sustain consumerist tendencies. As consumers, of course, our economic behaviour is dictated by our desires. But what is the basis of those desires? Is it possible that our desires are, in some sense, "programmed" into us by the economic systems in which we live—that we are, in effect, socially engineered consumers whose "needs," wants, and wishes have been carefully shaped to serve the interests of an economic system that is upheld by the mutually supportive pillars of consumption, craving, and (last, but certainly not least) credit?!

It is, to be sure, an ingenious trick. Inasmuch as Wallace has some control over the emotional propensities of his replicant creations, he could have designed K in such a way as to not feel a need for romantic love. That would have made a lot of sense, given K's role as a cold-blooded killer of rogue replicants. But why respect the logic of optimal design, when a carefully crafted "flaw" promises to create (or, more plausibly, widen) a gap in the market? From this perspective, Wallace's preoccupation with the nature of Deckard's desire makes perfect sense. Wallace is not, in fact, concerned with Deckard's status as a replicant; he is more concerned with the cultivation of desire—the way in which capitalist economies till the psychosocial terrain so as to inculcate the needs, wants, and wishes that are the motivational mainstay of economic profligacy.

What, finally, of the issue of replicant birth? Wallace is clearly driven to unlock the secret of replicant reproduction, but it is far from clear that Wallace has anything to gain by discovering this secret. Given his mastery of synthetic farming, it is likely that Wallace's business interests extend to more than just the manufacture of replicant models. But why would Wallace be prepared to cede control over the means of (replicant) production for the sake of expanding the replicant population? There are two reasons why this makes no sense, at least from an economic standpoint:

(1) First, if replicants can reproduce, then Wallace is no longer in a position to profit from the sale of replicants.
(2) Second, inasmuch as replicant reproduction blurs the distinction between humans and replicants, this undermines the extent to which replicants can be regarded as slaves. As stated by Freysa, "I knew that baby meant we are more than just slaves. If a baby can come from one of us ... we are our own masters."

As the head of a corporation that trades in replicant slaves, neither of these outcomes is particularly favourable for Wallace, and it is thus unclear why he would support the possibility of replicant birth. From the standpoint of the personification hypothesis, however, Wallace's ambitions make perfect sense. From an economic standpoint, replicant birth is simply a means of reducing the costs associated with the manufacture of a commercial product. This deals with the first of the issues mentioned above: Replicant birth is not a problem for Wallace, for it amounts to little more than a form of outsourcing—a way of reducing the costs associated with a given productive (or, in this case, reproductive) process.

What about the second issue—the issue relating to the distinction between humans and replicants? For humans, the sterility of replicants is important, for it helps to preserve the distinction between humans and replicants, and it thereby enables the latter to be treated as slaves. The apparent "impossibility" of replicant birth is thus one of the foundation stones for a "wall" that, according to Lt. Joshi, separates replicants from humankind:

> LT. JOSHI: That's not possible.
> LT. JOSHI: She was a Replicant. Pregnant.
> LT. JOSHI: The world is built on a wall. It separates kind. Tell either side there's no wall, you bought a war. Or a slaughter. So, what you saw ... didn't happen.

The question to ask here is why Joshi's wall would be of any interest to Wallace (at least, from the standpoint of the personification hypothesis). This is, after all, a world where *both* humans and replicants appear to be in the service of capitalism. Crucially, Joshi's wall is *not* a wall that separates the human *free* from the replicant *slave*; it is merely a line drawn between two forms of economic subjugation. Replicant rebellion undoubtedly poses a threat to Wallace as the head of a major corporation. But as the cinematic embodiment of capitalism, it is far from clear that Wallace has anything to lose if replicants should be indistinguishable from humans. For this is *not* a world where either humans or replicants are free; it is, instead, a world where capital is king.

Touching the void

Wallace's power is sustained, at least in part, by the deployment of technological fixes. One such fix is synthetic farming. We learn that Wallace's mastery of synthetic farming helped to avert famine following the collapse of ecosystems in the 2020s. Synthetic farming is thus an example of an environmentally oriented technological fix: a fix that is intended to deal with a problem that afflicts the wider biotic environment of humanity.

Environmental fixes, however, are not the only sort of technological fix we see in *Blade Runner 2049*. It is possible that another kind of fix comes in the form of K's hologrammatic companion, Joi. In contrast to synthetic farming, I suggest Joi functions as a technological fix for problems of the social kind. She is, as such, a socially oriented technological fix. Despite the fact that Joi addresses a problem of a somewhat different kind than does synthetic farming, she is nevertheless indicative of a form of ecological collapse. In particular, Joi reminds us that the human ecological niche is one that straddles multiple kinds of ecosystem. Joi is, in short, a reminder that something has gone very wrong with society several decades into the twenty-first century—that the decay and degradation of the wider biotic environment is echoed by a similar deterioration in the structure of social relationships.

If Joi is a technological fix, then what sort of problem is she supposed to solve? Undoubtedly, given her state of undress in a number of advertising hoardings, there is a sexual component to Joi's functionality. This, however, is unlikely to be the only sort of "fix" she provides for her consumer base, since she is clearly capable of functioning in a more romantic manner, and sexual gratification is evidently not the basis of her relationship with K. In any case, her hologrammatic status precludes the possibility of physical contact, and this looks to be a particular disadvantage given the more substantive forms of carnal indulgence on offer at Bibi's bar. At the very least, the availability of replicant prostitutes raises a question about Joi's market competitiveness: sexual titillation is hardly a unique selling point for Joi, and I very much doubt it is the most alluring aspect of her service portfolio.

Joi's true purpose, I suggest, is revealed once we direct our attention to K. His problem is one of loneliness, social isolation, and a lack of intimacy, and this is precisely the sort of problem that Joi is intended to solve. In essence, I propose that Joi is a technological fix for an all-too-familiar feature of the human condition—one that undoubtedly stems from our status as social animals: she is a fix for the problem of loneliness, or, more generically, the problems of social connection and interpersonal attachment.

There can be little doubt that social connection is important to K, for it serves as one of the recurring elements of his baseline test:

INTERVIEWER: What's it like to hold the hand of someone you love? Interlinked.
K: Interlinked.
INTERVIEWER: Did they teach you how to feel finger to finger? Interlinked.
K: Interlinked.

INTERVIEWER: Do you long for having your heart interlinked?
Interlinked.
K: Interlinked.

Social connection also serves as one of the major thematic elements of *Blade Runner 2049*. When it comes to the matter of replicant birth, for example, what seems to matter most is not the fact that replicant birth represents some sort of technological breakthrough; rather, it is the fact that birth typically entails a default form of social connectivity—that, as a result of being born, one typically gets to enjoy some form of emotionally significant connection with another social being:

JOI: I always knew you were special. Maybe this is how. A child. Of woman born. Pushed into the world. Wanted. Loved.

Finally, consider that Joi, herself, comments on her ability to tackle the problem of loneliness. Towards the end of the movie, K confronts one of Joi's large, pink, hologrammatic adverts. Note how this particular version of Joi (Pink Joi) advertises her wares:

PINK JOI: Hello, handsome.
PINK JOI: What a day, hmm? You look lonely. *I can fix that* [emphasis added].

There are a number of reasons why Joi's status as a technological fix is important. First, Joi illuminates the adaptive capabilities of capitalism—the ability of capitalism to sustain itself even in the face of impending bio- and socio-ecological doom. It does so, not by addressing the cause of some problem, because that risks drawing attention to its own role in perpetuating whatever problems need to be fixed. Instead, capitalism does something quite remarkable: it transforms a crisis into a profit-making exercise, yielding fixes that provide new opportunities for capital accumulation. Joi is an example of precisely this sort of fix.

A second point of interest concerns Joi's status as a virtual slave. Joi is an intelligent agent who is manufactured to service the romantic, social, and sexual interests of those who purchase her. She is, in this sense, no different than a replicant pleasure model, such as Pris in the original

Blade Runner movie. If replicants are slaves, courtesy of the fact that they are born to serve, then why should we regard Joi any differently?

Finally, Joi's status as a socially oriented technological fix resonates with our current interest in resolving social problems via technological means. Of particular interest is Joi's apparent capacity to resolve problems of social connection. Loneliness is widely recognised as a problem for contemporary societies, and the advent of new communications technology (e.g. the Internet) seems to have done little to address this (see Turkle, 2011). In this respect, Joi serves as an example of the sort of fix that might be required to tackle the problem of social connection and curtail its social, psychological, and physiological sequelae (see Cacioppo & Patrick, 2008). Despite her fictional status, Joi arguably epitomises the ambitions of a number of increasingly prominent lines of research, including those associated with the development of artificial companions (e.g. Wilks, 2010), virtual romantic partners (e.g. Pettman, 2009), and, of course, sex robots (e.g. Levy, 2009).

As a means of bringing these various points together, let us consider the extent to which Joi qualifies as a benign technological fix, by which I mean a technological fix that causes little in the way of further problems. This issue is important, for technological fixes are seldom seen as a panacea for humanity's problems. More often than not, a technological solution to a problem creates a series of further problems that then require a further set of fixes. In the worst case, a technological fix can yield problems that are sufficiently severe as to pose an existential threat to humanity. Let us refer to these technological fixes as malign fixes. A malign technological fix is thus one that raises the spectre of an existential threat, while a benign technological fix does not.

So, what kind of fix is Joi? Relative to the way she is presented in Blade Runner 2049, there are a number of reasons to think that Joi is a relatively benign form of technological fix. For a start, Joi is one of the few characters in the movie who shows no sign of violence or malice. K, for example, kills Sapper Morton; Freysa, the leader of the replicant rebellion, instructs K to kill Deckard; Lt. Joshi orders K to kill the offspring of Rachael; Luv kills Lt. Joshi and Coco; and Niander Wallace brutally dispenses with a newly created (and thus entirely innocent) female replicant. Even Deckard shows something of a violent streak, as he relentlessly bludgeons K in a casino bar. Joi is different. Her primary concern is K's well-being, and we see no evidence of any sort of malign intent.

Joi's virtuality is also relevant to her benignant status. As a hologram, Joi is incapable of interacting with physical objects, and it is thus unclear to what extent she could pose a physical threat to others. In this respect, Joi is unlike the forms of AI that are the typical sources of our existential angst. She is, to be sure, a form of AI, but she is unlike the forms of AI that we see depicted in movies such as *The Terminator* (James Cameron, 1984), *The Matrix* (The Wachowski Brothers, 1999), and *Ex Machina* (Alex Garland, 2015). Perhaps, then, this is one case where technological virtuality goes hand in hand with humanitarian virtue. Courtesy of her hologrammatic status, Joi has limited abilities to effect changes in her physical environment, and this undermines the extent to which she could be seen to pose any sort of threat to humanity.

We thus have a number of reasons to think that Joi ought to be located in the category of benign technological fixes. That doesn't mean there are no negative consequences to her introduction, but it seems relatively clear that she poses little in the way of an existential threat to humanity. She is, to be sure, nothing like the forms of AI that both reflect and feed our fears about the existential impact of Matrix-style supercomputers and Terminator-like killing machines.

Threats, however, are curious things. Just like AI systems, they come in all manner of shapes and sizes. Joi appears both beautiful and benign. But let us not forget that even the most powerful of beasts can be slain by beauty, and, all too often, innocuity is the faithful servant of insidiousness. In fact, the rough outline of a more general worry about artificial companions is evident in the nature of K's relationship with Joi. Whatever else we might think about this relationship, such as whether Joi's love counts as authentic, or whether Joi herself ought to count as "real," it is clear that K is emotionally attached to her. Joi is real for K, even if others (e.g. Mariette) doubt her status as a "real girl."

It is here that we begin to confront a worry raised by Joi (and her technological ilk). For note that while intimacy appears important to K, there are a number of times in the movie where K appears to shun the advances made by other female characters. These include the advances made by Luv (in the memory vault), Mariette (outside Bibi's bar), and Lt. Joshi (in his own apartment). Admittedly, these may not be the sort of advances that K is looking for—the advances by Lt. Joshi and Mariette are of an overtly sexual nature, and the one by Luv is, to say the least, cumbersome. Nevertheless, the fact remains that K declines the opportunity to be "physically" interlinked, and he does so presumably because of his existing emotional connection to Joi. In the context of the movie, of course, K's fidelity (which, in an economic sense, amounts to a form of customer loyalty) is of little consequence; presumably K is an infertile replicant, so he was never going to be the father of lots of little "k's." In the real world, however, K's devotion raises the spectre of a *fertility problem*: In a world where artificial companions make perfect partners, why should we assume that humans will continue to participate in biologically basic forms of reproduction? Given the availability of romantic companions who are (to paraphrase Joi's advertising slogan) "whoever we want them to be," is there any reason to think that we won't end up like K: emotionally smitten, yet reproductively sterile?

The fertility problem is seldom at the forefront of debates about the ethical implications of AI technology. To my mind, however, the existential risk posed by Joi-like artificial companions is no less real. It may be that the path to artificial companions is littered by a greater number of technological obstacles than that associated with, let's say, the implementation of a Skynet-like supercomputer. But perhaps it is also the case that it is easier (or at least more enjoyable) to be loved out of existence than it is to succumb to a war of attrition.

Joi is thus a potent reminder of the problems associated with technological fixes. She reflects humanity's prodigious capacity for technological innovation and, in that sense, she is a cause for optimism. At the same time, however, Joi is a cause for despair, reminding us that even the most brilliant and seemingly benign of (socio-) ecological interventions can, on occasion, sow the seeds of our own destruction.

Perhaps, however, I am being overly pessimistic. Before we consign ourselves to the conclusion that all roads lead to wrack and ruin, it is worth noting that some of the philosophical issues raised by Joi hint at a potential solution to the fertility problem. To help us appreciate this solution, it is worth asking ourselves what it is that underwrites Joi's effectiveness as a technological fix. The answer to that question, I suggest, is not so much that she is a form of *artificial* intelligence as it is that she is a form of *advanced* intelligence. The thing that makes Joi *real* for K is thus the nature of her behavioural responses—that she is behaviourally (and thus, perhaps, psychologically) isomorphic to a "real girl." At this point, however, a philosophical (and, more specifically, an ethical) tension starts to emerge. The thing that makes Joi an effective technological fix for loneliness (among other things) is the nature of her intelligence—the fact that she is so advanced as to be the sort of being that a typical human might be inclined to fall in love with. But aren't these precisely the sort of features that make us wonder about the status of Joi as a virtual person (or virtual human)? In the same way that *Blade Runner* encourages us to reflect on issues of personhood and thus question the moral legitimacy of replicant enslavement, so *Blade Runner 2049* encourages us to ask more or less the same questions about artificial (in this case, hologrammatic) companions. And, if we accept the idea that Joi counts as a virtual person, then she is surely entitled to some form of moral recognition. If so, then why should we condemn her to a life of romantic/sexual servitude? If we find the notion of replicant slavery morally repugnant, then shouldn't our moral sensibilities be similarly inflamed by the prospect of artificial companions? Do these two cases not count as a form of slavery, and is there a reason why one form of slavery is more acceptable than the other?

It is here that we begin to see the approximate shape of a philosophical argument that is intended to counter the existential threat posed by the fertility problem. Artificial companions are a threat inasmuch as they provide an alternative to conventional human-to-human relationships. But beyond a certain level of behavioural and cognitive sophistication, issues of moral standing start to come to the fore. The result is that technological progress in this area is likely to be self-limiting: We want our artificial companions to be real, but perhaps not so real as to raise concerns about their status as artificial persons and thus romantic/sexual slaves. The prophylactic efficacy of this philosophical fix to the fertility problem no doubt turns on the extent to which the criterial determinants of personhood can themselves be resolved. It is also possible, I suppose, that humanity will simply opt to ignore the ethical issues. Or perhaps the means by which something is produced (born vs. made) will be seen as the ultimate arbiter of moral entitlement. Perhaps, for example, issues of natality will be used to revivify the Aristotelian notion of a natural slave, with liberty reserved only for those who are pushed (as opposed to pulled) into the world. If so, then perhaps being loved out of existence is not the worst fate that might befall humanity. It is, perhaps, no more than we deserve: a perfectly appropriate (and suitably ironic) form of artificial justice.

Notes

1 As noted by Timothy Shanahan (personal communication), it is relatively easy to see how K qualifies as the provider of an economic service, but it is much harder to see how he qualifies as the producer of an economic good. This is relevant to K's ostensible status as an artificial prosumer, since the term "prosumption" is an amalgam of "production" and "consumption (as opposed to "provision" and "consumption"). Perhaps, then, K ought not to be regarded as a prosumer on the grounds that he fails to produce anything in the way of a tangible economic good, and he thus fails to qualify as an economic producer. There is, no doubt, much that could be said about this issue. In the interests of brevity, however, I suggest that an agent's status as a provider or producer has no bearing on their status as a prosumer. In essence, I suggest that all forms of economic activity (i.e., activity that generates an income) ought to be regarded as productive, in the sense that such activities produce something of economic value. This applies as much to the work of, let's say, a dentist (who provides a service) as it does to the work of a dental technician (who manufactures a dental prosthetic). Clearly, the dentist and the dental technician are involved in the production of different things, but is there any reason to regard the labour of the dentist as any less productive than the labour of the dental technician? True, dental technicians produce a tangible good as a result of their labour (e.g. a denture), while the dentist provides something that more closely resembles a service (e.g. the restoration of dental functionality). But does this mean that the dental technician is involved in productive labour, while the dentist is not? Similarly, is it only the dental technician who ought to be regarded as an economic producer? To my mind, both the dentist and the dental technician qualify as economic producers, and they do so because they are both involved in some form of productive labour. What it means to be an economic producer, I suggest, is to be an agent who produces something as a result of some form of activity. Whether that activity culminates in something tangible (or intangible) is of no material consequence to an agent's status as an economic producer and, thus, their candidacy as an economic prosumer.
2 We could, of course, dispute the idea that replicants ought to be characterised as a form of AI. Given that replicants are described as "bioengineered humans," it might be thought that their intelligence is no more artificial (or, perhaps, no less natural) than is the intelligence of conventional human beings. I am grateful to Timothy Shanahan for raising this particular issue.

3 This way of defending the notion of artificial economics provides a clue as to its philosophical pedigree. In short, artificial economics appeals to concepts that are spread across a number of fields of philosophical enquiry. This includes work relating to functionalism (Polger, 2009), multiple realisability (Aizawa & Gillett, 2009), and mechanistic realisation (e.g. Wilson & Craver, 2007). The defence is also one that appeals to the role of economic mechanisms in realizing economic phenomena (e.g. economic processes). This speaks to a growing interest in the philosophical study of mechanisms (Glennan, 2017), including economic mechanisms (Marchionni, 2018).

References

Aizawa, K., & Gillett, C. (2009). The (Multiple) Realization of Psychological and Other Properties in the Sciences. *Mind & Language* 24(2), 181–208.
Cacioppo, J. T., & Patrick, W. (2008). *Loneliness: Human Nature and the Need for Social Connection*. New York: W. W. Norton.
Glennan, S. (2017). *The New Mechanical Philosophy*. Oxford: Oxford University Press.
Levy, D. (2009). *Love and Sex with Robots: The Evolution of Human–Robot Relationships*. New York: HarperCollins.
Marchionni, C. (2018). Mechanisms in Economics. In S. Glennan & P. M. Illari (Eds.), *The Routledge Handbook of Mechanisms and Mechanical Philosophy* (pp. 423–434). New York: Routledge.
Pettman, D. (2009). Love in the Time of Tamagotchi. *Theory, Culture & Society* 26(2–3), 189–208.
Polger, T. W. (2009). Computational Functionalism. In J. Symons & P. Calvo (Eds.), *The Routledge Companion to Philosophy of Psychology* (pp. 148–163). New York: Routledge.
Ritzer, G., Dean, P., & Jurgenson, N. (2012). The Coming of Age of the Prosumer. *American Behavioral Scientist* 56(4), 379–398.
Turkle, S. (2011). *Alone Together: Why We Expect More from Technology and Less from Each Other*. New York: Basic Books.
Wartenberg, T. E. (2009). Film as Philosophy. In P. Livingstone & C. Plantinga (Eds.), *The Routledge Companion to Philosophy and Film* (pp. 549–559). Abingdon: Routledge.
Wilks, Y. (Ed.). (2010). *Close Engagements with Artificial Companions: Key Social, Psychological, Ethical and Design Issues*. Amsterdam: John Benjamins Publishing Company.
Wilson, R. A., & Craver, C. F. (2007). Realization: Metaphysical and Scientific Perspectives. In P. Thagard (Ed.), *Philosophy of Psychology and Cognitive Science* (pp. 81–104). Oxford: North-Holland.

Chapter 11

Nigel Shadbolt and Paul Smart
THE EYES OF GOD

Introduction

OF ALL THE VISUAL ELEMENTS presented by Denis Villeneuve's cinematic spectacle, none is perhaps more significant than the eye motif. Eyes play an important role in each of the *Blade Runner* movies. Both films' opening scenes feature a dramatic close-up of an eye. The original *Blade Runner* appealed to the status of eyes as "windows to the soul." In particular, ocular responses (e.g. involuntary dilation of the iris) formed a crucial part of the Voight-Kampff test, the means to tell humans from replicants. In *Blade Runner 2049* (BR2049), different methods are employed to distinguish humans from replicants. Yet, despite the seeming obsolescence of the Voight-Kampff test, the thematic, narrative, and symbolic significance of eyes is undiminished in BR2049. Older (NEXUS 8) replicants continue to be identified by their eyes, albeit by indelible serial numbers printed below their corneas. But BR2049 extends the optic symbolism of the original *Blade Runner* film in new and interesting ways. By introducing augmented vision technology, for example, the film raises important questions about how we see ourselves and how we are, ourselves, seen in a world that is hurtling at breakneck speed towards an era of surveillance capitalism (see Zuboff, 2015).

This chapter will examine three issues, two of which have as their locus the character of Niander Wallace. One of the things that makes

Wallace interesting as a character is his eyes. Wallace is biologically blind, but he is able to see thanks to a prosthetic vision system consisting of six artificial drone "eyes."[1] Such forms of biotechnological pairing, bonding, and merger raise many interesting issues, including those relating to human enhancement, embodied cognition, brain–machine interfaces, and the technological transformation of the self.[2]

The second issue concerns the surveillance capabilities of new technologies. Issues of surveillance surface at a number of points in BR2049. Initially, the holographic Artificial Intelligence (AI) avatar, Joi, appears to serve as a surveillance device for Wallace Corporation, providing information about the location of her replicant companion, K. The link with the surveillance capabilities of contemporary computing devices (e.g. smartphones, ubiquitous Internet of Things technology, and so on) is all-too-clear: Just as Joi's portable emanator enables Luv to track K's movements, so contemporary mobile devices enable corporate agencies to track the behaviour of their customer base. This link is further reinforced by the character of Niander Wallace: As we witness Wallace enjoying a panoptic view of his surroundings, courtesy of his six artificial eyes, we cannot help but be reminded of our present-day concerns about the all-powerful, all-seeing commercial organisation and the surveillance potential of its technological offerings.

Which brings us to the third, and final, issue. Despite the thematic preoccupation with surveillance, both *Blade Runner* films have at their heart the possibility of deceptive manipulation, false memories, forgetting, and the elimination of experience through death or the degradation of digitally stored content. The visual technology systems and data stores of the *Blade Runner* universe are enormously powerful. Yet they are also revealed to be highly fragile, capable of being destroyed in an instant (as detailed in the prequel *2022: Black Out*). In both films, there are fundamental gaps in informational omniscience, and the plot lines achieve much of their power through what is *not* known—what remains opaque and obscure.

The eyes of God, Part I: the augmentation of Niander Wallace

Wallace is, to say the least, an unusual character. He evidently regards himself as a god of sorts. But he also acknowledges his limitations, especially when it comes to his capacity to emulate the achievements of his predecessor, Tyrell:

> WALLACE: I cannot breed them. So help me, I have tried ... Tyrell's final trick: Procreation. Perfected, then lost.

Wallace also shows little in the way of empathy (or, indeed, any emotion) for his replicant creations. In this respect, Wallace matches the description of the archetypical replicant, as envisioned by Philip K. Dick. As noted by Davies (2015),

> [a] lack of empathy is described as one of a replicant's defining conditions—it "ha[s] no regard for animals ... [and] possess[es] no ability to feel empathic joy for another life form's success or grief at its defeat" (Dick, 2007: 30) [and] "no ability to appreciate the existence of another" (ibid. 40).
>
> (Davies, 2015: 137)

Does this mean that Wallace is a replicant? That seems unlikely. But what is he then? A human psychopath and narcissist? A cyborg? A personification of our concerns about corporate power and control? It is, perhaps, hard to say for sure, for Wallace defies our attempts at conventional categorisation. Indeed, it is not obvious that Wallace is *any* sort of being that we humans can relate to. Wallace is perhaps intended to represent something new, strange, or different, but exactly what he represents is far from clear.

The idea that Wallace represents something new, strange, or different receives support from an etymological analysis of his name. "Niander" is close to the Greek word Νέανδρος, or "new man," while "Wallace" is an Anglo-Saxon word whose origin denotes "stranger."[3] "Niander" could also be a reference to the Neander Valley where Neanderthals were first uncovered, the Neanderthals being an extinct species (or subspecies) in the *Homo* genus that were contemporaneous with *Homo sapiens*. In contrast to the aforementioned notion of Wallace as the "new man," this interpretation highlights the distinctive (and, perhaps, regressive) nature of Wallace's character—the fact that Wallace is portrayed as a barely human brute (although recent archaeological evidence shows that Neanderthals had bigger brains, were more powerfully built, and were better adapted to their particular environment). The surname "Wallace" may also have something of an evolutionary pedigree. It is, perhaps, a reference to one of Charles Darwin's contemporaries, namely, Alfred Russel Wallace (ARW). Support for this idea stems from one of ARW's contributions to evolutionary biology. In particular, ARW developed the idea that natural selection increases the reproductive isolation between two populations within a species, thereby contributing to the process of speciation (and thus divergence). Interestingly, this is known as the "Wallace Effect" (Johnson, 2008).

No doubt the source of much of what is new, strange, or different about Wallace stems from the nature of his prosthetic visual system. Wallace is biologically blind, yet he is able to see via a technological implant that enables his brain to interface with the six independently manoeuvrable floating drones. The upshot is that Wallace views the world not through his own biological eyes but through the lenses of technology. In this respect, Wallace is similar to Eldon Tyrell in the original *Blade Runner* film (Tyrell, recall, was required to don thick-lensed spectacles to remedy his extreme myopia). Interestingly, neither Wallace nor Tyrell can see the world unaided; they view the world through synthetic lenses, and this perhaps alters their view of it, providing them with a technologically inflected view of reality. Wallace's technological prostheses are, of course, radically unlike Tyrell's spectacles. Tyrell's spectacles worked as bidirectional lenses, providing us with a magnified view of his natural human eyes. Wallace's floating drones, by contrast, afford no such insight. Wallace's biological eyes are, in fact, opaque, and his technological prostheses yield no insight into the nature of his humanity, if, indeed, he has any.

The peculiar form of biotechnological bonding exemplified by Niander Wallace speaks to our contemporary concerns with technological augmentation, human enhancement, and the ethics of brain–machine interfaces. It also speaks to issues concerning the extent to which technologies are apt to effect a change in the nature of our embodiment, thereby altering our perceptual and cognitive contact with reality (see, for example, Smart et al., 2017: 36–40).

Inasmuch as Wallace's floating drones are intended to gather information from the surrounding environment, his view of the world will be profoundly different from anything that we are familiar with (or could perhaps even imagine). For a start, there are six "eye" drones associated with Wallace's visual system, so he must be able to process at least six streams of visual information. It is clear from the movie that these streams need not be focused on the same part of the visual field, since, in one scene, Wallace is able to direct one of the drones to keep an "eye" on Luv, who is standing behind him. He therefore has a panoptic view of his surroundings; he can see all around him. In a functional (if not quite a literal) sense, Wallace has eyes in the back of his head!

The distinctive character of Wallace's visual system is also evidenced by the so-called "halo" devices that he uses to interface with the drones. In one scene, Luv opens a small wooden container to reveal a multi-coloured array of halos. It is not entirely clear how these halos affect Wallace's visuo-cognitive capabilities. Do they enable him to have perceptual access to different parts of the electromagnetic spectrum? Is the relevant "visual" input modulated and/or augmented with additional information about the objects being interrogated? The fact that there are seven halos, each of which is uniquely identified by a combination of colour and labelling, is strongly suggestive of some sort of functional differentiation, but the precise ways in which the halos influence Wallace's perceptual capabilities is left unspecified.

There are clearly reasons to think that Wallace sees the world in a way that is radically different from our own. But, in addition to altering the nature of Wallace's perceptual reality (i.e., the content of his visual experiences), there are also reasons to think that Wallace's technological prosthesis may also alter the nature of his conceptual reality. That is to say, Wallace's visual system may not just impact the way he sees the world, it may also alter the way he thinks about the world, perhaps by enabling him to entertain concepts that would otherwise lie beyond the purview of his (technologically non-augmented) biological brain. Kirsh (2013), for example, argues that new technologies provide opportunities to change the nature of our embodiment and thereby alter the conceptual ingredients and infrastructure of human cognition:

> Change our body enough and maybe we can even think what is currently unthinkable. For instance, a new cognitive prosthesis might enable us to conceptualize things that before were completely out of reach.[4] And not just the 10^{20} digit of pi! It would be a new way of thinking of pi; something unlike anything we can understand

now, in principle. If modern cognitive theories are right, bodies have greater cognitive consequences than we used to believe.

(Kirsh, 2013: 2)

Courtesy of his technological prostheses, then, it is likely that Wallace sees the world in a way that is distinct from humans (and replicants), and this perhaps extends to include the way that Wallace thinks about the world. This may be the source of much of what is new, strange, or different about Wallace. Perhaps, for example, Wallace's visuo-cognitive capabilities are such that it no longer makes any sense to regard those capabilities as compatible with our traditional notions of *human* vision. We might thus confront something of a technologically mediated rift in the existing cognitive order. Wallace undoubtedly started out as a human, and clearly his biological blindness posed no impediment to his membership of the human cognitive club. As a result of his peculiar form of biotechnological bonding, however, Wallace has perhaps acquired a capacity that is radically unlike anything that we can understand or relate to. The result is that his status as a human being is rendered problematic because he no longer satisfies the conditions of what we might call our *cognitive humanity*, that is, the set of criteria that define what it means to be human courtesy of an appeal to the characteristic features of the human cognitive system.[5]

In this sense, Wallace's onscreen persona resonates with the notion of a *posthuman god*: the idea that technological enhancement may one day lead to the emergence of beings so powerful as to be god-like in comparison with present-day humans. There is, to be sure, ample evidence that Wallace regards himself as a god, and of all the characters in BR2049, he is perhaps the least human-like. He is certainly one of the more "detached" characters of the movie, expressing little in the way of emotion, even as he brutally murders one of his replicant "angels."

Before leaving this topic, it is worth noting the way in which Wallace's visual system may alter the way he sees himself, in both a literal and a metaphorical sense. Consider, for example, the way Wallace is able to observe himself from a third-person perspective. This peculiar ability stems from the fact that his drone eyes are able to move independently of his biological body. The result is that Wallace can manoeuvre the drones so as to see himself pretty much as he would any other part of his environment, and he does so through the very same technological filter that shapes (and, in a sense, defines) the nature of his perceptual (and, perhaps, conceptual) reality.

What might be the effect of this rather unusual, albeit not entirely alien (think of out-of-body experiences), ability to observe oneself from a third-person perspective? How does Wallace feel, for example, when he observes himself killing a female replicant? Does he, perhaps, experience the same sort of alleged detachment that occurs when we watch the bombing of military targets through the eyes of a remotely piloted drone?[6] Or does the sense of detachment run deeper? Does Wallace's technologically mediated view of himself lead to a profound shift in his sense of self—his sense of who (and perhaps what) he is? To be sure, Wallace witnesses himself committing various atrocities, but perhaps such actions merely serve to reinforce a view of himself that was already established by his technological add-ons: a view of himself as something external to himself, as something that is perhaps *not* himself. This is an admittedly awkward idea, but the basic point is that Wallace has a rather unique capacity to engage in a form of self-observation or self-surveillance.[7] By viewing himself from an external perspective, we might wonder whether he begins to lose sight of who he is, in the sense that he begins to see himself in the same way that you or I would see someone else.

To help us understand this in a bit more detail, suppose that your sole source of visual access to the world was a big screen that encompassed your entire visual field. Also suppose that what you saw on the screen was, among other things, yourself. Every action you perform, everything you say or do—everything is depicted on the big screen, in the manner, perhaps, of a movie—your life cinematised! Now consider how you might feel after watching yourself from this third-person perspective, perhaps from multiple angles. Would you, after a while, continue to view that person, who is perhaps just one of many individuals you see on the big screen, as the real you, or would you begin to regard that person as someone else, someone that you were able to place under constant surveillance? Would you, in this situation, continue to regard your act of watching the screen as a form of *self*-surveillance, or would it become something else: the surveillance of another person, perhaps—the surveillance of someone who was not "you"? And what of your affective responses to what you see on the screen? Do you like what you see? Does the person you observe occasionally do things that you do not like? Perhaps you have good reason to cognitively disassociate yourself from yourself. And if you can't do that, then there is no denying the reality of who and what you are: for the person you see before you is the real you, and your sense of who and what you are needs to follow suit.

This sort of idea dovetails with a body of recent work concerning self-tracking, self-surveillance, and the quantified self. Of particular interest is the idea that by monitoring our own activities and physiological responses through a growing array of digital devices (e.g. smart watches, activity trackers, and so on) we are able to re-encounter ourselves through the "eyes" of the technological devices that we use. In other words, self-tracking presents us with a technologically inflected view of ourselves—a digital self, which may or may not correspond to the self that exists in the absence of such data. The question, then, is which self is the *real* self? Is that the real you reflected in the digital data, or are you someone else? And if the two selves do not align, then what source of information ought to inform your sense of self? Digital devices do not lie, so perhaps your best route to self-related knowledge is to accept whatever it is you see on the digital dashboard.

At this point, it should be clear that the transformative potential of technological prostheses is not limited to what we see or what we think—it strikes at the heart of who and what we are. And once we see ourselves via the technological lenses that promise (or, perhaps, threaten) to ferry us forward into our posthuman future, then who knows what we may become. Do cyborgs still see themselves as human? Does Wallace? Will we?

The eyes of God Part II: the panopticon of Niander Wallace

In Greek mythology, Argus Panoptes, is a many-eyed giant whose epithet "Panoptes" (meaning "all-seeing") resonates with fears about the surveillance potential of technologies. The term "panopticon" was, in fact, used by the philosopher and social theorist, Jeremy Bentham, to describe the architecture of the perfect prison—a prison in which all the inmates (pan-) could be observed (-opticon) by a single watchman without the inmates being able to tell whether or not they were being watched. In this section, we will consider Wallace's status as a many-eyed "giant": an individual whose "visual" capacity extends far beyond the confines of his watery, womb-like abode in Wallace Towers. We will also explore some of the surveillance-related issues raised by BR2049 and assess their relationship to current concerns about the surveillance capabilities of existing (or emerging) digital technologies.

A prominent cinematic element of the original Blade Runner film was the use of shaft lighting, that is, powerful beams of light that penetrated the murky gloom of a variety of interior spaces. These beams typically emanated from airborne vehicles that hovered above the city. The lights interrogated the darkness in much the same way that searchlights monitor a prison. They also penetrated spaces that we would typically deem to be private, such as the interior of Deckard's apartment. This is how Jordan Cronenweth, the American cinematographer, described the use of shaft lighting in the original Blade Runner movie:

> In the futuristic environment, they [airships] bathe the city in constantly swinging lights. They were supposedly used for both advertising and crime control, much the way a prison is monitored by moving search lights. The shafts of light represent the invasion of privacy by a supervising force; a form of control. You are never sure who it is, but even in the darkened seclusion of your home, unless you pull your shades down, you are going to be disturbed at one time or another.[8]

Surveillance and privacy violation were thus important, albeit subtle, thematic elements of the original Blade Runner movie, and they continue to be so in BR2049. How private can one be in the exterior world or, indeed, the interior world of one's thoughts? In BR2049, the searchlights of the original movie have been replaced by less obvious—although no less potent—forms of surveillance that speak to contemporary concerns about the capacity of the technological environment to monitor and model each and every one of us (O'Hara & Shadbolt, 2008). Perhaps it is only a question of time before the reach of surveillance technology is able to penetrate the inner sanctum of the mind and monitor our thoughts, feelings, desires, attitudes, and opinions (Shadbolt & Hampson, 2018).

A number of forms of surveillance are evident in BR2049. Throughout the film, the AI avatar, Joi, appears to monitor K's conversations, particularly conversations with female characters. Joi's portable emanator also provides the means by which Luv is able to track K's movements. Note, for example, that when K finally acquiesces to Joi's demands to break the emanator antenna, we switch to a scene of Luv sitting in front of a monitor. A marker on the display screen suddenly disappears, and Luv immediately stands up, looking frustrated. She subsequently visits K's apartment, where we see her retrieve the remains of the broken antenna. The juxtaposition of these scenes is no doubt intended to serve as a cinematic device that confirms the status of Joi (or, at any rate, her emanator) as a form of tracking device. This, no doubt, explains how Luv is able to monitor K's journey to the Morrillcole orphanage. After K's spinner crashes in the San Diego wasteland, he is attacked by Bedouin scavengers, and we see Luv intervening in the attack via a remotely controlled satellite/drone platform. We then see Luv issuing instructions to open fire on the attacking Bedouins from an office in Wallace Towers. It is clear from this scene that Luv has the capacity to track K's movements and monitor the progress of his search for the offspring of Deckard and Rachael. In fact, two kinds of surveillance device are pressed into operational service in this scene: Joi's emanator helps Luv to track K's movements, while the remotely controlled satellite/drone provides Luv with a bird's-eye view (perhaps a god's-eye view?) of events as they unfold on the ground below.

As the film progresses, additional forms of surveillance come to light. Lt. Joshi, for example, is able to monitor K's movements via a console in her office.[9] (This is presumably how the LAPD were able to locate and intercept K as he left Ana Stelline's laboratory.) The same console is later used by Luv after she discovers the broken antenna in K's apartment. The plot also makes use of a tracking device secreted by Mariette, a member of the replicant resistance, in K's coat. This is what enables K to be rescued from the Las Vegas casino after a violent confrontation with Luv. At this point, it becomes clear that all the women who have in some way expressed a sexual or romantic interest in K (namely, Lt. Joshi, Mariette, Joi, and Luv) are able to track K's movements, and that they do so via some form of surveillance technology: Joi monitors K's conversations with Mariette, Joshi, and (perhaps) Luv; Luv tracks K via Joi; Joshi tracks K via his spinner; and Mariette tracks K via a tracking device planted in his pocket.

Given the surveillance capabilities of technology in BR2049, are its denizens aware of the reality of surveillance, or are they oblivious? Perhaps they are aware but just indifferent. There are, as already noted, a number of parallels here with contemporary concerns about surveillance and privacy (O'Hara & Shadbolt, 2008). Portable devices, such as smartphones, enable companies to track our location and activities in unprecedented detail, and this tracking often occurs without our knowledge. Joi's emanator is perhaps similar to devices such as the Amazon Echo, which is, in effect, a networked microphone that is always on, always "listening." While such technologies are visible, it is not always clear that people are fully aware of their surveillance capabilities. In this respect, the transition from *Blade Runner* to BR2049 might be seen to reflect a shift in the "visibility" of surveillance capabilities—from overt to somewhat more covert forms of surveillance. The surveillance potential of the searchlights in the original *Blade Runner* movie is, for example, relatively explicit; in BR2049, however, surveillance is undertaken in a much more surreptitious manner. As with our ever-growing arsenal of portable, networked devices, the technological artefacts of BR2049 often serve a multiplicity of purposes, and their surveillance potential is seldom appreciated by their user base.

In our world, there are a number of forces and factors that contribute to the widespread adoption of surveillance technologies. A very large part of our digital economy is predicated on turning personal data into marketing insights and opportunities. It is data that can be repurposed in a multitude of ways. Personal data can, for example, be used to ensure our safety and well-being. It can also be used to support the creation of personalised services that speak to our individual interests and concerns. Finally, personal data is a prominent target for national governments, providing new opportunities for social-policy formulation. The sheer scale of the capitalist surveillance society we are building is not widely appreciated or understood by either consumers and citizens, or politicians and regulators. The concentration of data in a few powerful platforms is just now being estimated, the variety of pathways our data take as they flow from our phones just now being visualised (Van Kleek et al., 2018). And it shows hyper concentration: A few organisations with phenomenal oversight—Wallace-like in their extent.

Surveillance of our exterior selves is one thing, but surveillance of our inner mental lives is quite another. In BR2049, we see technologies being used to "look inside" K—to survey his cognitive innards. In the scene with Ana Stelline, for example, Ana uses a memory-scanning device to visualise K's memories. She appears able to access the content of K's (implanted) memories simply by asking him to recall the memory while she observes him via the scanner:

> ANA: Now, think about the memory you want me to see. Not even that hard. Just picture it. Let it play.

This suggests that the technology of BR2049 is able to access the inner cognitive states of test subjects ... at least when the test subjects are replicants.

A similar form of surveillance is perhaps evident during the course of the second baseline test. Here, the baseline test appears to provide some insight as to what K looks like on the inside. Note, for example, what Lt. Joshi says in the aftermath of the test:

> LT. JOSHI: Scan said you didn't look like you *on the inside*. Miles off your baseline [emphasis added].
> LT. JOSHI: Do you know what that means?

From a surveillance perspective, this suggests that the technology of BR2049 has advanced to the point where it is possible to penetrate the cognitive innards of a test subject—to peer inside their "soul" (or at least their inner selves).

Neuroscience has always been fascinated by the notion of being able to "read out" our neural and mental states. Dramatic recent advances originate from Jack Gallant's lab at the University of Berkeley. In a series of papers, his team have shown how characteristics of images and movies shown to human subjects can be reconstructed at the time of viewing and also in the act of recall (Kay et al., 2008; Naselaris et al., 2015; Naselaris et al., 2009; Nishimoto et al., 2011). These remarkable studies rely on high-resolution fMRI and Bayesian algorithms that learn the associated encodings. Gallant himself is circumspect about the ability to decode neural signals with enough resolution to be useful in legal or forensic contexts. Nevertheless, advances in neural recording technology and machine learning are likely to improve our capacity to penetrate the inner realm of percepts and mental pictures—to look not just into the biological eye (as was the case with the Voight-Kampff test), but to go deeper: to peer into the inner eye, the mind's eye, the true window, perhaps, to a person's "soul."

It thus seems that science is about to provide the means for particularly intimate forms of what might be dubbed *cognitive veillance* (see Smart et al., 2017: 83–85)—forms of surveillance that are able to "look inside us" and provide public access to previously private mental states and processes. The implications are, perhaps, as disconcerting as they are striking. Scientific and technological advances appear to portend an era in which it will be possible to reveal something about our innermost thoughts and feelings—the erstwhile private realm of our mental lives stands to be revealed as a public space, available for observation, analysis, and scrutiny by all manner of external agencies.

Of course, to some extent, our fears about surveillance do not rely on future forms of technological innovation; for many of our surveillance-related fears are fuelled by technologies that are available in the here and now. The Internet and Web are particularly prominent in this respect. Because of the role that such technologies play in a variety of cognitive, epistemic, and social activities, they provide ample opportunities for surveillance, including the forms of surveillance suggested by the notion of cognitive veillance. Consider, for example, the claim that the informational and technological elements of the Web may form the basis for the emergence of so-called Web-extended minds (Smart, 2012). In this case, there is no need for technologies to probe the intracranial realm in order to gain access to the machinery of the mind, because some of the components of that "cognitive machine" are already situated in the online realm and are thus available for public scrutiny. The upshot is a rather worrying vision of the surveillance capabilities of the Internet and Web, as well as the various digital devices that are connected to them. It is a worry that is perhaps best captured by the following remark of Eric Schmidt, CEO of Google: "We don't need you to type at all. We know where you are. We know where you've been. We can more or less know what you're thinking about."

We should, of course, note that surveillance-related fears are often the flipside of a technological coin whose opposing surface reveals a multitude of cognitive and social benefits. The capacity of the Web to support the emergence of Web-extended minds, for example, speaks to issues of epistemic expansion and extended knowledge (see Carter et al., 2018). If we accept the idea that cognitive extension entails a form of epistemic expansion, and we also accept the possibility of Web-extended minds, then the scene is set for a remarkable transformation: Web-based forms of cognitive extension are apt to lead to the emergence of supersized knowers—individuals who are able to enjoy various forms of epistemic omniscience courtesy of their access to an online realm that comprises the sum of human knowledge (see Bjerring & Pedersen, 2014; Ludwig, 2015).[10]

The Web also provides important opportunities for the enhancement of socio-cognitive and socio-epistemic capabilities. Indeed, with regard to the contemporary Web, there are two ways of reading the phrase "many eyes." It could refer to the surveillance potential of the Web, or it could refer to the fact that the Web supports a capacity to harness the collective resolving power of the "many eyes" of humanity. This latter idea is epitomised by research into so-called *social machines* (Shadbolt et al., 2019). The central idea, in this case, is that the technological (and perhaps social) fabric of the Web can be used as the basis for delivering new forms of collective intelligence, including new "insights" into otherwise intractable problems, such as those posed by climate change, incurable diseases, and large-scale humanitarian crises (Hendler & Berners-Lee, 2010). In this respect, it is interesting to note that many (although not necessarily all) social machines rely on a form of collective "perception" that harnesses the visuo-cognitive capabilities of multiple human individuals (e.g. Lin et al., 2014).

The upshot is a contrasting vision of contemporary (and emerging) technology. With the advent of the Internet and Web, and the emergence of the sorts of brain-reading technology discussed earlier, we seem to encounter a form of privacy violation that is potentially more disturbing than that envisaged in George Orwell's (2004) famous dystopia, *Nineteen Eighty-Four*. It is a vision in which technology is able to probe every aspect of ourselves, including the erstwhile private realm of our minds. Such, perhaps, is the danger of being "interlinked." The relentless march of networking technologies provides us with new opportunities to monitor both ourselves and the world around us and then share this information with countless other individuals. At the same time, however, such technologies open the door to forms of surveillance that are sufficiently potent as to portend the end of privacy as we know it. For better or worse, it seems, the many-eyed Argus is also a two-headed Hydra. On the one hand, our all-seeing eyes are the gateway to a potential transformation in our individual and collective capabilities, providing us with a form of epistemic omniscience—a capacity to see (individually and collectively) beyond the limits of our current knowledge. On the other hand, however, a technology of enlightenment is all too easily repurposed as a searchlight of the "soul"—a technology that threatens to bring an end to privacy as we know it. The path to epistemic omniscience, it seems, is only a few steps removed from the perfect prison of the global panopticon.

The eyes of God Part III: blind spots

Given that surveillance features as a common thematic element of both *Blade Runner* movies, it is perhaps surprising that both should also be concerned with issues relating to the fallibility of memory, of forgetting, data loss, and fragmentation. Indeed, the plots of both films rely on what we might call *blind spots*: gaps in the record caused by imperfect recall and disruptions to a digital infrastructure.

One of the main premises of BR2049 concerns the loss of data in 2022. An Electro-Magnetic Pulse (EMP) led to a blackout, resulting in the erasure (or corruption) of most (if not all) digital records, including the Tyrell Corporation's files on replicants. This is confirmed by the File Clerk, as he reminisces about the Blackout:

> FILE CLERK: Everyone remembers where they were at the Blackout. You?
> K: That was a little before my time.
> FILE CLERK: Mm. I was home with my folks, then 10 days of darkness.
> FILE CLERK: Every machine stopped cold.
> FILE CLERK: When the lights came back, we were wiped clean.
> FILE CLERK: Photos, files, every bit of data, pfft, gone. Bank records too. Heh.
> FILE CLERK: Didn't mind that. It's funny it's only paper that lasted.
> FILE CLERK: I mean, we had everything on drives. Everything, everything, everything. Heh.
> FILE CLERK: My mom still cries over the lost baby pictures.

As noted by the File Clerk, the results of the Blackout were catastrophic—although, as later revealed by Deckard, the Blackout did come with some benefits: it helped to cover the tracks of rogue replicants, and probably reestablished some degree of privacy via practical obscurity:

K: You didn't even meet your own kid? Why?
DECKARD: Because that was the plan. I showed them how to scramble the records, cover their tracks. Everyone had a part. Mine was to leave. *Then the Blackout came, paved over everything. Couldn't have found the child if I tried* [emphasis added].

As a result of the Blackout, the world Wallace inherits is incomplete, at least from an informational standpoint. Although Wallace is a data hoarder, his memory vaults contain little more than the fractured remains of what has gone before. Wallace's view of the present may be hyper-acute, but his view of the past is occluded. In the movie, we see that records of the past, most notably those pertaining to the events of the original *Blade Runner* movie, are stored on glassy, crystalline spheres, called "memory bearings." These objects are clearly intended to provide a link to the past, and they thus speak to the theme of memory, which is prominent throughout both *Blade Runner* movies. In addition to this, however, memory bearings are an important reminder of the links between memory, technology, and vision. Note, for example, that memory bearings are roughly the same shape and size as human eyeballs, and their crystalline structure is somewhat reminiscent of a window or lens. The result is both beautiful and brilliant: a form of thematic convergence that is revealed (or, at any rate, brought into sharper focus) as a result of the film's utilisation of the eye motif.

On the one hand, memory bearings remind us of the observational and recording capabilities of technology—the capacity of technology to (in this case) "crystallise" our connection to the past by capturing specific moments in time. On the other hand, however, the memory bearings remind us of the fragility of memory and the hazards of data loss. As a result of the Blackout, the memory bearings are not the perfect "windows into the past" that they might otherwise have been. "All our memory bearings from the time," Luv comments, "[t]hey were all damaged in the Blackout." Such damage appears to take the form of internal fractures, which transform an erstwhile limpid "lens" into something that more closely resembles a "cataract." As noted by the File

Clerk who works for Wallace Corporation, the Blackout contributed to a form of collective amnesia or, at any rate, a loss of mnemonic connection with the past. For the inhabitants of the BR2049 world, memories of the past are fragmented and imperfect, obscured by incomplete records and the clouded appearance of the memory bearings. "Not much from then," the File Clerk says when K asks him to check Rachael's serial number. "And what's there is ... thick ... milky."

In the real world, our susceptibility to an event resembling the Blackout has been much discussed within both scientific academies and by national governments (House of Commons Defence Committee, 2012). Damaging EMPs could arise through extreme space weather, such as mass coronal ejections and so-called Carrington events,[11] or the detonation of a nuclear device at high altitude. Such events could disable or disrupt the elements of our contemporary computing infrastructure, leading, in the worst cases, to something of a digital Dark Age.

A different kind of digital Dark Age is envisioned by the Internet pioneer, Vint Cerf.[12] His concern is the relentless obsolescence built into so many of our hardware, software, and regulatory systems.[13] The worry is that countless datasets might be rendered inaccessible by changes to our recording technology or the introduction of software that fails to maintain backwards compatibility.

A not-altogether unrelated concern is highlighted by Rick West, a data manager at Google.

> We may [one day] know less about the early 21st century than we do about the early 20th century. The early 20th century is still largely based on things like paper and film formats that are still accessible to a large extent; whereas, much of what we're doing now—the things we're putting into the cloud, our digital content—is born digital. It's not something that we translated from an analog container into a digital container, but, in fact, it is born, and now increasingly dies, as digital content, without any kind of analog counterpart.[14]

This notion of data loss as contributing to a loss of the past, or, at any rate, a form of mnemonic disconnection with the past, resonates with the thematic and artistic concerns of both *Blade Runner* movies, particularly in relation to issues of death, decay, and the ephemerality of experience.

In the original movie, such a concern is amply demonstrated by Roy Batty's "tears in rain" monologue, which has to qualify as one of the most moving and memorable scenes in sci-fi cinematic history. As Batty sits opposite Deckard on the roof of the Bradbury building, he reminds Deckard, and us, of the fleeting character of experience—the fact that death entails the erasure of our first-person experiences, experiences made available to us by our senses:

> BATTY: I've seen things you people wouldn't believe ... All those moments will be lost in time, like tears in rain. Time to die.

BR2049 extends this sense of experiential loss to the realm of technology. A particularly interesting example of such loss comes in the form of Joi. When Joi is disconnected from the console, all her "memories" are stored on a single device, namely, the emanator. There is, as such, a single point of failure for Joi. If Joi's emanator is damaged—if her digital traces of the past are in any way corrupted—then there is no backup repository that can be used to recreate her: she is gone forever, "Like a real girl."

Ultimately, of course, the emanator is destroyed, and with it are all the digital traces of Joi's past. The result is that Joi cannot be resurrected, for there is no way to recreate the particular patterns of data that marked the trajectory of Joi's digital life and that (via learning) made her unique. Joi is, in this sense, special; for she is no longer the sort of thing that can be replaced or duplicated. The Joi we see for much of the movie has been individualised as a result of the particular and peculiar experiences she shared with K, and these experiences cannot be easily recreated or reconstructed. They are, instead, like Batty's tears in rain: moments from the past that are now lost in time.

This notion of data loss as contributing to a loss of the past, or, at any rate, a form of mnemonic disconnection with the past, dovetails with the wider narrative of experiential erasure in both of the *Blade Runner* films. A drowned world is one that offers the prospect of loss. The incessant downpour that we see in *Blade Runner* and the ferment of the ocean in BR2049 are reminiscent of the capacity of water to purify but also to inundate, erode, and literally wash away. Even if the past can be replicated, can it ever be authentic?

The challenge of authentic replication is present in Wallace's corrupted memory bearings. Such memory bearings contain traces of the past, including those pertaining to Deckard's encounter with Rachael. Ultimately, however, these records are revealed to be inadequate. Just as K's Joi is no longer the sort of thing that can be resurrected, neither can Deckard's Rachael be replicated. Despite his best efforts, Wallace is unable to produce a convincing replica of Rachael because the things that made Rachael unique, including the moments she shared with Deckard, are lost in the mists of time. As is indicated by Deckard's response to the Rachael facsimile ("Her eyes were green"), the mists in question are ones that not even the eyes of God can penetrate.

Notes

1 These are referred to as "barracudas" in the final shooting script by Hampton Fancher and Michael Green.
2 It would be a mistake to think that this potential to change ourselves through our technology is anything new. For at least 3.3 million years we and our hominid ancestors have been making tools and progressively altering the nature of the physical, biological, and cultural environments in which our minds develop. The tool-making culture that first surfaced in Lomekwi (Harmand et al., 2015) and elsewhere over the course of 300,000 generations changed our bodies, cultivated our capacity for fine motor control, shaped our cortex, and probably acted as a driver for the emergence of language and planning. We did not just make our technology, our technology made us (Shadbolt & Hampson, 2018). And so it continues into the present day. BR2049 invites us to imagine how far this capacity for technology-mediated transformation might take us.
3 See http://broethr.wikia.com/wiki/Anglo-Saxon_Male_Names.
4 Language may also work to effect a similar shift in our conceptual and cognitive capabilities. Indeed, language has, at times, been characterized as the "ultimate artefact"—a form of cognitive technology that profoundly alters the shape of the human cognitive economy (see Clark, 1997: chap. 10). This is a topic that is explored in one of Denis Villeneuve's earlier movies, namely, *Arrival*.
5 This appeal to cognitive humanity contrasts with the notions of biological and evaluative humanity, as discussed by Gaut (2015).
6 In fact, recent research with human drone operators shows that far from exhibiting a sense of carefree detachment, most operators reported feeling grief, remorse, and sadness (Chappelle et al., 2018). Many experienced these "negative, disruptive emotions" for a month or more.
7 This is the technologically mediated equivalent of what is sometimes called autoscopy (Blanke & Mohr, 2005). Autoscopy literally means "self watcher."

Interestingly, given the nature of Wallace's character, it is often associated with some form of psychiatric disorder, such as delirium, depression, or psychosis (Dening & Berrios, 1994). In this sense, Wallace's eye drones might be seen as a form of *technological psychotomimetic*—a technology that, in the manner of a psychotomimetic drug, yields a state of psychosis.

8 See https://www.diyphotography.net/blade-runner-cinematography-jordan-cronenweth/.
9 In all likelihood, Lt. Joshi is tracking K's movements via his spinner, although it isn't entirely clear from the movie. After Luv dispenses with Lt. Joshi, she asks the LAPD computer to locate K ("Location: Officer KD6-3.7"), but we aren't told whether it is K's location that is revealed, or simply the location of his spinner.
10 It is, of course, unclear how such claims stand to be affected by worries about information manipulation, fake news, and the emergence of a post-truth world.
11 Named after the 1859 solar storm observed by British astronomer Richard Carrington.
12 See https://www.itnews.com.au/news/internet-is-losing-its-memory-cerf-495854.
13 See https://www.economist.com/leaders/2012/04/28/bit-rot.
14 See https://theweek.com/articles/747424/scientists-warn-entering-digital-dark-age.

References

Bjerring, J. C., & Pedersen, N. J. L. L. (2014). All the (Many, Many) Things We Know: Extended Knowledge. *Philosophical Issues* 24(1), 24–38.
Blanke, O., & Mohr, C. (2005). Out-of-Body Experience, Heautoscopy, and Autoscopic Hallucination of Neurological Origin: Implications for Neurocognitive Mechanisms of Corporeal Awareness and Self-Consciousness. *Brain Research Reviews* 50(1), 184–199.
Carter, A. J., Clark, A., Kallestrup, J., Palermos, O. S., & Pritchard, D. (Eds.). (2018). *Extended Epistemology*. Oxford: Oxford University Press.
Chappelle, W., Skinner, E., Goodman, T., Swearingen, J., & Prince, L. (2018). Emotional Reactions to Killing in Remotely Piloted Aircraft Crewmembers During and Following Weapon Strikes. *Military Behavioral Health* 6(4), 357–367.
Clark, A. (1997). *Being There: Putting Brain, Body and World Together Again*. Cambridge, MA: MIT Press.
Davies, D. (2015). Blade Runner and the Cognitive Values of Cinema. In A. Coplan & D. Davies (Eds.), *Blade Runner* (pp. 135–154). Abingdon: Routledge.
Dening, T. R., & Berrios, G. E. (1994). Autoscopic Phenomena. *The British Journal of Psychiatry* 165(6), 808–817.
Dick, P. K. (2007). *Do Androids Dream of Electric Sheep?* New York: Ballantine Books.

Gaut, B. (2015). Elegy in LA: *Blade Runner*, Empathy and Death. In A. Coplan & D. Davies (Eds.), *Blade Runner* (pp. 31–45). Abingdon: Routledge.

Harmand, S., Lewis, J. E., Feibel, C. S., Lepre, C. J., Prat, S., Lenoble, A., et al. (2015). 3.3-Million-Year-Old Stone Tools from Lomekwi 3, West Turkana, Kenya. *Nature* 521(7552), 310–315.

Hendler, J. A., & Berners-Lee, T. (2010). From the Semantic Web to Social Machines: A Research Challenge for AI on the World Wide Web. *Artificial Intelligence* 174(2), 156–161.

House of Commons Defence Committee. (2012). *Developing Threats: Electro-Magnetic Pulses (EMP)*. London: The Stationery Office.

Johnson, N. A. (2008). Direct Selection for Reproductive Isolation: The Wallace Effect and Reinforcement. In C. H. Smith & G. Beccaloni (Eds.), *Natural Selection and Beyond: The Intellectual Legacy of Alfred Russel Wallace* (pp. 114–124). Oxford: Oxford University Press.

Kay, K. N., Naselaris, T., Prenger, R. J., & Gallant, J. L. (2008). Identifying Natural Images from Human Brain Activity. *Nature* 452(7185), 352–355.

Kirsh, D. (2013). Embodied Cognition and the Magical Future of Interaction Design. *ACM Transactions on Computer-Human Interaction* 20(1), 1–30.

Lin, A. Y.-M., Huynh, A., Lanckriet, G., & Barrington, L. (2014). Crowdsourcing the Unknown: The Satellite Search for Genghis Khan. *PLoS One* 9(12), e114046.

Ludwig, D. (2015). Extended Cognition and the Explosion of Knowledge. *Philosophical Psychology* 28(3), 355–368.

Naselaris, T., Olman, C. A., Stansbury, D. E., Ugurbil, K., & Gallant, J. L. (2015). A Voxel-Wise Encoding Model for Early Visual Areas Decodes Mental Images of Remembered Scenes. *Neuroimage* 105, 215–228.

Naselaris, T., Prenger, R. J., Kay, K. N., Oliver, M., & Gallant, J. L. (2009). Bayesian Reconstruction of Natural Images from Human Brain Activity. *Neuron* 63(6), 902–915.

Nishimoto, S., Vu, A. T., Naselaris, T., Benjamini, Y., Yu, B., & Gallant, J. L. (2011). Reconstructing Visual Experiences from Brain Activity Evoked by Natural Movies. *Current Biology* 21(19), 1641–1646.

O'Hara, K., & Shadbolt, N. R. (2008). *The Spy in the Coffee Machine: The End of Privacy as We Know It*. Oxford: Oneworld Publications.

Orwell, G. (2004). *Nineteen Eighty-Four*. London: Penguin Books.

Shadbolt, N., & Hampson, R. (2018). *The Digital Ape: How to Live (in Peace) with Smart Machines*. London: Scribe Publications.

Shadbolt, N., O'Hara, K., De Roure, D., & Hall, W. (2019). *The Theory and Practice of Social Machines*. Basel: Springer.

Smart, P. R. (2012). The Web-Extended Mind. *Metaphilosophy* 43(4), 426–445.

Smart, P. R., Clowes, R. W., & Heersmink, R. (2017). Minds Online: The Interface between Web Science, Cognitive Science and the Philosophy of Mind. *Foundations and Trends in Web Science*, 6(1–2), 1–232.

Van Kleek, M., Binns, R., Zhao, J., Slack, A., Lee, S., Ottewell, D., et al. (2018). X-ray Refine: Supporting the Exploration and Refinement of Information Exposure Resulting from Smartphone Apps. In R. Mandryk, M. Hancock, M. Perry & A. Cox (Eds.), *Conference on Human Factors in Computing Systems*. New York: Association of Computing Machinery.

Zuboff, S. (2015). Big Other: Surveillance Capitalism and the Prospects of an Information Civilisation. *Journal of Information Technology* 30(1), 75–89.

Chapter 12

Timothy Shanahan

WHAT AM I TO YOU?

THE DECK-A-REP DEBATE AND THE QUESTION OF FICTIONAL TRUTH

Introduction

NO PHILOSOPHICAL EXAMINATION OF *BLADE RUNNER* 2049 would be complete without considering its bearing on the question of whether replicant-killer Rick Deckard is himself a replicant. Ever since the original *Blade Runner* premiered in 1982, fans have scrutinised that film and other sources for clues to solve the puzzle.[1] There are intriguing hints (especially in later versions of the film) that Deckard *might* be a replicant; but the truth is never made explicit.[2] Many hoped that BR2049 would resolve the issue once and for all. As it turns out, the sequel is just as enigmatic on this score as the original (Butler, 2018).

Thus, the "Deck-a-Rep debate" remains stubbornly deadlocked. *Unless*, that is, we believe Ridley Scott, who directed the original film and served as executive producer of BR2049. For Scott tells us, "The idea that I always insisted on from day one, because I directed the fucking movie [i.e., *Blade Runner*], is that Harrison Ford, Deckard, is a replicant. *He had to be. So for this story to function today* [i.e., in BR2049], *he has to be a replicant; otherwise, there's no story*" [emphases added].[3] Some have taken such directorial declarations to be decisive.[4] After all, if *Ridley Scott* says that Deckard is a replicant, well, that definitively settles the matter, doesn't it?

Maybe not. There is more to Scott's assertion than at first meets the eye. Considered closely, his assertion raises a host of questions about (among other things) the identity of fictional characters across fictional representations, the scope of directorial authority, the nature of fictional truth, and our ability to know it. Indeed, taken at face value, there are at least *seven* distinct claims asserted or implied in Scott's declaration; namely: (1) Deckard is a replicant in *Blade Runner*. (2) If Deckard is a replicant in *Blade Runner*, then he *must* be one in BR2049 as well. (3) Unless Deckard is a replicant, there is "no story" in BR2049. (4) As the director of the original film, Scott occupies an epistemically privileged vantage point regarding the truth about Deckard's nature in both it and its sequel. (5) More generally, a fictional work's creator is, by virtue of *being* its creator, uniquely qualified to reveal the truth about that work's story, characters, meaning, and so forth. (6) There are truths about fictional characters. (7) At least some of those truths are *made true* by factors extrinsic to the fictional work(s) in which those characters appear.[5]

My aim in this chapter is to examine these and related claims to assess the extent to which they are credible. I will argue that claims (2) through (5) are at the very least questionable, and that even if one grants claim (6), claim (7) is false—yet its acceptance has far-reaching implications for our attempts to make sense of fictional narratives and, indeed, of the nature of fiction itself. Exploring these issues will require not only careful attention to the narrative details of the two *Blade Runner* films, but also a focused foray into the metaphysics and epistemology of fiction.

I hasten to add that my purpose in the following discussion is *not* to attack Sir Ridley Scott—a visionary filmmaker, who has brought us some of the greatest films of all time. Rather, my aim is to use Scott's provocative comment about BR2049 as the point of departure for *deepening* the often-superficial Deck-a-Rep debate, for thinking more broadly about the nature of truth within works of fiction (especially films), and for assessing our ability to know whatever fictional truths there may be. Let me also assure readers that I am sympathetic to the complaint that the Deck-a-Rep debate has occupied a disproportionately large place in (popular) discussions of *Blade Runner*. It would be understandable if one assumed that there is now nothing else worth saying about that issue. However, in light of Scott's striking statement, the topic deserves reconsideration because, if *Scott is right*, the viability of BR2049 as a sequel, perhaps even as a film, crucially depends on the truth of a particular position in the Deck-a-Rep debate. So, it is worthwhile investigating whether he is right, beginning with perhaps the easiest issue to resolve.

Deckard has to be a replicant; otherwise, there's no story

First, consider Scott's claim that unless Deckard is a replicant, there is "no story" in BR2049. Whereas, manifestly, there is a story in BR2049, presumably he means that unless Deckard is a replicant, there is no *coherent* or *compelling* story in the film. The most straightforward way to evaluate this claim, so understood, is to bracket the question of whether Deckard is a replicant and then see whether the film thereby becomes narratively eviscerated, or even unintelligible.

K's quest to discover his true identity and to understand its significance is arguably the film's central narrative. Through a series of startling developments, he first comes to believe, and then is stripped of the belief, that he is the child of Rachael (a replicant) and Deckard. The significance of this belief for him resides, not in the fact that *Deckard* is his *father*, but rather that *a replicant* is his *mother*. That is the fact that "breaks the world," as Lt. Joshi worried (without, it seems, having any idea who or even what the father might be). Eventually, K is disappointed to discover that he is not what he had hoped he was. But his disappointment has nothing to do with Deckard's nature as replicant or human.[6] Had he learned that Rachael was his mother after all, but that someone other than Deckard was his father, his hope that he is special would have been undiminished. Hence, the film's central narrative holds up whether or not Deckard is a replicant.

Arguably, the same is true for the film's secondary narratives involving: Niander Wallace's quest to find the child born of a replicant (because he believes that it holds the key to unlocking the secret of replicant procreation); Lt. Joshi's worry that if it became widely known that a replicant gave birth, the wall separating humans and replicants would collapse (because humans are *born*, whereas replicants are *made*); and Freysa's ambition to recruit Rachael's daughter as a messiah for her nascent resistance movement because (she thinks), "If a baby can come from one of us ... we are much more than slaves, we are our own masters." None of these secondary narratives requires that Deckard be a replicant. Indeed, some make more sense if he is a human.[7]

The same can be said for an especially striking scene that merits close examination.[8] In his quest to track down Deckard, K questions Gaff, Deckard's old brown-nosing LAPD partner, now living (and/or working) in a retirement community. In a series of cryptic but suggestive remarks, he tells K that his former partner "was not long for this world," that "there was something in his eye," and that Deckard was "retired." Fans of the original film could be expected to recognise the potential significance of these remarks. After all, replicants, produced by the Tyrell Corp. as slave labour for the off-world colonies, were literally *not for this world*. They were identified using an *eye*-scanning device (the Voight-Kampff machine). When detected on earth, they were summarily *retired*. Gaff may be dropping not-so-subtle hints that *Deckard is a replicant*. K does not visibly react to those clues. But for those with ears to hear, the deeper meaning of Gaff's words may seem plain.

Well, perhaps. Such an interpretation presupposes that Gaff knows the truth about Deckard's nature. But we cannot be sure that even his old partner knew what he was.[9] Moreover, even if Gaff sincerely *believed* Deckard to be a replicant and was slyly communicating that belief to K (who, not having seen the original film, might not be expected to pick up on Gaff's subtle innuendos), it wouldn't follow that his belief about Deckard was *correct*. Besides, an alternative and equally reasonable interpretation is readily available. By saying that Deckard "was not long for this world," Gaff may have been noting that by fleeing with Rachael (a replicant he had been ordered to kill), Deckard had brought upon himself a death sentence; that the "something in his eye" was Rachael, his love interest; and that he had *literally* retired as a blade runner. (In voice-over narration in the theatrical release of *Blade Runner*, Deckard repeatedly refers to himself as "retired"—while obviously still very much alive.) Finally, we may presume that Gaff knows that K is a replicant. As a former blade runner, he may still take a dim view of that kind. By uttering his cryptic remarks, Gaff may have been having a little fun at K's expense, just as he may have been doing at Deckard's expense in the original film (e.g. by making little origami figures). In short, we do not need to suppose that Deckard is a replicant to make sense of Gaff's remarks.

To sum up, recall that the question being considered here is *not* whether the evidence in BR2049 makes it *more likely than not* that Deckard is a replicant, nor whether it shows that he *might* be a replicant, nor even whether it could possibly be viewed as *supporting* that interpretation.

Those are precisely the sorts of questions that characterise the Deck-a-Rep debate. Rather, the question here is whether BR2049's story becomes hopelessly compromised *unless* Deckard is viewed as a replicant. I've argued that such a sweeping claim cannot be sustained. The narratives in BR2049 are no less coherent if we simply leave the question of Deckard's nature unresolved. We can thus turn our attention to some of the presuppositions that draw upon broader considerations to see if, taken together, they provide grounds for judging Scott's claim about Deckard to be correct.

Don't you know what I am?

Ridley Scott insists that because Deckard is a replicant in *Blade Runner*, he must be one in BR2049 as well. In a previous book (Shanahan, 2014) I critically examined ten arguments commonly advanced to demonstrate that in the original film Deckard must be a replicant, showed why each of those arguments fails, and suggested that an alternative view has as much, and probably more, to recommend it.[10] Space prohibits revisiting those arguments here. Suppose, however, for the sake of argument, that Deckard is judged to be a replicant in the original film. Would it follow, as Scott assumes, that he *must* be a replicant in its sequel as well?

Not necessarily. Scott appears to be relying upon what we might dub the principle of Trans-Fictional Identity—namely, the claim that the identity (and/or essential properties) of any fictional character is necessarily transitive across works of fiction in which "they" are named. The truth of this principle is not self-evident.

Consider James Bond. A character with that name first appeared in Ian Fleming's novel *Casino Royale* (1953). Over the subsequent sixty years, "James Bond" has appeared in numerous other novels and films. It is tempting to think of James Bond as necessarily the same character in all of them. Yet each of those fictional works stands on its own. We can make sense of the 2015 film *Spectre* with no knowledge whatsoever of Ian Fleming's novel *Casino Royale*, or indeed of any of the James Bond novels and films that have appeared in the interim.[11] Moreover, what is true of Agent 007 in Dr. No, the first James Bond film, in which he was played by Sean Connery as swarthy, urbane, and polished, need not be true of the character with that code name in the most recent instalment (to date) in which he is played by Daniel Craig as fair-haired, somewhat coarse, and decidedly rough-around-the-edges. Likewise, what might be true of the Deckard in *Blade Runner* need not be true of the Deckard in BR2049—not even whether he is a replicant. After all, there have been at least equally dramatic alterations in a character bearing the same name from one fictional representation to another.[12] Besides, a consistent application of the principle upon which Scott implicitly relies would entail that because the Deckard character in *Do Androids Dream of Electric Sheep?* (the fictional work in which he was first named) is explicitly *not* a replicant, he *could not* be one in either of the two *Blade Runner* films. It is hard to see what could justify such a categorical dismissal of what seems like a real possibility. But if so, then the assumption that if Deckard was a replicant in *Blade Runner*, he must be one in BR2049 as well, is unsupported.

I directed the movie

So far, we have been assessing the assertion that Deckard must be a replicant in BR2049 by considering evidence internal to the fictional works in which a character with that name appears. We can now turn our attention to external evidence. Recall Scott's statement: "The idea that I always insisted on from day one, *because I directed the fucking movie*, is that ... Deckard is a replicant" (emphasis added). The idea seems to be that because he directed the original movie, Scott occupies a uniquely privileged epistemic position with regard to knowing the truth about Deckard's nature in that film and, by implication, in BR2049 as well. More generally, according to this Authorial View of fictional truth, "what is true in the story is just what the author intended to be true in the story, and the author's intentions are formed with reference to what he has imagined" (Phillips, 1999: 276).[13] Thus, if Scott imagined and thereby intended Deckard to be a replicant in *Blade Runner* then, necessarily, Deckard must be a replicant, full stop.

Despite its popular appeal, this Authorial View suffers from at least two crippling problems. First, although it may be natural to think of the director as a film's creator, it is usually the case that a number of individuals contribute significant creative input to the final artistic product, thereby engendering the possibility of opposing interpretive views. Philip K. Dick deliberately made Deckard human in *Electric Sheep*.[14] Harrison Ford—who is so closely associated with the character he plays that Scott can write, "Harrison Ford, Deckard, is a replicant,"—has

Figure 12.1 Ridley Scott, right, directs Harrison Ford in *Blade Runner* (1982)

always said that he considers the character he plays to be human.[15] Hampton Fancher, who co-wrote the screenplay for both the original *and* the sequel, has said that he considers it an open question whether Deckard is a replicant[16]—an opinion that is consistent with director Denis Villeneuve's explicit statement that in *his* film he did not want to resolve that issue.[17] *Whose* view should be taken as authoritative? To make matters worse, in some interviews Ridley Scott has referred to Deckard as "a Nexus-6" (Sullivan, 2012). On other occasions, he has hinted that Deckard is "a Nexus-7" (Sammon, 2017: 517). *Which* view should we trust?

A second issue concerns the fact that most of us would be unwilling to docilely accept just *any* statement by a writer or director about their literary or cinematic creation, as the Authorial View would require us to do. If Samuel Taylor Coleridge insisted that his *Rime of the Ancient Mariner* is *really* about a failed jewel heist, we would be justified in rejecting that claim as ludicrous (Phillips, 1999: 277). Likewise, if (absurdly) Ridley Scott were to insist that Deckard is, in fact, the xenomorph of the *Alien* films (albeit in a clever disguise), the interpretive cost of accepting such a claim would be prohibitive. In this case, we would reasonably weigh other considerations against the director's surprising insistence, and reach our own conclusions based (among other things) on the narrative integrity of the film itself. That same principle applies equally in less dramatic cases in which a director's gloss on their own film conflicts with what we encounter in the film itself. Phillips (1999: 275) is right: "The author's intentions play a role in how the story is constructed, but once this work is completed it is the product of this labour, and not the author's intentions, which determines what propositions [i.e., truths] are in the story." Hence, Ridley Scott may insist that Deckard is a replicant; but that insistence cannot *make* it so.

All the courage in the world cannot alter fact

So far, we have been assessing Ridley Scott's claim that Deckard *must* be a replicant in BR2049 by considering evidential considerations bearing on that claim. We now need to turn our attention to deeper philosophical issues that are implicated in, but transcend, that specific issue. Scott's insistence that Deckard is a replicant can be given a weaker or a stronger reading. In the weaker reading, he can be understood as saying merely that BR2049—and *Blade Runner*, for that matter—are *narratively intelligible* only if we view Deckard as a replicant. This reading is addressed above and in my book on the original film (Shanahan, 2014), where I argue that such a judgment cannot be sustained. Scott's insistence that Deckard is a replicant also can be given a stronger reading according to which he is claiming that it is *true*, in some sense, that Deckard is a replicant.[18] That claim, in turn, entails the thesis that *there are truths about fictional characters*.

Difficult questions follow from that stronger interpretation: *Are* there, in fact, truths about fictional characters? If there are, what is the *nature* of such truths? How *far* do such truths extend? What *makes* those truths ... true?[19] A vast (and often highly technical) scholarly philosophical literature explores such questions. Space prohibits engaging with that literature in depth here. But by selectively drawing upon that work we can hope to make at least a little headway in exploring those questions.

To get started, we need an account of "truth" in general that can then be further specified. Following Armstrong (2004), truth may be understood as a binary relation requiring a *truth-bearer* (i.e., a statement, proposition, belief, or thought) that has the property of being true, as well as a *truth-maker* (i.e., facts) that makes it the case that the truth-bearer has that property.[20] Truth in this view consists in a particular kind of *correspondence* between statements and facts. Truths about the actual world are made true by actual facts. Likewise, truths within fiction—*fictional truths*—are made true by *fictional facts*.[21] The questions previously posed about the existence and nature of fictional truth then become dependent on answers to even more basic questions: Where are fictional facts to be found, and how might they be constituted?

First, consider the simplest, most austere, and most uncompromising view:

(F1) Fiction, by definition, deals in make-believe worlds, and fictional characters are not actual persons; hence, there are no facts (and thus there are no truths) concerning them.

According to (F1), because fictional characters do not actually exist, there are no facts that could serve as truth-makers for any statements ostensibly made about them. Hence, there can be no truths about them. It follows that we cannot *know* anything true about them. Consequently, there is no truth about Deckard's nature, and of course therefore none that can be known.[22]

Judging from its paucity of defenders, this seems to be a deeply unpopular view. Despite being fictional, it seems to many manifestly true that *within the film* in which these characters appear, Officer KD6-3.7 is a NEXUS 9 blade runner, Niander Wallace is a brilliant industrialist, Luv is his ruthless lieutenant, and Freysa is a passionate freedom fighter. Besides, a *fictional truth* requires only that there be relevant *fictional facts* to make certain statements about fictional characters, objects, events, and the like, true.[23] None of these, of course, needs to be actual.

For the sake of argument, let's suppose that the foregoing statements about BR2049 *do* express fictional truths. What determines the relevant fictional facts and thereby the fictional truths they support? Answers to *those* questions distinguish the remaining views worth examining.

A natural place to begin is with facts that just seem to be handed to us in a fictional work:

(F2) The only fictional facts are those explicitly given within a fictional work itself.

A fictional fact is explicitly given, we might suppose, if it is *stated* or otherwise *shown* to us within a work of fiction. For example, early in BR2049 we are *told*, "The collapse of the ecosystems in the mid-2020s led to the rise of industrialist Niander Wallace, whose mastery of synthetic farming averted famine." According to (F2), it is therefore true, within BR2049, that Wallace's mastery of synthetic farming averted famine.[24] Likewise, it is true that K reports to Lt. Joshi, that Joi is his digital girlfriend, and so on, because in each of these cases we are *shown* relevant facts within the film that support those statements.[25] By contrast, because we are *not* explicitly told or shown what Deckard really is, there is simply no truth about that.[26]

This view might strike some as rather ... miserly. Surely, we are entitled to *infer* certain facts from those that are explicitly given, aren't we? As David Lewis (1978: 41) observes, "Most of us are content to read a fiction against a background of well-known facts, 'reading into' the fiction content that is not there explicitly but that comes jointly from the explicit content and the factual background."[27] So, from the fact that Wallace's corporate headquarters displays an abundance of wood, and the additional fact that (as we learn from the character Doc Badger) wood is a rare and precious commodity in 2049, we can conclude that Wallace is stupendously wealthy.

Note that the foregoing inference is *not* what would *make* the statement "Wallace is stupendously wealthy" true. That inference would simply *reveal* to us a fictional fact that already exists, as it were. But since that fact is not directly given to us in the film, it would have to exist (if it exists at all) as an ungiven but inferable feature of the *fictional world* (partially) depicted in the film. How else could it exist? This suggests a considerably more expansive view of fictional facts:

(F3) Fictional facts include those explicitly given within a fictional work, plus other facts that collectively constitute the fictional world (partially) depicted in a work of fiction.

This view invites us to think of fictional characters as inhabiting *fictional worlds*, either chock-full of facts, or as partly stocked with facts. A fictional world is *complete* if every statement about it is either true or false. Such a world would need to be *fully factually determinate*—there would need to be a fact determining the truth of every statement about it—even if no one could know every fact (and hence truth) about it. A fictional world is *incomplete* if only some, but not all, statements about it are either true or false. Such a world will not be fully factually determinate. Some statements about it will lack a truth value. They will be indeterminate.

Either way, in order to make sense of a work of fiction, we may have to assume (unless given compelling reasons to think otherwise) that the fictional world (partially) depicted in the work operates according to the same principles as the actual world. Unsupported heavy objects fall; water is wet; people have private mental states; and so on. Thus, some fictional facts will be explicitly given in the fictional work itself, others will be such that they can be inferred from those explicitly given facts, others will comprise the fundamental structure of the fictional world, and yet (possibly countless) others may not be epistemically accessible at all, but will exist nonetheless.[28] Thus, if the fictional world of BR2049 is *incomplete* there may not be a truth of the matter about whether Deckard is a replicant. If the fictional world of BR2049 is *complete*, then, necessarily, there is a fact of the matter about whether Deckard is a replicant, but it might be such that we can never know what that fact is. We can, of course, attempt to *infer* some facts from other facts explicitly given in the film, but we may never know for sure if we are right.

Unless, that is, we can rely on sources *external* to a work of fiction to supplement the fictional facts explicitly given in the work, those whose existence we can infer, and those required for the fictional work to be intelligible at all. Suppose, for example, that the creator of a fictional work can know vastly more about its fictional world than we can because the creator's imagination and intentions *constitute* the facts that comprise that fictional world. Hence, a fourth view:

(F4) Fictional facts include those explicitly given within a fictional work, plus others that collectively constitute the fictional world (partially) depicted in that work, all or some of which are *constituted by the imagination and intentions of the fictional work's creator*.

For example, suppose that: Ridley Scott directs a film called *Blade Runner* that depicts a fictional Los Angeles in 2019; there is a character in that fictional world named "Deckard;" and Scott tells us in interviews that he imagined and intended Deckard to be a replicant. According to view (F4), therefore, it is a fact that Deckard is a replicant in that fictional world, even if (let us suppose) this fact is not explicitly given in, nor inferable from, anything in the film itself.[29]

But why stop with the imagination and intentions of those few who receive formal credit as a fictional work's creator(s)? After all, what would any work of art, including any film, be without its audience? Eric Kandel (2012) discusses the notion of "the beholder's share," according to which a work of art is "completed" by its beholders. In this view, those who apprehend a work of art are, in some sense, co-creators of that work. But if so, then perhaps their imaginations and intentions should also be understood to have the power to populate a fictional world with facts. Hence, the most expansive view of fictional facts, and truth, that we have space here to consider:

(F5) Fictional facts include those explicitly given within a fictional work, plus others that collectively constitute the fictional world (partially) depicted in that work, all or some of which are constituted by the imagination and intentions of (a) those who receive formal credit for the work *and* (b) those who apprehend or behold it.[30]

In this view, nothing but the imaginations of a work of fiction's co-creators limit the number of fictional facts constituting a given fictional world—or rather, *worlds*, because there is no reason to assume (and plenty of reasons not to) that different beholders will imagine different worlds, thereby resulting in different and incompatible fictional truths. Consequently, in what could be considered a *reductio ad absurdum*, Deckard both is, and equally is not, a replicant in BR2049.

Even he didn't know what he was

It is time to begin drawing this discussion to a close. We've identified five different answers to the question, "What determines the fictional facts that make claims about fictional characters true?"[31] Rather than trying to decisively settle the issue of which (if any) of those answers is correct, we can summarise their epistemological consequences for the debate with which we began: What can we really *know* about whether Rick Deckard is a replicant in BR2049?

As we have seen, even if we assume, pace (F1), that there *are* fictional truths, BR2049 does not, as specified by (F2), present us with any explicit fictional facts requiring that Deckard be viewed as a replicant. Moreover, a fact of that sort, located somewhere in a fictional world, cannot be cogently inferred from the explicit fictional facts that are given, as (F3) would require. Appealing to the imagination(s) of a fictional work's creator(s), as (F4) and (F5) would bid us to do, is fraught with difficulties. As argued previously, we can't even rely on the Principle of the Transitivity of Fictional Identities to transfer to BR2049 Deckard's (supposed) nature as a replicant in *Blade Runner*. Consequently, even if there *is* a truth of the matter about whether Deckard is a replicant (which is questionable), neither we nor even Ridley Scott has epistemic access to that truth.[32] Hence, we cannot know whether Deckard is a replicant.

Such a rejection of *claims to knowledge of fictional truth that outrun both evidence and logical inference* invites predictable complaints. Doesn't this conclusion severely limit our ability to *understand*, not to mention *enjoy*, works of fiction? As Lamarque (1990: 335) observes, "Both literary critics and ordinary readers take it for granted that inferences beyond what is explicit are not just permissible but indispensable in understanding fiction." Of course. But inferential permissibility and indispensability do not entail knowledge of fictional truths any more than they entail knowledge of scientific truths. It is scientifically *permissible* to infer from observations that the universe is ultimately simple, unified, consistent, and so on. Such heuristic posits may also be *indispensable* for the scientific quest to understand nature. But these posits can be viewed as scaffolding that assists us in imaginatively relating otherwise disparate facts to one another so that we can thereby achieve a coherent understanding of those facts—one of the key aims of scientific inquiry. Whether such posits can be known to be true is a distinct issue. Likewise, with respect to a work of fiction, we can, and no doubt should, make inferences on the basis of various assumptions to assist us in achieving a coherent understanding of that work. Whether any conclusions based upon those assumptions can be known to be true is a distinct issue.

Such a conclusion might *seem* to rob fiction of much of its richness, but it need not. Although a fictional work may contain far fewer knowable truths than some have supposed, it remains a perfectly appropriate *response* to fiction to freely *imagine* all manner of fictional facts in order to fill in one's conception of the work. After all, a fictional work's creator(s) can't supply every detail of the fictional world they have partially sketched, and therefore must count on their audience to render the work whole *for themselves* to whatever extent the audience desires. Indeed, in the second section of this chapter I generously helped myself to this imaginative license. But from the fact that well-wrought fiction invites diverse *imaginings*, it does not follow that it demands unlimited truths.[33]

Such complaints aside, such agnosticism may be deeply upsetting to some. The fact that the Deck-a-Rep debate has persisted for over three decades suggests something about the importance many fans associate with there being (and with someone knowing) *the* truth. Some are emotionally invested in a particular interpretation. BR2049 co-screenwriter Michael Green attempts to offer some consolation with respect to the film he helped to create:

> I suspect that the people who love to debate this [issue] will come out [of the theatre] vehemently believing they have their confirmation [about Deckard's nature] and then will be shocked to find others disagree just as hotly. But, you know, this is *Blade Runner*—no one can be wrong."
>
> (Vilkomerson, 2017)

If Green just means that partisans on both sides can find evidence in the film to support their respective views, then he is undoubtedly correct. But if he means that both sides in the Deck-a-Rep debate can *be* correct, then his claim is incoherent insofar as they embrace incompatible claims to knowledge. The only justified consolation here consists in realising that *the other side's* claim to knowledge is false.

If you don't get it, you're a moron

At the end of BR2049, when Deckard asks K, "Who am I to you?" he might as well be asking "*What* am I to you?"—*to us*. In Dick's (1968) novel, Deckard is presented as human. *Blade Runner* provides clues that he *might* be a replicant, but never makes that explicit. BR2049 is even more non-committal. Consequently, Deckard's nature as a replicant *could have been*, but as a matter of fact *isn't*, revealed in any of these works of fiction. *Blade Runner* director Ridley Scott, citing Deckard's unicorn reverie in later versions of his film as proof that Deckard must be a replicant, has remarked: "Can't be any clearer than that. If you don't get it, you're a moron."[34] Perhaps. But as I've argued in this chapter, a more reasonable view is that there is no knowable truth of the matter about whether Deckard is a replicant. We are perfectly free to imagine all manner of facts and truths that go beyond those explicitly given in a work of fiction. Enjoying and making sense of fiction typically requires doing precisely that. But we should not confuse what *we* bring to a fictional work with what the fictional work itself explicitly provides—or provides justification for asserting. Happily, this may be precisely what we should want from works of fiction, namely, the depiction of partially realised worlds that permit their beholders to imaginatively fill in the details as they each might imagine them to be.

Notes

1 Fodder for the seemingly insatiable desire to know the truth about Deckard crops up regularly. For example, the Internet Movie Database tells us that: "a newly-assembled narrative of 24 deleted and alternate scenes from the film *Blade Runner* [provides] additional clues to *the true nature* of Rick Deckard" (emphasis added). https://www.imdb.com/title/tt1165254/. Retrieved 12 August 2019.
2 Director Ridley Scott's view seems to be that, although Deckard *is* a replicant in *Blade Runner*, that fact was not explicitly *revealed* to the audience. Two years after the film came out, he confided: "At one stage, we considered having Deckard turn out to be, ironically, a replicant. In fact, if you look at the film closely, especially the ending, you may get some clues—some by slight innuendo—that Deckard is indeed a replicant" (Peary, 2005: 54—55). More recently he has said: "We don't know for sure that Harrison Ford [in *Blade Runner*] was a Nexus. Harrison himself refused to believe it, and I said, 'Harry, you're a Nexus'" (Lapointe, 2017: 13). Paul M. Sammon, who had a fly-on-the-wall vantage point during the filming of *Blade Runner*, has remarked: "Is he [Deckard] a replicant, is he not.... The question on set was 'maybe.' It was never he is or not. Ambiguity was the key word, always" (University of California Television [UCTV], air date 28 May 2019 https://www.youtube.com/watch?v=HV3bw3LAHKM). Accessed 12 August 2019.
3 Emphases added. http://www.denofgeek.com/uk/movies/ridley-scott/51999/ridley-scott-interview-blade-runner-2049-alien-and-more Retrieved 19 June 2018. Scott has made similar remarks on other occasions. See, for example, Sammon (2017: 515–516).

4 See https://screencrush.com/ridley-scott-blade-runner-2049-script-too-long/. Retrieved 12 August 2019.
5 By a *fictional work* I mean a work of *fiction*, not a work that is fictional in the sense of itself being non-actual.
6 I will treat *replicant* and *human* as mutually exclusive categories—which, of course, in some understandings of those terms, they are not. The replicants may be human in all the ways that matter (Shanahan, 2018). Indeed, BR2049 informs us that replicants are bioengineered *humans*. Thus, the distinction at issue here really concerns whether or not Deckard is a *synthetic* human.
7 After all, Freysa does say, "If a baby can come from *one* of us ..." (emphasis added). This is *not* to say that the film's other narratives can only be understood in this way. The point here is just that none of the film's narratives *depends* on Deckard being a replicant, *or* human.
8 It is not hard to imagine this scene with Gaff playing the same confirmatory role for some viewers of BR2049 that the unicorn reverie and Gaff's origami unicorn figure play for viewers of *Blade Runner: The Final Cut* (2007) who are convinced that Deckard must be a replicant. Nonetheless, neither scene provides the confirmation those viewers seek.
9 In an alternate (unused) scene from *Blade Runner*, Gaff yells to Deckard across the rooftop of the Bradbury Building, "You've done a man's job, sir. But are you sure you *are* a man? It's hard to tell who's who around here." This is usually interpreted as Gaff sowing seeds of doubt in *Deckard*, and/or tipping off the audience. But perhaps he was expressing his *own* uncertainty.
10 Paul Salamoff (2018) provides additional (and in my view, compelling) reasons for concluding that the Deckard-is-a-replicant interpretation is far too problematic to be complacently accepted.
11 This is *not* to claim, of course, that our acquaintance with earlier works in which "James Bond" appears cannot or should not inform our reading or viewing of later works in which a character with that name appears. The point here is just that such acquaintance is not *required*.
12 In "The Final Problem" (1893), Sherlock Holmes is *killed* in a struggle with his nemesis, Professor Moriarty, yet reappears ten years later—no worse for wear—in "The Adventure of the Empty House" (1903).
13 As we shall see below, Phillips *rejects* this view.
14 As Dick explained, "*Sheep* stemmed from my basic interest in the problem of differentiating the authentic human being from the reflexive machine, which I call an android" (Sammon, 2017: 18).
15 See, e.g., Sammon (2017: 412–413).
16 "Is Deckard a replicant? *Blade Runner 2049* writers discuss that and other mysteries" https://www.latimes.com/entertainment/movies/la-et-mn-blade-runner-screenwriters-20171009-htmlstory.html. Retrieved 12 August 2019.

17 Blade Runner 2049 director Denis Villeneuve: Deckard is human. https://www.thenational.ae/arts-culture/film/blade-runner-2049-director-denis-villeneuve-deckard-is-human-1.661092 Retrieved 12 August 2019.
18 This stronger interpretation is supported both by the original quotation from Ridley Scott that is the point of departure for this chapter, as well as by similar remarks he has reportedly made in other interviews. For example, before shooting commenced on BR2049, he is reported to have met with Harrison Ford, where he told the actor: "[I]f you weren't a replicant, the film you're about to do wouldn't exist. So when [audiences] see the film, it's essential [to know] that in the present film, he's a replicant." (https://theplaylist.net/ridley-scott-deckard-alien-20171017/). Retrieved 12 August 2019.
19 Such questions presuppose what Brock (2002: 1) calls the Ontological Thesis, namely, that there *are* fictional characters, where: "A fictional character is an individual (or role) picked out by a name or description which (i) is first introduced in a work of fiction, and (ii) does not pick out a concrete individual in the actual world."
20 Moreover, for the sake of this discussion I will assume *truthmaker maximalism*, i.e., the doctrine that for *every* truth, there is a truth-maker. For a defense of this doctrine, see Jago (2018).
21 Fictional truths are thus truths *about* fictional characters, objects, events, and the like. An important yet distinct issue not addressed here concerns truth *via* fiction, i.e., often profound truths about the *actual world* that are powerfully conveyed to us by works of fiction.
22 Consider another application of this view. To the question, "What did James Bond *really* drink?" the authors of "Shaken and Stirred: What James Bond Really Drinks" soberly answer: "Nothing. He's not a real person." (see Sandham & McFarland, 2014). *Irrealism* of this sort is defended by Walton (1990), who argues that metaphysically dubious statements about the existence of fictional characters and their properties should be recast as metaphysically unobjectionable pretense. For a defense of *realism* concerning fictional characters, namely, the view that fictional characters *exist*, albeit as abstract objects, see van Inwagen (1977).
23 For simplicity, I will focus on the nature of fictional truths concerning fictional *characters*; but virtually all of the points made here apply equally to fictional objects, events, etc.
24 Alex Byrne (1993: 24) rejects this view on the grounds that, "Well, in some fictions there are deluded narrators, and so they speak falsely." But we need not take everything a character (or a narrator) says at face value. If K tells Lt. Joshi, "What you asked. It's done. No trace left. Just like you wanted," we do not need to *believe* him. Rather, in the view we are considering, the fictional *fact* in this instance is that K lied to his boss. We know, because the film has *shown us* that he knows perfectly well that he didn't do what Lt. Joshi ordered him to do.

25 Or are we? Strictly speaking, we are *given* in a work of fiction less than we might initially suppose. We see Luv abruptly jump up, apparently alarmed, when Joi's antenna is broken. We then naturally infer that, "The Wallace Corporation uses some of its products to keep tabs on some of its customers." But both the statement of what we "see" and the inference we make on that basis are at bottom *interpretations* of what we are given, namely, certain images and sounds.

26 Cf. Parsons (2011: 34): "What should we say about the question of whether [Sherlock] Holmes is bald, or not? I think there is no answer to this question … Notice that I am not saying that Holmes is neither bald nor non-bald … [T]hat is a definite answer, not a rejection of an answer … I want to say instead that there is no answer at all."

27 Cf. Dorothy Sayers (2004: 40–41): "In what sense is the unwritten past of the characters in a book less true than their behaviour in it? … If it is deducible from the evidence, self-consistent, and recognisable in its effects, it is quite real, whether or not it was ever actual."

28 Note that insofar as we think of fictional characters as inhabiting complete fictional worlds, there will be as many fictional facts about each fictional character as there are actual facts about any real person inhabiting the actual world. For example, there will be facts about Deckard's siblings, where he takes his dry cleaning, the number of hairs on his head the day he first met Rachael, what he did *each and every day* for thirty years while hiding out in Vegas, and about countless other things associated with living a life. Indeed, there will be as many truths about Rick Deckard as there are about Harrison Ford. But one must wonder: Is there *really* a fact of the matter about what Deckard ate for lunch on 22 December 2034? How *could* there be such a fact?

29 It is undeniable that such a view can seem quite attractive. No work of fiction can answer every question we might have about its fictional world. How wonderful to be able to suppose that there *is* a correct answer to every such question, *and* (if we are lucky) that we can learn those answers from the very person whose imagination and intentions *make* them so! Nevertheless, recall that when we considered the Authorial View above, we encountered reasons to conclude that there are limits to how far we should be willing to go in accepting a creator's claims about their fictional work, especially when such claims conflict with facts explicitly given *within* the work of fiction in question. Note as well that no merely human creator can imagine or have intentions about *every* aspect of a fictional world they create. Consequently, either the fictional world will consist of all and only those fictional facts explicitly given in the fictional work, plus those additional fictional facts the creator has imagined, *but no others*, or some undisclosed fictional facts will remain epistemically inaccessible. Moreover, when more than one creator of a fictional world imagines that world differently, or when the same creator does so at different times, some statements about that fictional world will be literally true *and* false.

30 A view like this may be what Livingston and Sauchelli (2011: 356) have in mind when they write: "[A]gents use their imaginations in certain kinds of ways and end up endowing the [fictional] work with a determinate content, where the term 'content' refers to what is to be imagined in engaging appreciatively with the work qua work of fiction."

31 But consider an even more epicyclic view that we have neither space nor desire to critically examine here: "It is true in fiction F that p iff it is reasonable for the informed reader to infer that the fictional [N.B.: not the actual!] author of F believes that p" (Currie, 1990: 80).

32 Note that the claim is not that there could not be a truth of the matter about whether Deckard is a replicant, but only that, as a matter of fact, given the contents of BR2049 and its relationship to other works in the "Blade Runner universe," claims to knowledge of such a fact are unjustified.

33 A useful distinction is between the *metaphysics and epistemology* of fiction, on the one hand, and the *aesthetics and critical appraisal* of fiction, on the other. The former are concerned (among other things) with the nature and existence of fictional entities, and the grounds of truth-claims about fictional entities. The latter are concerned (among other things) with the generation of meaning through the application to fiction of interpretive principles and frameworks. Both involve "reasoning to what is true in fiction" (Lamarque, 1990), but the sort of "truth" each activity seeks is different enough to merit drawing a distinction between them.

34 Scott's comments appear in the Enhancement Archive DVD (included in the Five-Disk Ultimate Collector's Edition of *Blade Runner*).

References

Armstrong, D. M. (2004). *Truth and Truthmakers*. Cambridge: Cambridge University Press.

Brock, S. (2002). Fictionalism about Fictional Characters. *Noûs* 36(1), 1–21.

Butler, N. P. (2018). Building a World Without Breaking It: Why Unasked Questions Are Answered but Our Most Enduring Question Is Not. In L. Tambone & J. Bongiorno (Eds.), *The Cyberpunk Nexus: Exploring the Blade Runner Universe* (pp. 336–353). Edwardsville, IL: Sequart Organization.

Byrne, A. (1993). Truth in Fiction: The Story Continued. *Australasian Journal of Philosophy* 71(1), 24–35.

Currie, G. (1990). *The Nature of Fiction*. Cambridge: Cambridge University Press.

Dick, P. K. (1968). *Do Androids Dream of Electric Sheep?* New York: Ballantine Books.

Jago, M. (2018). *What Truth Is*. New York: Oxford University Press.

Kandel, E. R. (2012). *The Age of Insight: The Quest to Understand the Unconscious in Art, Mind, and Brain, from Vienna 1900 to the Present*. New York: Random House.

Lamarque, P. (1990). Reasoning to What is True in Fiction. *Argumentation* 4, 333–346.

Lapointe, T. (2017). *The Art and Soul of Blade Runner 2049*. Los Angeles: Alcon Entertainment.
Lewis, D. (1978). Truth in Fiction. *American Philosophical Quarterly* 15(1), 37–46.
Livingston, P., & Sauchelli, A. (2011). Philosophical Perspectives on Fictional Characters. *New Literary History* 42(2), 337–360.
Parsons, T. (2011). Fictional Characters and Indeterminate Identity. In F. Lihoreau (Ed.), *Truth in Fiction* (pp. 27–42). Frankfurt: Ontos Verlag.
Peary, D. (2005). Directing *Alien* and *Blade Runner*: An Interview with Ridley Scott. In L. F. Knapp & A. F. Kulas (Eds.), *Ridley Scott: Interviews* (pp. 42–55). Jackson: University Press of Mississippi.
Phillips, J. F. (1999). Truth and Inference in Fiction. *Philosophical Studies* 94(3), 273–293.
Salamoff, P. J. (2018). Why the Theatrical Cut is the Truest Version of *Blade Runner*. In L. Tambone & J. Bongiorno (Eds.), *The Cyberpunk Nexus: Exploring the Blade Runner Universe* (pp. 100–110) Edwardsville, IL: Sequart Organization.
Sammon, P. M. (2017). *Future Noir: The Making of Blade Runner* (revised & updated ed.). New York: HarperCollins.
Sandham, T. & McFarland, B. (2014). "Shaken and Stirred: What James Bond Really Drinks," *The Telegraph* December 16, 2014; https://www.telegraph.co.uk/men/the-filter/11294189/Shaken-and-stirred-what-James-Bond-really-drinks.html. Retrieved 12 August 2019.
Sayers, D. L. (2004). *Letters to a Diminished Church*. Nashville: W Publishing Group.
Shanahan, T. (2014). *Philosophy and Blade Runner*. Houndsmills: Palgrave Macmillan.
Shanahan, T. (2018). Mirrors for the Human Condition. In L. Tambone & J. Bongiorno (Eds.), *The Cyberpunk Nexus: Exploring the Blade Runner Universe* (pp. 143–160) Edwardsville, IL: Sequart Organization.
Sullivan, K. P. (2012). Ridley Scott Gives "Prometheus 2" and "Blade Runner 2" Updates. http://www.mtv.com/news/2442388/prometheus-2-blade-runner-2-updates/. Retrieved 12 August 2019.
van Inwagen, P. (1977). Creatures of Fiction. *American Philosophical Quarterly* 14(4), 299–308.
Vilkomerson, S. (2017). "Blade Runner 2049 Screenwriter Michael Green Answers Our Burning Questions." Entertainment Weekly. https://ew.com/movies/2017/10/08/blade-runner-2049-ending-explained/. Retrieved 12 August 2019.
Walton, K. L. (1990). *Mimesis as Make-Believe: On the Foundations of the Representational Arts*. Cambridge, MA: Harvard University Press.

Index

Note: Page numbers in *italics* indicate figures on the corresponding pages.

2022: Black Out 2, 10, 24n5
2036: Nexus Dawn 2, 10–11, 76
2048: Nowhere to Run 2, 11, 14

Alien 27–28, 30, 234
Alien: Covenant 31
Allen, C. 56
Arendt, H. 71
Armstrong 235–236
Arrival 32–34, 46, 182
art, Blade Runner 2049 as 135–136
artificial intelligence (AI) 16–19, 109–110, 207; advanced 202; cinematic 144, 145; philosophical questions raised by 127–128; in the social domain 118–119; see also holograms
Atterton, P. 70
augmentation of Niander Wallace 207–213
authentic humans: being-in-relation 75–77; bioengineered 68–70; characteristics of 19–22, 50, 52–53, 83–85; cloning of 72–74, 80; death in 70–71; human agency in 110–112; moral agency in 55, 59–62; narrative experience of 77–80; natality in 71–75; see also personhood; replicant reproduction
authenticity issue in holograms 132–135, *133*
authentic memory 82–83
autonomy 131–132

baseline test 2, 75, 82, 114, 206; memory, literature, and 39–45; post-traumatic 115–117
Being and Time 71
being-from-birth 71–75
being-in-relation 75–77, 81
being-toward-death 70–71
bioengineered humans 68–70
Blade Runner 1, 2, 3, 7, 8; baseline test in see baseline test; death in 70–71; different versions of 27; plot of 9; replicant emotions in 55–56, 56–57
Blade Runner 2049: artificial intelligence (AI) in see artificial intelligence

(AI); cinematic implantation through directing and acting in 45–47; cinematic philosophy of *see* cinematic philosophy; death in 71; embodiment and miracle of birth in 34–39; holograms in *see* holograms; identity in *see* identity; importance of reality to characters in 22–23; intimate relationships in *see* intimate relationships; main story of 2–3; memories depicted in 87–88; memories as implants in 15–16; memory, literature, and the baseline test in 39–45; opening of 10; philosophical questions of 108–110; plot of 3–7, 11–12, 48; predecessors and backstory to 1–2, 8–23; premiere of 1; question of authentic humanity in 83–85; question of what it means to be human in 19–22; replicant emotions in 56–59; replicant moral status in 62–63; replicant reproduction in *see* replicant reproduction; sexism and misogyny in 174–176
blind spots 220–224
BR2049 *see* Blade Runner 2049
Bratman, M. E. 111, 112

Calhoun, C. 177
Cameron, J. 27, 28
capacity to communicate 55
Casino Royale 232
Cerf, V. 222
childbirth and children *see* replicant reproduction
cinematic AI 144, 145
cinematic philosophy 127, 137–143, 139, 142; cinematic AI and 144, 145
Clark, A. 152–153
cloning 72–74, 80, 86n7
Clowes R., 4

Cogito 50, 63–64
cognitive psychology 99
cognitive veillance 218
Coleridge, S. T. 234
Conclusive Human Self-Ownership Thesis 52
Conclusive Person Self-Ownership Thesis 53
constrained agents 112, 117–118, 119
Critique of Pure Reason 27

Darwin, C. 209
Dasein 71–72
Davies, D. 208
death 70–71
De Civitate Dei 182
Deck-a-Rep debate 228–230; Deckard must be a replicant argument 230–232; deeper philosophical issues in 235–239; "If you don't get it, you're a moron" in 241–242; Rick Deckard's own knowledge of the situation in 239–241; Scott's statement as director of the movie and 233–235, 234
Defeasible Fruit Principle 51–52
Descartes, R. 50, 63–64
Dick, P. K. 2, 8–9, 12–14, 208, 233
Dilthey, W. 71
DNA 69–70, 78
Do Androids Dream of Electric Sheep? 2, 12–14, 233
domestic life 120–122

economics, artificial: artificial prosumers and 185–191, 203–204n1; environmental fixes in 197–198; personification hypothesis in 192–197; saviour paradox in 191–192; social connection and 198–200; technological fixes in 199–203
Electro- Magnetic Pulse (EMP) 220
Elliot, R. 79–80
embodiment and miracle of birth 34–39

emotionality 55
emotions, replicant 55–59, 85n3
empathic love 177–179
empathy 20
emplotment 94
evaluative humanity 90
evocative objects 98–99
expansionism 191
explicitness objection 135–136
eyes: artificial 206–207; augmentation of Niander Wallace and 207–213; blind spots and 220–224; of drones 209–210; panopticon of Niander Wallace and 213–220

fertility 29–30
fictional truths 236–241
flashbacks 34
flashbulb memories 104n2
flashforwards 34
Fleming, I. 232
folk psychology 119–120
Ford, H., Scott's direction of 233–234, 234
Frankfurt, H. 110–112, 113, 122
Fruit Principle 50–54

Gallant, J. 217
Gaut, B. 138
Generation Problem 51–54
genetic engineering 29, 85n2
God 182
Google 222

halo devices 210
Heersmink, R. 3
Heidegger, M. 71
Heinlein, R. A. 177
hierarchical generative model (HGM) 152–153
hologrammatically extended minds 144, 146–148
holograms 127–128, 160–161; art, ambiguity, and intrinsic value in 135–137; authenticity in 132–135, 133; autonomy in 131–132; as cinematic AI 144, 145; cinematic philosophy and 127, 137–143, 139, 142; hologrammatically extended minds and 144, 146–148; predictive processing and 151–156, 153; sentience in 128–131; as virtual companions 144, 145–146; virtual vs. non-virtual environment and 156–160; *see also* artificial intelligence (AI)
human, what it means to be *see* authentic humans, characteristics of
human agency 110–112
humanhood 88–90

idem-identity 77–78
identity 77–78, 86n7; memory, narrative, and 91–98; personal 181–182; personhood and 88–89; of replicants 80–83
implanted memory 15–16, 39, 82–83, 97–98, 101, 105n7
Internet of Things 207
intimate relationships 165–166; love in 132–135, 133, 177–183; romance and 166–170; sex in 34–39, 149–150, 170–174; sexism and misogyny in 174–176; *see also* replicant reproduction
intrinsic value response 136–137
ipse-identity 77–78
Ishiguro, K. 72

James, W. 169–170
James Bond novels 232

Kandel, E. 239
Kant, I. 27
Kirsh, D. 210–211
Kundera, M. 84

legal ownership 67n1
light refraction 32–33

Locke, J. 94, 105n4
love 177–183; authentic 132–135, 133; empathic 177–179; *see also* intimate relationships

McCarroll, C. J. 3
mediated memories 99
Meditations 63–64
memory: authentic 82–83; baseline testing of 40–45; depicted in *Blade Runner 2049* 87–88; flashbulb 104n2; implanted 15–16, 39, 82–83, 97–98, 101, 105n7; mediated 99; narrative, identity, and 91–98; quasi- 40, 96–98, 102–103; shared 103–104; spread of personal 98–101; vicarious 101–103
mental states: capacity to reason about 112–114; human agency and 110–112; mindshaping and 119–122; in the social domain 118–119
Metzinger, T. K. 5, 150
Microsoft HoloLens 141–143, 142
minds, hologrammatically extended 144, 146–148
mindshaping 119–122
moral agency 55, 59–62
moral sense 52
moral status, replicant 62–63
mortality 70–71
Mulhall, S. 2

Nabokov, V. 42, 93–94, 104n3
Nancy, J.-L. 71
narcissism 30, 44
narrative: memory, identity, and 91–98; natality and 77–80
natality 71–75; narrative and 77–80
Natality and Finitude 71
neuroscience 217
Never Let Me Go 72
New York Post 173
Nineteen Eighty-Four 219

O'Byrne, A. 3, 71–74
Oneself as Another 85–86n7
Ontological Thesis 244n19
Orwell, G. 219

Pale Fire 42, 85, 93, 104n3
panopticon of Niander Wallace 213–220
Parfit, D. 85–86n7, 97
personal identity 181–182
personal memory, spread of 98–101
personhood 55, 88–90; Cartesian argument for replicant 63–64; having command of one's own will and 122–124; human agency and 110–112; *see also* authentic humans
personification hypothesis 192–197
phenomenal selves 150–151
Phillips, J. F. 235
post-traumatic baseline test 115–117
predictive processing 151–156, 153
privacy violations 214–215
Prometheus 27, 28–32
property, offspring as 50–54
prosumers, artificial 185–191, 203–204n1

quantified self 213
quasi-memory 40, 96–98, 102–103

reality 22–23
reason 55
Reasons and Persons 85–86n7
Red Dead Redemption 2 143
Reeve, C. D. C. 56, 61, 63
relationality 72–73, 75, 81
remembering 98–99
replicant, Deckard as *see* Deck-a-Rep debate
replicant emotions 55–59, 85n3
replicant reproduction 29, 34–39, 65–67; introduction to 48–50; owning offspring in 50–54; replicant emotions and 55–59;

replicant moral status and 62–63; significance of capacity to reproduce and 65
replication vs. recreation 182
reproduction, replicant *see* replicant reproduction
Ricoeur, P. 77–78, 85–86n7
Rime of the Ancient Mariner 234
robot evolution 68–70
romance 166–170; *see also* intimate relationships

Sacks, O. 94–95
saviour paradox 191; personification hypothesis in 192–197
Schechtman, M. 94, 122
Scott, R. 1–2, 8, 27–28, 47, 228–229, 232, 233–235, 234
self-awareness 55
self-hatred 30
Self-Model Theory of Subjectivity 150–151
self-surveillance 213
self-tracking 213
sentience 55, 128–131
sexism and misogyny 174–176
sexual activity 34–39, 149–150, 170–174; *see also* intimate relationships
Shadbolt, N. 6
Shade, J. 42
Shanahan, T. 2, 5, 6, 203–204n1
shared memory 103–104
Smart, P. 4, 5–6
social connection 198–200
social machines 219
Sterelny, K. 109
Stewart, S. 173
strong agency 111, 117–118
surveillance technologies 207, 213, 214–220

Terminator, The 200–201
Tolstoy, L. 70
Transitivity of Fictional Identity Principle 232, 240
Treanor, B. 3
truth 235–239
Turkle, S. 98

van Dijck, J. 99
van Inwagen, P. 182
vicarious memory 101–103
Vilkomerson, S. 241
Villeneuve, D. 1, 2, 8, 28, 46–47, 182, 206; *Arrival* directed by 32–34
virtual companions 144, 145–146
virtual reality (VR) technology 149–150, 154–155
virtual vs. non-virtual environment 156–160
Voight-Kampff test *see* baseline test
Vygotsky, L. 120

Wallace, A. R. 209
Wallace effect 209–212
Warren, M. A. 52–53, 55, 56, 59, 62
Wartenberg, T. E. 135–136
Web-extended minds 218–219
Wegner, D. M. 99–100
West, R. 222
Weyland, P. 28–32
Wiese, W. 5
will: becoming a strong agent and having one's own 117–118; personhood and having command of one's own 122–124; structure of the 110–112
Woollard, F. 2–3

Zaner, R. 73
Zawidzki, T. W. 121